"Operation Tune-up was a well-oiled m

"Before the WooSox in Worcester, there was Operation Tune-Up. An adventurous true crime story with feel-good results, this book hits it out of the park!"

– Steve Lyons, former MLB player, Boston Red Sox analyst, and author of *Psychoanalysis*

"*A Peek Under the Hood* is a fascinating look into DEA's Operation Tune Up, which dismantled several international drug operations in the depressed Main South area of Worcester, Mass. in the mid 1990s when heroin reigned supreme. Michael Pavarnik was an undercover DEA agent who was personally involved in this operation, with the invaluable assistance of an intrepid and street-savvy confidential informant from Vietnam by way of Canada where he honed his expertise.

Pevarnik describes in minute and engrossing detail the colorful Hispanic, Vietnamese, and South Asian drug perpetrators who had all migrated to Worcester, which became the epicenter of regional drug dealing during that era. There was intense competition among these groups, and occasional betrayals and violence.

He also carefully describes the perpetrators' connections to the various sources of the drugs in places like Puerto Rico, Panama, Columbia, and Thailand, and how and where the drugs were transported and distributed, ending up in Worcester.

And he meticulously describes the development and execution of Op-plans designed to interdict the drug flow and bring the perpetrators to justice, some successful and some not, working from the street level up to the kingpins, all leading to the dramatic denouement.

A great read."

–Dean B. Pineles, retired judge and author of *A Judge's Odyssey: From Vermont to Russia, Kazakhstan, and Georgia, Then on to War Crimes and Organ Trafficking in Kosovo*

A Peek Under the Hood

A Peek Under the Hood

Heroin, Hope & Operation Tune-Up

Michael Pevarnik

Montpelier, VT

First Printing: September 2023

Release Date: September 26, 2023

Hardcover ISBN: 978-1-57869-149-4
Softcover ISBN: 978-1-57869-148-7
eBook ISBN: 978-1-57869-150-0

Published by Rootstock Publishing
an imprint of Ziggy Media LLC
32 Main Street #165
Montpelier, VT 05602 USA

www.rootstockpublishing.com

info@rootstockpublishing.com

Interior and cover design by Eddie Vincent, ENC Graphic Services
(ed.vincent@encirclepub.com)
Cover art credit: Shutterstock
Author photo by George Loring Studio
Map and flow chart by Tim Newcomb (www.newcombstudios.com)

For permissions or to schedule an author interview, contact the author
at michaelpevarnik@outlook.com.

Printed in the USA

DEDICATION

To the Main South neighborhood of Worcester, Massachusetts.

Main South Neighborhood, Worcester, Massachusetts

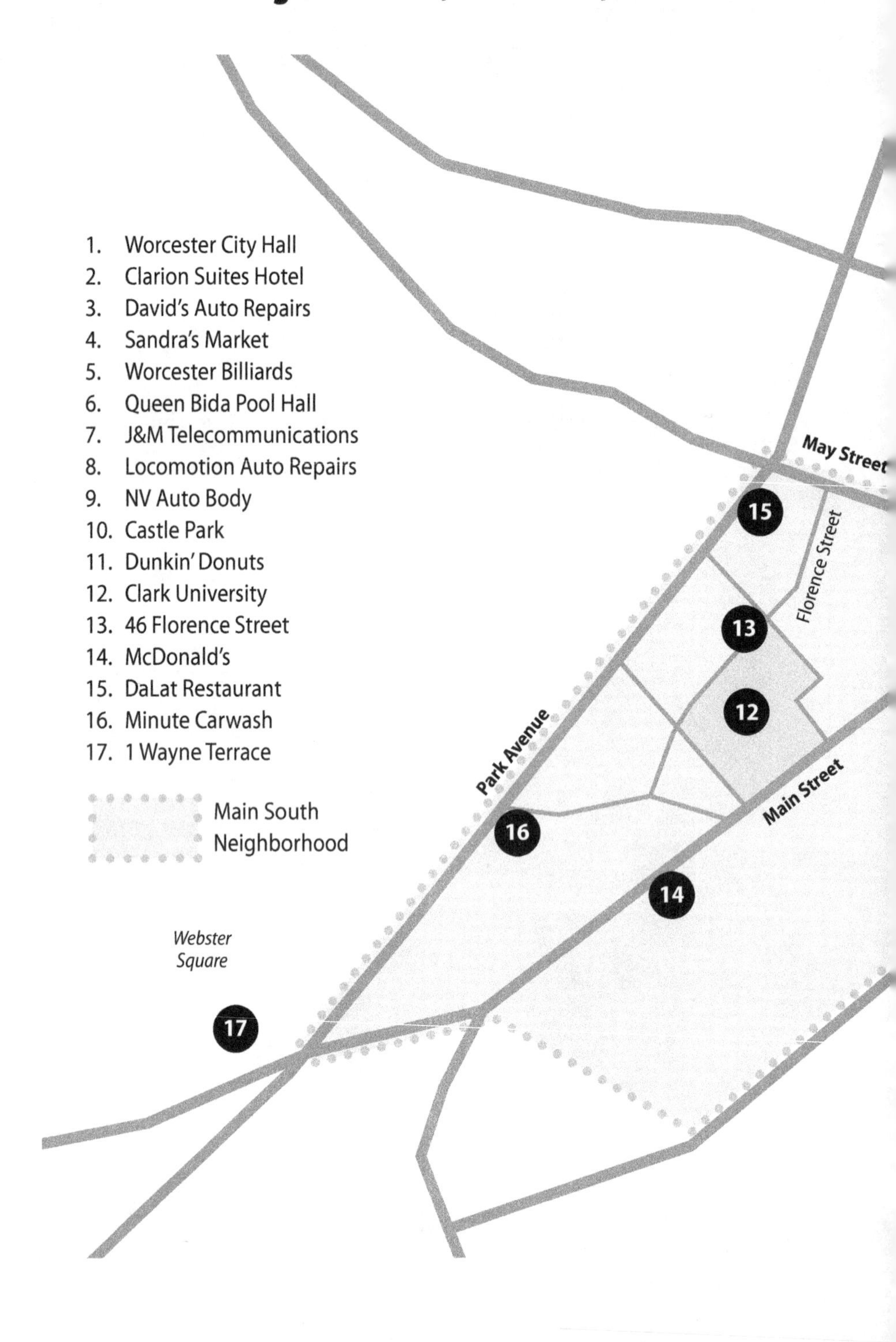

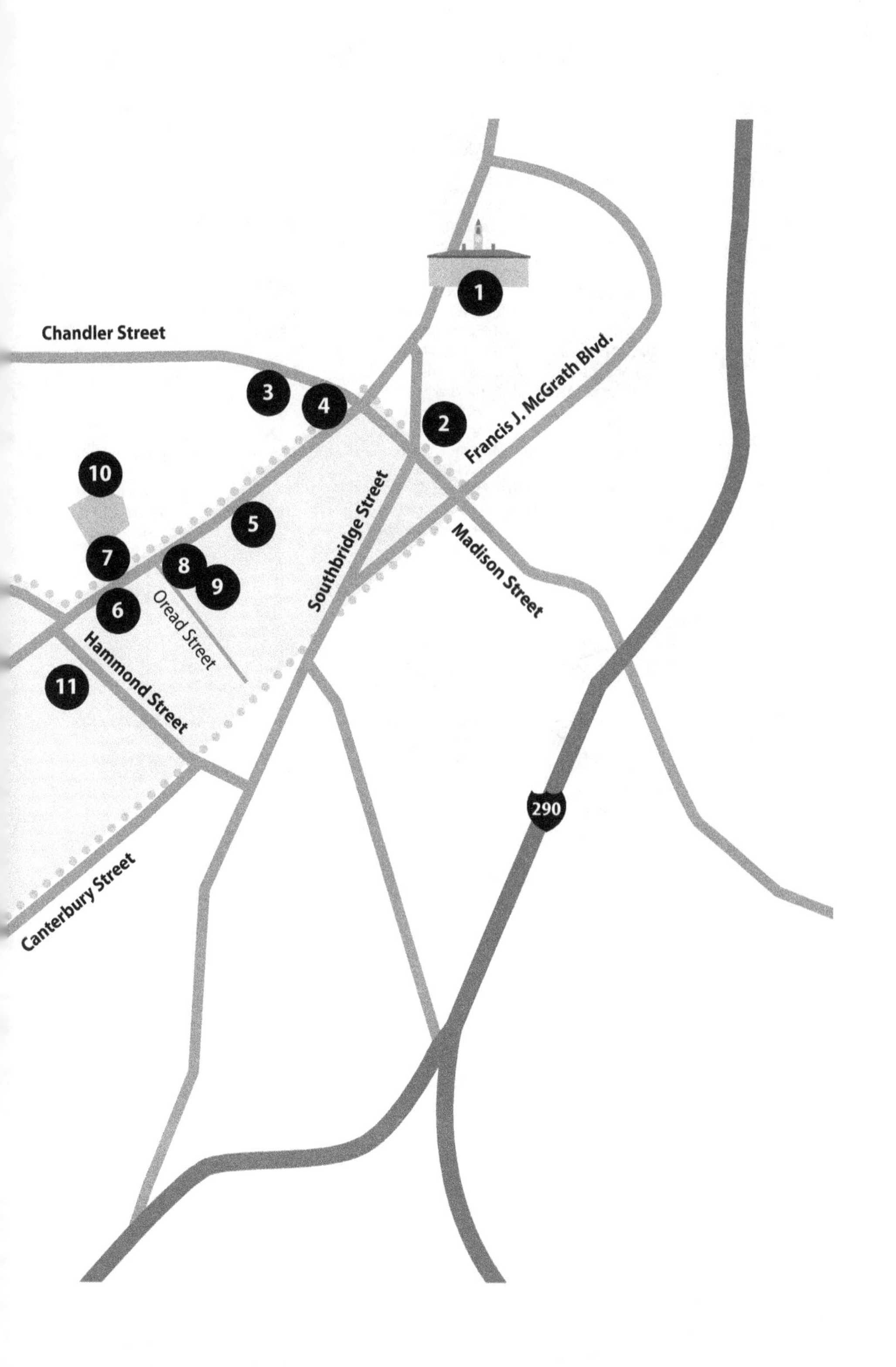
Chandler Street
Francis J. McGrath Blvd.
Southbridge Street
Madison Street
Oread Street
Hammond Street
Canterbury Street
290
1
2
3
4
5
6
7
8
9
10
11

Operation Tune-Up

PROLOGUE

The blue bubble on the dashboard spun wildly as the unmarked car raced through the streets of Old San Juan. Spanish style row houses blurred in a kaleidoscope of pastel colors, distorting the cultural beauty of a bygone era best savored at a slower pace. Red-Knuckled fists clenched a ten and two as I glanced in the rearview mirror, or, at least, that was my intention. Instead, I found myself mesmerized by the unexpected darkness that stared back. Alternating an intense focus between what lay ahead and what loomed behind, I watched as a massive black cloud rolled off the Caribbean Sea to consume the sixteenth century fortress of El Morro.

The swift-moving tropical downpour took pursuit and captured the government vehicle, which then began to rumble over rain-slickened cobblestones. The violent thunderstorm's sudden appearance added an eeriness to the atmosphere of danger that already existed. Under different circumstances, the flash of lightning illuminating the castle would have conjured the image of an old Vincent Price movie and given this baby boomer agent a chuckle.

But not now. Not as I neared *that* moment of truth I'd hoped to never encounter in my career. All the range practice, tactical maneuvering exercises, and legal instructions on the use of deadly force may have prepared me for the perils of the street, but not for the complexities of conscience, even if justified by law, when taking a life.

There was no doubt I'd be using my firearm today, only this time it wouldn't be aimed at a silhouette cardboard figure clipped to a metal target holder, its pointed spike firmly planted in the ground to hold it upright. There'd be nobody broadcasting, *'ready on the firing line,'* first ensuring the safety of all shooters as they donned eye and ear protection. Today, my sights would be set on human beings—all of whom would be aiming back with the intention of killing me.

Sluggish windshield wipers complained as they languished back and forth; flashing strobes of rotating blue created a rolling dance floor effect; all the windows fogged up from the exhaled breaths of foreboding and concern. As I accelerated toward whatever destiny had in store for us, a hypnotic presence swirled varying levels of heroism and fear through my mind.

Chapter 1

"Operation Tune-Up" Worcester, Massachusetts

August/September 1994

The Canadian controller insisted he be the one to set up a meet with his informant. Kept calling him the "little guy," a nickname that conveyed a hint of fondness, saying his relocated source only trusted one person to make the arrangements, and it wasn't the DEA agent on the other end of the line.

"Too many people want him dead," the controller whispered as if delivering a line in a spy film noir. "Calls me every day at the same time to tell me what's going on down there."

I waited for the part about synchronized watches, but it never came. A rendezvous site was agreed upon and a physical description good enough to make the ID given: Vietnamese male, late twenties, thin build, tattoos on both arms, and long, dark hair that fell over the collar.

"You can't miss him," the controller said in parting. "He stands out in a crowd."

But when I turned into the Dunkin' Donuts in the Main South neighborhood of Worcester, Massachusetts, the only thing that stood out was the irony of his assurance. There had to be a dozen Vietnamese men in front of the place, all of them squatting in a straight-line formation as though sitting on a low-rise, invisible bench. Each smoked a cigarette and sipped a cup of coffee while remaining perfectly balanced in their alley cat pose.

None had long hair.

It was a beautiful late-summer day with clear blue skies and bright sunshine, but the non-conforming New England weather was too chilly for the date. So cool that everybody in the lot wore a long-sleeved shirt or jacket. If any of them sported tattoos on their arms, they were not to be seen.

I went inside the Dunkin' Donuts and took my place in a long, snaking line, a wait I'd normally grumble about, but today it gave me time to consider my dilemma. Ten minutes later, armed with my own cup of coffee and a plan, I emerged from the building, leaned up against its brick façade, and flipped open the perforated wedge of plastic on the cup's lid. Steam plumed into the crisp morning air, fogging the dark sunglasses sitting on the bridge of my nose. Here I was, a six-foot four, clean-cut, white male propped up against the wall with twelve crouching Vietnamese men.

Since I couldn't pick the little guy out of a line-up, I was hoping the informant would pick me out of one.

He did.

Nonchalantly, the little guy approached and said my first name in a soft voice. I nodded and whispered for him to start walking along Main Street, then announced in a voice loud enough for the others to hear, "Sorry, no change." I hung around to finish my coffee and reinforce the lack of association before departing in my G-car, a Lexus seized and forfeited from a South Boston associate of Irish mob boss James "Whitey" Bulger.

I caught up with the informant as he traipsed along the city's central thoroughfare, still sipping what had to by then be a cold cup of coffee. As I pulled to the curb just beyond his deliberate stroll, he casually approached the car, looked around to make sure nobody was watching, then quickly got into the backseat, and lay down so as not to be seen. His laid back demeanor suddenly changed as he snapped, "Go! Go!"

It was obvious he'd done this before.

* * *

My meeting with "Lanh," a Vietnamese national with recently shorn hair, was the result of being the DEA duty agent that week. It's a dreaded assignment that can't pass fast enough, as investigations take a backseat to administrative tasks and distasteful grunt work. All day long you're tethered to the office while fielding a flow of inquiries ranging from the mundane to the bizarre. It seems that every duty agent week, a former CIA operative visits or calls with deep concerns about a massive governmental conspiracy with aliens.

Nighttime and weekend hours bring a new element. Whether it's something as serious as a death threat to an undercover agent or simply the drunken tomfoolery of a barfly, every incoming call fielded by an answering service is forwarded to the duty agent beeper — the communicative device of choice just prior to the era of the ubiquitous cell phone — which required an immediate response. The assignment is akin to pitching "mop-up" in a baseball game your team is losing by a mile — somebody has to do it, but you can't wait for the game to be over.

At the time, DEA's New England Field Division office was based in a professional building just up the street from the Boston Garden. The building's mostly medical offices served the health needs of the elderly. It was an odd location for a federal law enforcement agency, making for incongruent scenes of armed agents escorting handcuffed prisoners in shared elevator space with geriatric patients guiding their walkers. However, it was an improvement over the prior DEA location: rodent infested, basement accommodations in the low-rise section of the JFK Federal Building.

I was sitting at my desk when the group secretary yelled across the cavernous room, "Duty agent…line 2!" Grimacing, I lifted the receiver and greeted the caller with a curt but very official, "DEA." The response from the other end was just as official.

"Corporal Larison, RCMP, Kitchener Detachment." After proffering my name and title, the Royal Canadian Mounted Police corporal galloped on an explanatory path, first stride saying he had an informant now living in "the States" who was willing to assist DEA. He outlined an impressive resume, rather effusively, about several successful investigations Lanh worked at his direction in Ontario. But after too much regional exposure, he had to be moved out of the province.

"Ottawa decided he was too good a resource to give up and shipped him around to other detachments," Larison said, referring to RCMP's National Headquarters by its geographic location. "He continued making cases for the Crown, but when the death threats piled up, the little guy was relocated to a city in your state called Worcester."

The corporal butchered the pronunciation of the Central Massachusetts city.

"Go on."

"I kept in touch with him, or I should say he kept in touch with me. He doesn't want to stop working. Calls every day and says there's a lot going on down there. A lot of drug stuff. When I told him there's nothing I can do in another country, he said, 'then find someone for me.' That's why I called DEA."

"Give me his name and number and I'll see what he has to offer."

"He wants me to set up a meet," Larison insisted. "Nothing personal. It's simply a matter of not trusting someone he doesn't know."

I understood. I felt the same way about Corporal Larison. After hanging up the phone and getting the main number for the RCMP in Kitchener, Ontario, I asked for the corporal's extension. When the same voice answered, I was satisfied this wasn't a set-up or crank call and continued the conversation without missing a beat.

"So, how'd this guy become an informant?"

"He came to our attention during a homicide investigation."

Here we go...duty agent call.

But my cynicism was unfounded. Lanh was never considered a suspect in the case; he was only interviewed as a matter of course because the victim was his roommate. A drug-dealing gang member was eventually charged with the murder — an unintended result of the little guy's roomie getting caught in the crossfire of a drug feud. He was simply in the wrong place at the wrong time.

"We have a major problem with violent Vietnamese organizations up here, but no way to infiltrate them ... no Vietnamese snitches. Ottawa encouraged us to recruit whenever we had the opportunity."

"What's his motivation for working? Money?"

"Yes ... well, that and something else he told me." With a sympathetic undertone, Cpl. Larison explained that after Lanh settled into the Crown's territory, the little guy began to feel the same kind of anguish he thought he'd left behind in Vietnam. But instead of the pain and suffering caused by an incoming brutal regime, it was heroin, crack and ecstasy that were killing people and destroying lives. Then when his roommate got murdered because of drugs, it was the proverbial last straw.

"So, he became a source to seek out moral justice for others?"

"Never thought of it that way, but I guess you could say that."

"What's his criminal history like?"

"He has none, he's clean."

"Nothing in Vietnam?"

Larison paused to reflect. After gathering his thoughts, he said that Lanh had lived a tough life. Seen a lot of horror from the war. When he was a kid, his father put him on a packed boat, the last space available, leaving both parents behind to escape the army that had overtaken Saigon. It was a rickety vessel, by the corporal's account barely seaworthy, that drifted for days until a cargo ship saw it and brought them all to Hong Kong, only then to be caged in a refugee camp with an unsafe atmosphere and deplorable living conditions. They were the lucky ones, though. Other boats never made it that far and those people died at sea. There was a worldwide humanitarian outcry about the treatment of these so-called "boat people," and several countries, including Canada, granted a select few asylum and citizenship.

Lanh was one of them.

"Set it up," I said.

* * *

Lanh's hardships in life and high marks by the RCMP may have gotten him a debriefing, but the information he provided was not that impressive. His only viable target was a low-level crack dealer who failed to pop up on any of DEA's intelligence screens. That's not enough to open a federal drug investigation. After getting back to the office in Boston, I gave Cpl. Larison a courtesy call.

"Hi Bill, I met your guy."

"I know. He told me. How did it go?"

"Well, he doesn't have much. Only an auto body shop owner selling small amounts of crack. Might be able to get him a gun, too. I think we'll pass, but I'll refer him to the Mass State Police and see if ATF is interested in the gun angle. They handle federal firearms violations."

Cpl. Larison was not pleased, and his reaction surprised me. This Mountie wasn't going to be satisfied until DEA got his man.

"That won't work. He won't trust them. I told him your agency is the one he wants to work for. I told him you're the best."

"I'm sorry, Bill, but our resources are limited. We have to target the highest-level organizations that'll result in the greatest local impact. I'm sure you can appreciate that. I'm not going to abandon the little guy. The state police are a good agency."

"No good. You *have* to give him a chance. He's the hardest working source I've ever had. He *will* develop a case that's worthy of your federal standards. The Crown holds him in the highest regard … I'd rather not go over your head."

I'd exercised due diligence with Cpl. Larison; given him the courtesy of fully exploring what his informant had to offer and responded back with honesty and diplomacy. The heavy-handed threat left me inclined to say, *'do what you have to do,'* or even, *'go fuck yourself,'* and hang up the phone.

But I didn't.

Fact was, this Canadian cop only wanted to get as many bad guys off the street as possible, no matter what country that street lay in. He felt strongly that Lanh was an effective law enforcement tool whose instincts and acquired skills shouldn't go to waste. Though his dedication to duty was brusquely worn upon his hash-marked sleeve, he only wanted to convince another cop to do the right thing.

I liked that.

"I'll see what I can do."

* * *

Worcester (locally pronounced "Wuss-tah") is a blue-collar city with a prosperous past. In the mid-nineteenth century, the Worcester & Boston Railroad transformed the city into a transportation hub during the economic boom of the American Industrial Revolution. Manufacturing plants producing items such as shoes, clothing, wire products and machinery parts sprouted up and flourished. The good times attracted a sea of immigrants from all over the world, a swelling population that settled into the burgeoning number of triple-deckers being built in the city.

But like so many other once thriving New England mill towns, as manufacturing shifted overseas, Worcester's industrial area gave way to drugs and crime. The old textile and loom manufacturing plants, once symbols of success, had become extinct, lumbering behemoths — graffiti-streaked buildings with windows shattered by neighborhood youth or the strung-out.

One of the city's many neighborhoods is Main South, a small but thickly-settled square mile of urban decay that abuts downtown Worcester. Its busy Main Street bustles with the business of blight, as drug dealers, users, prostitutes, and other criminally-inclined characters, along with the surviving stores, some of which perpetuate the illegal activities, keep the area alive. Roving gangs of thugs and stationary dregs of society had commandeered its public parks and gathering spaces, littering these once safe, inner-city sanctuaries with hypodermic needles, broken booze bottles and used condoms.

With a population approaching two-hundred thousand in the mid-1990s, Worcester was in dire need of some federal drug enforcement attention. At the time, DEA had twelve offices strategically situated throughout the six states of New England, in areas most affected by drug distribution and its related violent crime. Yet the region's second most-populated city with one of its highest crime rates wasn't one of them. Several attempts were made to open an office in the central Mass city known as the "Heart of the Commonwealth," but each ended in failure, successfully blocked by a territorially-obsessed Worcester County District Attorney's Office.

The district attorney, a man who'd been in power for almost twenty years, bristled at the perception of usurped authority whenever DEA attempted to conduct an investigation in the city, or for that matter, any other community in Worcester County. Some of that animosity derived from the seizure of drug-related assets— as though the feds were coming in and stealing illegally gotten gains that rightfully belonged to him.

Under federal law, the vast majority of forfeited net proceeds from drug seizures augment the budgets of other law enforcement agencies participating in a DEA investigation. Typically, it's a greater percentage than those shares received had the seizure been processed through the state system. These were boons to local departments that the DA couldn't control. He wanted to be the one who decided how much money was being divvied out.

The district attorney's iron-fisted management style had an intimidating effect on the state police unit attached to his office—known then as a Crime Prevention and Control Unit (CPAC)—who were careful not to tread on his overbearing psyche while conducting drug investigations he discretionarily decided whether to prosecute or not. But the fear factor had an even greater effect on the local police departments operating within the county, some of whom fretted about losing state funding overseen by the DA if they got on his bad side.

And they all knew one way of doing that was to work with DEA.

DEA agents deciding to follow promising leads and make the fifty-mile plus trip from the nearest office in Boston or Springfield quickly felt the chill. It deterred most from doing drug cases in Worcester County, opting instead to conduct investigations in closer, more accommodating communities. Few federal pioneers dared to venture into the hostile territory often referred to as the "Wild West."

* * *

With a little cajoling to convince my supervisor it was worth pursuing federally—not a state case with a distributor unaffiliated with an identified organization, which in truth, it was—Lanh was documented as a confidential informant (CI), and I initiated an investigation targeting the owner of NV Auto Body on Oread Street in the heart of Main South. With the new case came a new title—in DEA parlance, "the case agent"—a position of leadership with additional authority and responsibilities somewhat analogous to those of a film director. Only instead of making a movie to be shown on the silver screen, the goal was producing a prosecutable case to be proven in a court of law.

On August 29th, 1994, Lanh arranged the purchase of a $300 piece of crack, also known on the streets of Worcester as "rock," and a handgun from the shop's owner, Thanh Nguyen, another Vietnamese national who'd taken a different path in life after also granted asylum and citizenship (in the US) following the atrocities of war. DEA and ATF conducted the controlled buy; the city's Vice & Narcotics Squad didn't participate in the operation.

They weren't even told about the investigation.

About a year earlier, altruism mixed with a touch of naivety convinced me to dip my toes into the icy waters of Worcester. I'd heard the stories about the city's attitude toward the feds — DEA in particular — but decided not to prejudge based upon the opinion of others. I started a case with the police department's vice squad. Unfortunately, my firsthand experience gave merit to the bad reputation that preceded the unit.

With a limited budget and resources relegating the vast majority of drug cases to swiftly completed "all or nothing at all" search warrants or "buy/busts" — often on lower-level targets — detectives assigned to the case had a hard time exercising patience in the federal long-term goal of identifying and dismantling an entire organization. I understood that thinking. I was a local cop before becoming a DEA agent. What I couldn't accept was despite being advised otherwise, they got a state search warrant behind my back using probable cause generated from DEA funded informant buys and made an arrest. I complained, but this defiant act was apparently supported by three levels of local supervision. The betrayal resulted in little dope on the table and lots of compromise to the federal case, which had to be prematurely closed.

That treacherous act combined with the lack of a welcome mat at the county line made my decision to operate in a vacuum this time around a no-brainer.

Surveillance of the garage, which sat on the periphery of the Main South business district, had been established prior to Lanh's arrival. Typical of most urban neighborhoods, it was difficult setting up in the area without being noticed. Foot traffic was heavy from the shoppers, loiterers, and illicit street merchants hawking their respective products or services. The rest of the block was residential with mostly dilapidated triple-deckers — some abandoned and boarded up; some supposedly vacant but used by junkies or squatters; others occupied by honest citizens who feared the predators and distrusted the police.

Lanh met Nguyen in a small lot in front of the garage, a compact square filled with vehicles in various states of repair or alteration. I listened and recorded the conversation through the "Kel" from about a block away. In fed-speak, referring to a body wire as a Kel is comparable to calling a cotton swab a Q-Tip.

Nguyen was thinner than Lanh — if that was possible — with a sunken face, wispy mustache and wild hair that gave him the look of a mad scientist. The shoulder holster containing a .380 caliber revolver beneath his mechanic's shirt left a bulging imprint. He was authorized by the Worcester PD to carry the weapon, stating in his application he needed it because his business was in a dangerous neighborhood.

He failed to mention being part of the problem.

They went inside the garage, part of a contiguous row of attached brick buildings originating on Main Street, where Nguyen proceeded to smoke a small piece of crack he'd just cooked. His addiction satisfied, at least for the moment, he then handed a substantially bigger piece to Lanh, took the drug money, then told the informant to sit tight and wait for the second part of the deal.

The gun was on the way.

Lanh patiently waited and observantly watched as one user after another came and went, each purchasing rocks of various sizes depending upon how much money they'd scrounged up, until somebody finally walked in who was selling instead of buying. The street vendor reached beneath his brightly colored, baggy shirt and pulled out a handgun wrapped in a rag. He gave the stolen weapon to Nguyen, who unfolded the greasy piece of cloth and showed it to Lanh. With a nod of approval, the exchange was made without a word being spoken. Nguyen shoved a bill in his pocket and gave the rest of the money to the vendor, who scurried back out to the busy Main Street and disappeared into the crevices like a cockroach.

* * *

The first drug exhibit of many in the case — an inauspicious beginning on the federal scale, but one that would crack open creaky inner-city doors with rusty hinges — was a little light in weight, at least according to local market standards. I viewed it as a ground floor invitation to enter an underworld and swiftly take a step up the stairs of distribution.

Lanh was sent back to the garage immediately after the exhibit was weighed and instructed to voice his displeasure about being shorted. Perhaps it wasn't a good idea calling the cracked-out, gun carrying drug dealer a "loser" and an "asshole"—a dangerous decision that was not part of the plan—but the impulsive, no-filter informant made his point without being shot. However, the little guy did stay on script when he told the reprimanded shopkeeper he'd make another crack buy the following week—a bigger one—but *only* if his source delivered it personally and added on what was owed.

* * *

Lanh greeted the scolded shopkeeper in the parking lot out front before both went inside NV Auto Body to do the second deal. Called out after the short sale—a verbal lashing that would have angered a reasonable mind, much less one addicted to a drug that crazes with violent side effects—Nguyen agreed to Lanh's stipulations without apparent animosity. Nevertheless, when he slipped through an interior doorway to "get (his) guy," leaving the vulnerable informant alone with over a thousand dollars in his pocket, the little guy decided it might be wiser to wait outside under the watchful eyes of surveillance.

As soon as the bay door opened, the sounds of the city rushed through the Kel and into my ears, followed by a measured cadence of gravelly footsteps on the parking lot surface. When the steps stopped, the whispering began. Lanh stood still in the middle of a vehicular assemblage transmitting Nguyen's actions and words (translated from Vietnamese to English), along with an interior layout of the garage and license plates of cars in the lot. Given a small window of opportunity, he was relaying real time intelligence to his new controller, who he knew was listening on the receiving end.

It was then I appreciated the breadth of experience Lanh had acquired with the RCMP.

The news brief ceased when Lanh's peripheral vision spotted Nguyen emerging not from his garage, but from an adjoining brick building housing another auto repair shop he'd accessed via an interior double-door. The second garage also had a small, indented parking lot littered with vehicles in various states of repair or alteration. Its white exterior façade was spray painted with the words "Mazda" and "Toyota", assumed specialties of the shop. It wouldn't be long before I learned that "crack" and "heroin" would have been more apropos.

Nguyen was in the company of a lanky, scruffily bearded man with short dreadlocks that popped out below the rim of a cowboy hat. Openly smoking a "blunt"— marijuana wrapped in a cigar casing — the Rasta gaucho strutted from one lot to the other with an easy, carefree manner, clearly someone comfortable in his criminal environment. He introduced himself to Lanh as "Rey" with a handshake that held a piece of crack wrapped in clear plastic.

"Sorry 'bout last week, mon ... little extra this one," Rasta Rey assured the fleeced informant in broken English before shooting a daggered look at Nguyen, who stood in silence after being chewed out for skimming the product during the first deal.

But once bitten, twice shy.

Taking the small DEA provided, portable scale out of his pocket and placing it on the hood of a car, Lanh weighed the drug exhibit for accuracy. Rey seemed to be taken aback by the act of distrust yet was impressed with the customer's business savvy. After confirming the weight to be a heavy ounce, Lanh completed the transaction. Rey peeled off fifty bucks for Nguyen, pocketed the rest, and then handed a business card to the informant.

"Call *me* from now on," Rey said with a cocksure smile. Then with a puff of the blunt and no sense of urgency, he sauntered back to his garage.

In bold letters the card spelled out: "Locomotion Auto Repairs," with a motto that proudly proclaimed, "We Do it All." The owner's name was listed as "R. Barnes," but it was handwritten over another name that had been whited out. After learning more about Rey's background, I wondered what happened to the guy buried beneath the dried liquid.

Reginaldo "Rey" Barnes was a Panamanian national married to an American citizen living in Worcester. He had a criminal history that included disposition pending, felony arrests for cocaine trafficking (state) and illegal possession of a firearm (federal). The handgun he was nabbed with was one of twelve stolen during a burglary in Roanoke VA, confiscated just days apart from the recovery of another weapon taken during the same heist. That gun was used to murder Newark, New Jersey undercover Detective John Sczyrek. Barnes was questioned about the homicide by the Essex County Prosecutor's Office, but proof of involvement was inconclusive.

There is no drug case worth making if your undercover gets killed. The role is inherent with danger and its stage rife with unconscionable characters. Any warning sign that something's not right shouldn't be ignored. Whatever precautions can be taken while still doing the job, should be. Or maybe you should just walk away from doing a deal. There's always another day.

Every case agent must constantly be aware of potential safety issues, especially when red flags pop up while making life and death operational decisions. Several now flew in my mind.

Was Rey Barnes complicit in the murder of an undercover officer? Did he still possess any of the unrecovered stolen guns? No fear of doing a drug deal out in the open — was a dirty, local cop protecting Rey and his garage?

I didn't know the answers to these questions. I only knew that a crack smoking, gun slinging Vietnamese dealt drugs for a pot toking Panamanian, who's somehow connected to a weapons burglary and a cop killing.

And both owned auto repair shops in the Main South neighborhood of Worcester.

* * *

Lanh nurtured his newfound relationship with Rasta Rey by becoming a regular at Locomotion Auto Repairs. The informant hung out for a spell most days while watching the parade of customers come and go. Automobile repairs were mildly involved in the activities. He wasn't the only one who whittled away the hours at the criminal den of iniquities. It was an open house all day long. And Rey wasn't the only drug distributor there, either. The garage was a well-known marketplace for the purchase of heroin, crack, powder cocaine, marijuana, and stolen weapons.

Every drug dealer at Locomotion had his own independent business, but it was clear that Rey ruled the roost, and nobody wanted to upset him. Perhaps they knew more about his role in the cop killing than law enforcement did. Each valued their customers and offense might be taken if somebody messed with the company assets. But that didn't mean they wouldn't branch out whenever the opportunity arose to stealthily steal a client from one of their business buddies at the firm.

There is no honor amongst thieves.

Lanh's time spent at Locomotion was a worthwhile investment, as he built up trust and established the foundation of DEA's undercover story. Claiming to be a fugitive now living in Worcester under an assumed name — a believable fabrication because it rang true for others at the garage — he maintained contact with the Canadian organization that employed him before going on the lam. The group's alleged bread and butter product was heroin, but with the financial backing of organized crime, there was always an interest if the right deal came along for a bulk shipment of cocaine. He told them the crack purchased from Rey was used to start up a business of his own in Lowell, another old mill town about forty miles northeast of Worcester, saying he preferred "not to shit where you sleep."

Lanh so impressed the crew at Locomotion that I had a hard time keeping up with all the positive developments. Not only were the bad guys meeting my operational objectives, new opportunities and additional targets routinely exceeded them. Even the hard-to-impress US attorney's office in Boston was taken aback by each overachieving venture.

The pushy Mountie with the abrasive approach was right: Lanh *did* develop a case worthy of DEA's attention and resources. The little guy paved a smooth road straight to an inner-city drug distribution center, which then intersected with an avenue of DOJ funding administered through the US attorney's Organized Crime Drug Enforcement Task Force ("OCDETF"). A requirement of this special program was creating a code name for the investigation — typically related to some element in the case and usually thought to be clever, although often eliciting nothing but a groan, "Operation Tune-Up" was born.

But then the case hit a pothole.

A big one.

* * *

Kel affixed to the skin of his torso and buy money deep in his pocket, Lanh placed the off-white chunk on the portable scale. "We good," he declared from the concrete echo chamber of Locomotion Auto Repairs. The ounce of crack then filled the void previously occupied by the cash, which found a new home in Rey Barnes' pocket.

I didn't have Lanh purchase this latest exhibit just because he could. Every time an agent dips into the taxpayer's pocket, it'd better be for the purpose of creating growth in a federal investigation. One of those returns on investment is the identification and future forfeiture of drug-derived assets, which, in essence, often results in the bad guy footing the bill for the buy. Other returns include strengthening proof of criminal intent; tying in co-conspirators; revealing sources of supply; pinpointing possible stash sites; and setting up the seizure of drug shipments.

Rasta Rey provided all the above as incentives to make this buy.

During a recent unmonitored hangout session at the garage, Rey boasted to Lanh about having a connection capable of arranging the purchase of kilograms of pure cocaine straight out of Panama. I wasn't present to hear the details of his lofty claim, but the talk-induced trafficker had my full attention now.

Rey reiterated that he'd set up deals for others in the past, all of them "mule" trips, advising the client to use "an American or somebody old" to avoid suspicion and smuggle back no more than five kilos at a time. The price per key varied depending upon the existing market conditions in Panama, but usually ranged between two and three thousand dollars each — a far cry from the $30,000 price tag for one kilo in the Boston metropolitan region. The buyer was responsible for hiring the courier, paying the purchase price and travel expenses, and assuming all the risks connected with the drug's transportation. Rey simply set up the exchange for a fee.

"You got interest?" Rey inquired.

But before Lanh could answer, there was a yell from the parking lot.

"Hey Rey! I need you out here!"

"What they do without me?" Rey sniggered with an inflated sense of self-importance. "Be right back, mon," he said to Lanh, leaving behind the proposition of buying kilos of coke wafting in the air along with the skunky smell of burnt pot.

No sooner had the bay door closed behind him than a high-pitched voice hissed through the stale air from the loft above, its owner obviously someone who didn't care to differentiate between Asian nationalities.

"Yo, Chinaman."

The voice didn't match the body as a dark skinned, bespectacled Dominican wearing a backwards baseball cap and built like a nose tackle lumbered into view. Like so many other drug dealers in Massachusetts, Alex Guerrero had taken advantage of a state system that unwittingly lets some of the bigger fish swim away. Arrested for cocaine trafficking in the North Shore city of Lynn and released on bail with his illegally-gotten gains, he promptly picked up a new identity at the Registry of Motor Vehicles and continued the cycle of distribution elsewhere, specifically the drug-dealing consortium known as Locomotion Auto Repairs.

"You want heroin?" He'd apparently paid attention to Lanh's cover story. "Meet me around the corner in ten minutes."

"Give me twenty," Lanh replied, eager to explore the possibilities, but knowing he needed the extra time to pass the crack exhibit just purchased from Rey to me before taking another snap on the playing field.

"By the way, I can get you a better price on the rock, too."

An audible called by the nose tackle in quintessential, cutthroat fashion.

Lanh left the garage, uttering a farewell to Rey who was under the hood of a car with another drug dealer, and walked down Oread in the opposite direction of Main. Far enough away not to be heard, he started barking to me through the Kel.

"Hey! You hear me? He want bring me to heroin! You pick me up! Hey! You hear me? You pick me up!"

Turning off Oread onto Beacon Street, the informant saw the already parked Lexus and lackadaisically made his approach. He stopped and furtively gazed around, then quickly ducked into the government vehicle, lying down on the back seat.

"Go! Go!"

I hit the gas while spitting out instructions to surveillance over the air. One unit was directed to meet me at the "safe site," a predetermined location to discreetly coordinate operations and effect law enforcement functions, while the rest of the team was told to remain in place around the garage and prepare for a takeaway.

After chemically field-testing the drug exhibit to ensure it wasn't sham, and searching the informant to safeguard the buy's integrity, I raced back to Beacon. No sooner had the backdoor slammed shut, than a sporty Mazda RX-7 turned off Oread and pulled up to where the little guy had just been deposited. I watched in the rearview mirror while driving away knowing there wasn't a second to spare.

A heavily tinted window hummed open to reveal the nose tackle's full, fleshy face.

"Let's get something straight before we start this thing. This is just between you and me. Rey doesn't need to know we're working together. Got it?"

With a nod of the informant's head reciprocated by a rapacious smile, the pact was signed. Lanh got into the car borrowed off the Locomotion lot and the Mazda sped off, closely followed by a conga line of trailing surveillance units.

Followed to Chandler Street on the outskirts of Main South, the Mazda turned into an expansive, fenced-in parking lot filled with vehicles in various states of repair or alteration, as the automotive underbelly of Worcester's wide world of drugs broadened. Lanh was introduced to the owner of David's Auto Repairs, who just like the nose tackle, had a Massachusetts driver's license saying he was somebody else. But it really didn't matter what name he used. Everybody on the street still referred to the slick Puerto Rican trafficker by his well-deserved nickname, which in Spanish means "skinny" or "the thin one."

"Flaco."

* * *

After yet another overachieving buy operation in Worcester — this one opening the door to a cocaine trafficking route from Panama, exposing a third Main South drug dealing garage and identifying a local network of heroin distributors — I met with the surveillance team behind a gas station on Chandler to collect their notes before setting off on the fifty-mile trek into Boston to process the evidence.

On Main destined for the Mass Pike, I began to hear the sounds of sirens wailing in the distance; a cacophony of warble and whoop that gradually grew louder until two Worcester police cars came into view from the opposite direction I was heading. I pulled the Lexus to the curb, giving the emergency vehicles wide berth as they screamed past me. Not far behind them two more cruisers rapidly approached, their sirens also crying out in ear-piercing pain.

Something big is happening.

The screeching of tires drew my attention to the side view mirror, as the police cars that had just gone by me abruptly stopped and reversed course. My eyes then refocused forward when I heard the two trailing units coming to a skidding halt. The driver of the first car on the opposite side of the street jumped out with a shotgun in hand and racked one into the chamber. His partner and the two officers in the car behind them also emerged with handguns drawn.

All four weapons were aimed at me.

The intimidating sight and terrifying sound of the shotgun being loaded demanded my full attention. It's an effective control device, not one I ever expected to experience from the wrong end of the barrel. But what really worried me was the officer holding the gun. Weapon wedged into his shoulder and forefinger poised inside the trigger guard, his whole body visibly shook. There was a gritty determination on the cop's face that said he was summoning all the courage he could muster to overcome the fear he was feeling.

I was scared, too, but remained calm. Outwardly at least. In no position to ask why I was facing a firing squad, I placed my hands on the dashboard, palms up, explicitly showing them what I'd demanded others to do so many times in my own career.

There is no weapon in my hands.

A set of verbal commands was issued, but a spacey, floating feeling filled my head and froze my body. I dared not make a move thinking it might be taken the wrong way, remaining perfectly still for what felt like an eternity, but was only a matter of seconds, my gaze fixated on Shaky Jake and the quivering shotgun. Then the driver's side door opened, someone from behind me, and a pair of hands made an extraction in well-executed felony stop fashion.

I was dragged out of the car and thrown onto the trunk of my government vehicle, held there while another officer conducted a pat down. When I raised my head and looked up, I saw that a large, inner-city crowd had amassed and was watching the show. Behind the horde of gawking spectators, I noticed the cross-street sign.

Oread.

Then I saw him.

Standing in the crowd was Rey Barnes.

And then it hit me.

The ounce of crack he'd just sold to Lanh was inside the Lexus.

I had no idea what the hell was happening or why I was part of it — although the thought did cross my mind that the district attorney's dislike for DEA might have something to do with it — but I knew what had to be done right there and then.

"I'm a DEA agent," I whispered to the officer holding me down. "My creds are in the inside pocket of my jacket." Feeling a slight release of pressure, I quickly added: "Don't let me up! You've got to place me under arrest! If you openly verify who I am in front of all these people, you'll blow an ongoing investigation!"

The cop was stunned but remained cool. Using my jacket as a shield, he examined the US Department of Justice photo ID and the gold badge etched in cobalt blue that declared, "Drug Enforcement Administration Special Agent." He was confused — that made two of us. Nevertheless, he cuffed me behind my back and forcefully folded my long, lanky body into the backseat of an idling patrol car.

The surreal scene continued when I asked the cop if he minded grabbing a black bag in the Lexus that contained an ounce of crack and my handgun. *How I could have thought about chain of custody at such a moment, I don't know.* With shocked silence, the cop complied, and then without any further delay, I was transported into Worcester Police Headquarters.

Chapter 2

"A Little Piece of the Dead Zone"

October/November 1994

During the mid-1980s and lasting the better part of a decade, the "Crack Wars" were fought on the streets of America. At the heart of these campaigns was the freebase form of cocaine that crackles when heated and smoked (hence the name), a far more potent and faster acting illicit drug than its powdered cousin. Feeling an intense but short-lasting euphoria, users tried to recapture that initial sense of bliss immediately after the first high faded. But the brain couldn't keep up with demand. Subsequent "hits" increased in size and frequency, resulting in a sliding scale of diminished returns rather than a return to pure nirvana. Binging for days without sleep, addiction came fast, as did psychosis, hallucinations, bizarre, violent behavior, and death.

Death was a side effect for the other half of the crack equation, too, as warring organizations viciously fought for control of lucrative distribution points. This dark era of drugs and violence produced many battlefield casualties, none greater than in New York City, where according to the Disaster Center's Crime Rate Statistics from 1987 to 1994, the homicide numbers ballooned to average more than 2,300 murders per year. Of the city's seventy-seven precincts, the 75th, which primarily covers the East New York section of Brooklyn, had the dubious distinction of recording the most murders during this time span. With an annual homicide rate that exceeded yearly totals of entire countries, it ignominiously came to be known worldwide as "The Killing Fields," "Murder Capital of New York," and "The Dead Zone."

Milton Morales was one of many crack dealers who'd staked a claim in

Brooklyn's 75th, taking advantage of a booming new market by establishing a prosperous distribution point on Fulton Street. Often armed with a handgun to protect himself and his property, he had a reputation for violence and the resume to back it up. With three separate felony convictions for armed robbery, possession of a firearm, and drug distribution, he qualified as a career criminal before reaching the tender age of twenty-one.

Morales' brother, "Joey" Negron, also dealt drugs. But unlike his hard-charging sibling, he worked as a street peddler for the Santiago organization, a powerful, Queens-based band of Colombian brothers — supposedly seventeen in all. When Joey got arrested on the job, his employer promised to financially support him and his family for however long he remained in jail. It must have given the loyal foot soldier some measure of comfort ... the only problem was they didn't follow through. Either the Santiagos reneged on their promise or followed through on their lie, but the empty vow kept Joey's mouth shut long enough for them to make adjustments and render anything their weak-willed employee might tell the cops useless.

The Santiago brothers probably thought they'd covered all the bases, but they overlooked or underestimated another who also valued brotherly bonds. Screwing Joey may have been okay with the Colombians, but it infuriated Joey's brother Milton, whose revenge started a Hatfield/McCoy-like family feud ... Brooklyn style.

On June 19, 1992, Morales gunned down Angel Santiago in the confines of the 75th Precinct. It was the opening salvo in a conflict without conscience; the first move in a chess game of extreme indifference to human life, where pieces are silenced on the street rather than toppled and taken off the board.

Everybody knew that nobody messed with the Santiago boys and got away with it, so before the stunned Colombian family could make the next move on the big board, Morales preempted it by moving himself and his wife out of Brooklyn. It was a strategic defense, but not one that meant he was sacrificing his profits. Designating one of his workers to run the show during his hiatus, the crack boss continued making money while stealthily sneaking in and out of the borough to oversee the business he'd built up over the years.

The Santiagos' anger turned into frustration when they failed to find and eliminate their new number one enemy, so the organization pursued a different path of retaliation. Deducing the worker known as "Bocho" to be nothing more than a point guard for an absentee property owner, they figured if they couldn't kill Morales, at least they could kill his livelihood.

Bocho was murdered and the Santiagos took over the Fulton Street point.

The Colombians may have felt the score was settled, but the bloody takeover only poured fuel onto the white-hot fire burning within Milton Morales. With the silent swiftness of a jackal, the point-stripped crack dealer tracked down and snuffed out Javier Santiago.

Two down, fifteen to go.

The remaining brothers widened the net for their elusive antagonist by enlisting the aid of their expansive network, issuing $100,000 contracts on the lives of Morales *and* his wife.

Meanwhile, the guy whose betrayal inspired this eye-for-an-eye feud was released from prison. Joey Negron needed to make some money but knew he couldn't go back to working for the diminishing Santiago clan. Hooking up with a couple of old associates, Joshua Torres and Nicholas Libretti, the trio hatched a scheme to make a quick buck. But their plan backfired, leading to a most depraved crime, even by New York City standards.

Joey and Libretti abducted a young woman by the name of Kimberly Antonakos from the driveway of her Brooklyn home, threw her into the trunk of a car and took her to an abandoned building, where she was bound in the basement and left alone without food, water, or warmth in the dead of winter. Torres, an old acquaintance of Kimberly's who believed her family was wealthy, anonymously called her father to demand ransom, but when no one answered, he left a brief message with demands on the answering machine. Or so he thought … Torres finished speaking before the machine started recording.

After three days without a reply, the kidnappers returned to the vacant house to check on Kimberly. They found her dead. In an effort to hinder identification that might possibly connect them to the crime, they doused the body with gasoline and lit a match. However, the bungling trio had erred again. It was later concluded by a forensic pathologist that the victim was still alive when set on fire.

Kimberly burned to death.

The murder received widespread news coverage that outraged a city already reeling with homicidal numbness. This worried Joey; he didn't want to spend the rest of his life behind bars. Believing arrest inevitable, he decided to turn himself in and cooperate against the others in the hope of receiving a lesser sentence. But before acting on his intentions, he was confronted by a suspicious Torres. Whatever Joey said to him, he didn't like.

Joey Negron was murdered.

Joey may have avoided being the next victim in a family feud, but he couldn't escape the web of death spun in the Murder Capital of New York. Milton Morales, Joey's stealthy little brother continued to elude the Santiago organization, but he was still at war with the Colombian family, biding his time for the right moment to whack another brother. The distribution point he'd worked so hard to establish in Brooklyn was gone, but the enterprising crack dealer was able to carve out a new piece of territory in a different city.

Worcester, Massachusetts.

A little piece of the Dead Zone had come to town.

* * *

I've been in the back seat of a police car many times before, but never in handcuffs. As a local cop in New Jersey for eight years, I sat beside prisoners in cageless cruisers to prevent the driver from being head-butted; struggled to control drunk or drug crazed detainees trying to kick out windows; stopped during transport to "double-lock" hastily applied cuffs at the scene of a crime, thus preventing further tightening when true squelches of pain echoed in that enclosed chamber from cold metal biting into sensitive flesh and bone. Before every shift and after every arrest, I disjointed that back bench from its frame, at times finding tiny bags of drugs, razor blades, or other small, incriminating items dislodged and ditched before discovery during a more comprehensive bodily search at the station. A new experience with a different perspective was added to the list the day I was transported into Worcester Police Headquarters.

When the cruiser arrived at the rear of the station, I was guided out of the backseat and freed from my restraints. The still stunned "arresting officer" escorted me into the building, a Brutalist-style slab of concrete, where an ornery elevator took us up a few flights to the Vice & Narcotics squad room, a bleak, sprawling space filled with well-worn wooden desks, none of which were occupied, as all the drug detectives were out on the street at the start of a new shift. A year had passed since I'd last set foot in that room. Yet despite the staleness of time, the unpalatable taste of betrayal stirred fresh in my mind.

"Wait here for the lieutenant," sternly instructed the officer after conferring with someone on the phone. It was a scolding directive, as if given to a student brought into the principal's office for some schoolyard infraction. I was then left alone to ponder my punishment for a yet unexplained transgression.

I took a seat at a desk and tried to get an outside line on an internal phone system to notify my supervisor in Boston. A nervous twitch or an itchy finger and the notification could have come from someone other than me about an incident of friendly fire. With all the options in front of me, for some reason I chose a desk displaying the nameplate of one of the detectives who'd doublecrossed me back in 1993. I hung up when the door to a private office on the far side of the room opened and the lieutenant in charge of the unit's night shift came out.

Slightly hunched by age and a few extra pounds put on over the years, Lieutenant Phil Dussault still moved with the spryness of a rookie. His silver topped, bespectacled face had an avuncular quality — kind looking, the type who'd big-heartedly give his sister's son a quarter for penny candy at the corner store. It was etched with many deep lines of experience, each one surely telling a tale about a long career fighting crime and the politics of Worcester County.

He calmly explained why I was in this predicament. A citizen had reported that a group had gathered around a Lexus behind a gas station on Chandler; banal at first blush, until one of them took off his jacket and displayed a holstered handgun. Thinking it a prelude to an armed robbery, the concerned citizen called 911, but before any of the responding units arrived, the group dispersed in different vehicles. The caller couldn't say which car the guy with the gun left in, but he gave a description of my G-car as it turned onto Main Street.

"That's our story. What's yours?" the veteran squad leader sharply concluded; his facial kindness replaced by a steely stare that thinly veiled an inner fury.

As though transported through a portal of time, my mind raced back to the post-op meet after the crack buy from Rey at Locomotion Auto Repairs and the introduction to Flaco at David's Auto Repairs. There was a palpable excitement about the day's success, notably from a young Metropolitan District Commission Police (MDC) detective, who'd just participated in his first surveillance after his unit was invited into the case. Suddenly, his exuberance morphed into a lack of judgment, as he indiscreetly removed his jacket on the warm, early October afternoon to display a black, high-rise holster framed against his white shirt. I cringed, but refrained from saying something because I couldn't take the chance of offending his department. With no other options on the table, I needed them for state prosecutions.

Without the cooperation of a double-dealing city vice squad and state police unit beholden to the Worcester County DA, I had no avenue for the prosecution of defendants declined by the US attorney's office. In essence, a get out of jail free card for guilty conspirators dipping below the federally drawn violator line. The MDC — a soon to be defunct agency that patrolled state owned properties such as parks, beaches, and reservoirs, but which also had a unit to investigate drug crimes within those narrowly defined regions of authority — solved that problem for me. In the process of being merged into the Mass State Police — a consolidation that infuriated many "real troopers" — the MDC drug unit had overnight become statewide. With a caseload tried by a broader authority than the county DA — the Massachusetts Attorney General's Office — both the MDC and AG's office were made aware of the problems in Worcester and agreed to work with DEA.

Up until that moment, I thought the end-around was a brilliant call that gave me a wide-open field to run. Tackled from behind by a lack of deconfliction, it was ironic that I was now being grilled by the lieutenant because his own unit couldn't be trusted.

I told him all about the ongoing federal investigation, how it was progressing in several positive directions, providing details about the intelligence, the auto repair shops, the drugs, the guns, the surveillance photos, the recorded tapes — all that good stuff one in the law enforcement business might like to hear. But Lt. Dussault couldn't care less about the case. He just wanted to know one thing.

"Why wasn't the Worcester Police Department told that DEA was in *our city*?"

* * *

Three days later I returned to Worcester Police Headquarters, this time driving myself there in the company of my supervisor, Doug Ross. Lt. Dussault had set up a meeting between the two agencies, a "summit" he called it, which hinted that a diplomatic resolution to hostilities was possible. The Worcester County DA had already expressed his feelings to the DEA special agent in charge, a measured leader who oversaw operations in the six-state region, acrimoniously accusing the feds of "sneaking" into his territory. However, he did nothing to influence whatever direction the city police decided to go. The case was now too significant to quash without risking possible political repercussions with his constituency.

Both sides aired out the good, the bad and the ugly, and when the dust settled, an agreement was struck stipulating a liaison from each drug unit shift would be designated to coordinate case activities with DEA. It wasn't that the Vice Squad wanted to conduct a joint investigation with the feds — it was more of a *'we want to keep an eye on you'* pact, which was better than the *'get the hell of our city'* response I expected to hear.

The détente didn't bode well with detectives in the drug unit, who resented being forced into working with DEA — and particularly the cause of the distasteful directive — me. Deciding to take a path of least resistance by having a neutral face deal directly with the disgruntled group, not to mention being overwhelmed with work when the third garage popped up in the investigation, I sought out the help of another agent in my group.

"Brian" was relatively new to the Boston office after graduating from the DEA Academy in Quantico. The former Vermont state trooper, who still looked like one with his clean-cut, square jawed good looks, high and tight haircut, and powerful, perfectly postured build, had a positive attitude and respectful bedside manner from being raised the right way. He was itching to get involved in a case beyond that of a supportive role, so when presented with the opportunity to spearhead a splintered probe into Flaco's crew at David's Auto Repairs, he jumped at the chance. Gung-ho but methodical were the best descriptors of my new partner, whose hard work and fast results not only impressed the drug unit's reluctant liaisons, but also a leery Lanh, who didn't feel trust was an automatically transferrable thing.

With the nose tackle from Locomotion Auto Repairs vouching for the little guy's criminal righteousness, Lanh made a couple of one-ounce heroin buys from Flaco and his flunky, a wily character known as "Bibi." Brian quickly identified the dope's source of supply, a Dominican who called himself "Javier," although his Massachusetts driver's license said his first name was something else. He owned the Caribbean Express restaurant on Harrison Street in Worcester, which was also known as the Latin Taste Palace.

Even the bad guys' businesses had aliases.

Flaco ran a multi-faceted criminal enterprise that included the distribution of heroin, crack, and stolen firearms (it seemed every drug dealer in Main South also sold guns), along with the installation of vehicular hides to facilitate the movement of these illicit products and the money generated from their sales. His secret compartments ranged from a simple attachment behind the glovebox to electronically activated, hydraulic chambers secreted anywhere within the body's framework. The more sophisticated the hide, the greater the status symbol of achievement in the underworld of drug trafficking.

Flaco had been made aware of Lanh's cover story of running a fledgling drug distribution business in Lowell. The nose tackle had unwittingly acted on DEA's behalf by relaying Lanh's alleged resume. Flaco was also given insider information about how much Rey Barnes charged the little guy for crack supposedly sold in Lowell, intelligence that allowed Flaco to undercut the competition. When the skinny garage owner proposed the sale of a higher quality crack product at a better price than what Rasta Rey sold, then offered up one of two AK-47 assault rifles or a .45 caliber submachine gun he currently had in stock, the table was set for DEA's next course of action.

* * *

DEA informants are required by written agreement to testify in court if needed, but it's always preferable to have an agent or an officer on the stand. Credibility is the obvious reason, most informants having sordid backgrounds and/or self-serving motives for cooperating with the government. Not all informants are liars, which is what defense attorneys would have every judge and jury believe. Being a lawbreaker in life doesn't automatically mean you're not telling the truth in court. Nevertheless, discrediting an informant's integrity is the easiest way and often the only plausible defense that leads to a guilty client's acquittal.

Lanh wasn't your typical informant. In fact, he was an aberration. Whether picking apples in a Canadian orchard — his last job before recruitment by the RCMP — or intrepidly infiltrating a dangerous drug organization, the little guy performed his duties with dignity and honor. He took pride in his work, no matter how lowly that work was portrayed by some, once telling a defense attorney in court that any job worked hard and done honestly is a "noble" one. His principles were pure, and unlike most of his contemporaries who came with a lot of baggage, he didn't have a criminal history to provide ammunition to a sharpshooting legal mouthpiece. Still, attempts to impugn his truthfulness would be fired at him point blank, often as he endured the derogatory label of "rat" along with its profiling presumptions.

* * *

No advanced notice was given...the dark- colored undercover car that blended into the drabness of the day entered through the only access to David's Auto Repairs, a gap in an eight-foot high, chain-link fence with two-feet of barbed wire strung across the top. This security measure, bordering Chandler Street, stretched the length of the sidewalk between two brick buildings. An opened, hinged gate, which was a section of the fence padlocked shut during off-hours, was propped flat against a sidewall belonging to one of those anchoring buildings; a business that colorfully advertised itself on that exposed sidewall façade as a seller of copy machines and office furniture.

Neither operative in the car was wired up, nor did they have any money to make a buy. It was simply a meet and greet. No sense risking a pat-down discovery during an introduction. The timing of their arrival was anything but serendipitous. Surveillance, which had been set up on the shop for the past two hours, radioed that Flaco had just arrived a few minutes earlier.

Lanh emerged from the car with the first of several undercovers he'd weave into the case. Born and raised in the Dominican Republic before immigrating to America, the MDC detective was in great demand for these dangerous assignments in a field dominated by Spanish-speaking traffickers. His teddy bear body and amiable face — more prototype of a plush, life-sized FAO Schwarz toy than stereotype of a rough and tumble inner-city drug dealer — could win over the toughest crowd in the worst neighborhoods. Flaco and his flunky, Bibi, came out of the garage, where Lanh introduced "Jonny" as the partner from Lowell he had told them about.

The undercover's gregarious nature brightly shone no matter what language he used, but Jonny toggled his tongue to a more familiar taste and began raving about the quality of Flaco's *Manteca,* Spanish slang for heroin. Once finished solidifying the background foundation poured by the informant, Jonny then built upon it by saying that without his established client base in Lowell, Lanh, a newcomer in the city, didn't have the wherewithal to put Flaco's high-purity product on the street. Jonny's cordial confidence bordered on polite swagger with the well-timed, infectious smile of a mischievous child.

Talking about drug quality is risky business. A supplier knows his product and if somebody says an overly stepped-on, diluted compound is good stuff, he's either out of his league, or a cop pretending to be someone he's not. But Jonny spoke with confidence because DEA's Northeast Lab in New York had analyzed the previous buys from Flaco and determined each contained a high percentage of pure heroin hydrochloride.

"I understand you sell the rock, too," Jonny probed, segueing onto the next phase of the Op-Plan. "How about we do some bigger business together? Say, start off with an ounce of Manteca and two of the rock. I can be ready early next week." He then rubbed his fingers together looking for a price.

Up until then Bibi contained his general disdain for Dominicans, a bias exacerbated by one who'd brazenly invaded the sanctity of their little enclave without invitation.

"We'll tell the Chinaman. Have him come back tomorrow...by himself," the Puerto Rican flunky spat out with disgust while further mislabeling Lanh's nationality.

Jonny lifted an eyebrow and tilted his head in mock affront, then his chubby cheeks spread out into a broad smile that downplayed the intended slight. Addressing Flaco, he said he looked forward to doing business with him, but in civil fashion, he shook the hand of *both* traffickers before leaving with Lanh.

The flunky's dead fish grip sealed how he felt about the Dominican undercover.

* * *

"I don't like it ... he looks like a cop," Bibi loathingly announced in English when Lanh returned the next day, his hatred displayed on two levels.

Flaco and his flunky had already discussed the matter, so the declaration was nothing more than posturing meant to elicit a response from Lanh, but the unflappable informant just stared at Bibi as though he was crazy. Flaco looked on with indifference; paranoia and prejudice weren't going to interfere with his secret plan, especially since it was so close to fruition.

Almost a year and a half had passed since Jose "Flaco" Garcia was nabbed red-handed with a kilogram of cocaine, a serious state offense that carried a fifteen-year mandatory-minimum sentence. As if following protocol based upon frequency, he was released on bail, established a new identity through the Registry of Motor Vehicles, and continued the cycle of distribution elsewhere, in his case David's Auto Repairs, where with an alias unstained by criminal history, he registered the garage with the Massachusetts Division of Standards.

Flaco wasn't a fugitive...not yet anyway. Some said his decision to continue dealing in a different section of the same city where he'd been arrested was an audacious one. Others thought it just plain foolish, considering the unnecessary risk. But Flaco was a sly fox. He'd successfully deceived the criminal justice system into believing its decision to release him on bail was a good one. This lengthy hoodwinking was soon to end, proving to the court what a bad decision it had made.

Whereas most bail-jumping defendants skip town and are never seen again, the wily Flaco stuck around as a fugitive-in-waiting. He showed up for all his scheduled pre-trial appointments (under his true name) and had his attorney drag out the legal process by requesting and being granted one court continuance after another. His goal was simple: make as much money as possible from an established clientele in Worcester, then take off for safe haven in Puerto Rico when his delay tactics were exhausted to enjoy the fruits of his criminality. There was no concern about being tracked down, either; it was a well-known fact that the state seldom spent the money to look for drug fugitives beyond the boundaries of its own borders, much less outside the contiguous United States of America.

With a firm trial date looming on the horizon, Flaco had reached that point of no return. He wasn't sticking around to be convicted and sent off to jail. Nobody knew about his scheme — not his flunky, not the nose tackle, and certainly not DEA, who was about to purchase heroin and crack with federal funds from an alias out on state bail.

Bibi wanted nothing to do with the Dominican but was overruled by

Flaco. However, he did get his way on one point: Lanh was instructed to come into the garage by himself to do the deal while Jonny remained in the car. By avoiding a hand-to-hand transaction with a new player who *might* be an undercover, bad guys in general felt protected by the state's limited conspiracy law, rarely considering the possibility of being targeted by a federal agency with more statutory bite.

Of course, the flunky's hunch was right, but even a stopped clock is right twice a day. It was a baseless deduction built upon nothing but bias. To a paranoid drug dealer, everybody looks like a cop when your criminal vision is skewed by a constant fear of being arrested.

It was a narco-neurosis that makes some bad guys walk away rather than take the risk, real or imagined. But Flaco called the shots here. He had no intention of letting Bibi sour his avarice simply because he was seeing ghosts. Nevertheless, I couldn't ignore the possibility it was a warning sign that needed heeding.

* * *

November 29th, 1994

The undercover car slid into the lot at David's Auto Repairs. Jonny maneuvered through helter-skelter rows of customer cars after bearing left around the back of the office equipment business. The front of the multi-bay garage was straight ahead, tucked away in a corner beyond view of the heavily traveled Chandler; the shop shielded from the street by two brick buildings and a spanning stockade fence in front of a grassy area of open space. High, rocky terrain encircled the rest of the property; nature's contribution to a completely secured environment.

Lanh emerged from the passenger seat and moseyed towards the garage, leaving Jonny behind the wheel of the car equipped with a Kel transmitter secreted in its dashboard. Bibi stood out front, in anticipation of their arrival. He instructed the informant to go inside the shop, then remained outside a few seconds longer before joining him, taking a moment to glare with hatred at the Dominican driver.

Flaco wasn't there, only a couple of mechanics working on cars. Bibi made a few phone calls, then told Lanh to sit tight and wait.

The drugs were on the way.

Typical garage — one car on a lift over a floor spewed with tires, rotors, and brake pads. Another with a prone body lying on a blue mat beneath it, an outstretched hand reaching for a toolbox overflowing with wrenches, sockets, and bits. Off to the side stood a filthy utility sink with a bar of Lava soap still dripping foamy remnants of recent grease removal. On the wall a calendar displaying a leggy Latino bombshell from a long-ago month of a bygone year. Blaring from a portable boom box was the pulsating rhythm of salsa music; a bouncy beat that enlivened the otherwise gloomy, cement enclosure.

The surveillance team—strength in extra numbers just in case Bibi influenced an otherwise disinterested Flaco—hunkered down in stationary holes, parked in out-of-the-way spots along the perimeter of the property. The hum of a DEA plane could be heard flying through the crisp, clear skies of a fading fall season. Jonny discreetly relayed his observations to the Kel car, who in turn broadcasted a constant flow of information to the other units; each transmission satisfying a compelling need to know what they couldn't see in person.

Then the transmissions stopped…there was nothing new to report. Like a junkie itching for his next fix, the ground units nervously look elsewhere to fill the informational void, straining to see if a passing car was on the Op-Plan, or a familiar face was spotted in a vehicle that wasn't; all the while keenly aware of their own inner-city surroundings to avoid being spotted themselves. But the airwaves, once vibrant with voices, sometimes stepping on others trying to transmit more material observations, remained silent.

Ten minutes of dead air choked the radio before being resuscitated by the arrival of a brown Mazda Montero, its sole occupant the identified heroin source of supply, Francisco "Javier" Lendor. On its tail as though attached by a tow bar came a blue Jeep, an unfamiliar vehicle that Jonny reported was driven by Flaco. The flurry of sudden activity continued when two unknown Hispanic men walked into the parking lot from Chandler Street. The observant agent in a surveillance car on Chandler, near the entrance gate, gave a full physical description of each suspect from head to toe. He also reported that they'd gotten out of a red Pontiac Grand Prix parked further up the street and announced he was leaving his post to get the plate. Another unit took his place.

Both of the unknown Hispanic arrivals gave a long, hard look at the

Dominican behind the wheel of the UC car as they strode past him to join up with the others inside the garage, which including Lanh, totaled eight. Jonny bravely stared back with the best tough guy gaze he could muster.

When the information on the Grand Prix's plate was broadcast, one of the Worcester Vice detectives shared intel that the registered owner, "Luis Ramos," was a "known player in the city." What he didn't know was the name was now being used by Milton Morales; the adopted alias not intended to protect yet another fugitive released by the state on bail, but to help its user evade the wrath of the remaining fifteen brothers in the rival gang he'd left back in Brooklyn.

Milton Morales would be known by the name Luis Ramos throughout the investigation, just like Flaco was known by his alias, "Jose Negron." But whereas Morales had been given consent to use his pseudonym by his cousin in Worcester, Flaco's was acquired without the owner's permission, perhaps even chillingly for a price. Fortunately, the identity theft wouldn't affect the name's true owner because the real Jose Negron, who was better known as "Joey," didn't need it anymore.

Lanh emerged from the garage with Bibi, Morales, and the murderer's sidekick. He casually ambled towards the undercover car to get the money, while the three bad guys lined up shoulder-to-shoulder in front of the shop like the Clanton gang at the O.K. Corral. The trio focused their sights on the vulnerable driver, who took a gulp of courage and a chaser of reassurance feeling the handgun tucked in his waistband. He dared not move his lips to pass on further information, concerned it might trigger something other than an intimidating stare.

The spotter in the plane relayed what the undercover on the ground couldn't, radioing that Lendor had also come out of the garage. Walking to his Mazda, which was backed up to one of the bays, he lifted the hatch and stretched deep inside the dark recess, only the bottom half of his almost prone body visible from a magnified view high above. Fidgeting with something — deductively an obstinate secret compartment to access the heroin that finally yielded to his will — he shimmied back out and slammed the hatch shut. But instead of returning to the garage to do the deal, he went to the blue Jeep Flaco had arrived in, pulled a key out of his pocket, and started up the sturdy, four-wheel drive vehicle. Driving around the three watchdogs still baring their teeth at Jonny, he zigzagged his way through the littered lot towards the exit.

Lendor wanted to give the impression he had the heroin — a deke used by overly suspicious drug dealers just in case uninvited guests with dangling badges excitedly crashed their little party. Satisfied it wasn't a buy-bust, he was now going to get his part of the deal, switching up vehicles to confuse anybody who might be waiting on the other side of the fence, assuaging that part of his paranoia that still wasn't appeased.

I barked for two units to follow Lendor with a feeling of another overachievement in the making. That the heroin source was about to lead DEA straight to a previously unidentified stash site, or reveal a new co-conspirator, or maybe even both. But like an unscrewed plug beneath a car to do an oil change, the next transmission swiftly drained my optimism.

"Jeep's at the exit...indicating a right turn onto Chandler," matter-of-factly reported the pilot. "Stand by...now he's backing up. Looks like he changed his mind and wants to make a left." A few more confusing back-and-forth movements were relayed before the pilot saw the clarity of what was happening. "All units be aware...the Jeep's blocking the exit!"

Leaving the customer owned Jeep in for repairs at a forty-five-degree angle, which entirely filled the gap in the security fence made by the opened swing arm gate, Lendor had just sealed off the undercover operatives' only means of egress — but not before first grabbing the Colt Cobra revolver stored in the back of his own vehicle.

"Careful ground units! One of the other targets is climbing on the roof of a car in the lot. He's doing counter-surveillance!" A warning from the sky as Bibi mounted another customer's car to get an elevated view of Chandler over the stockade fence.

It's a rip!

My fear was felt by everyone else on the ground, too, as they mentally and physically geared up for action: strapping on bulletproof vests, reaching for raid jackets, one unzipping a nylon carrying case to remove a submachine gun. Each prepared to barnstorm the barricaded property once told to move in. The driver of the biggest vehicle out there, a GMC Yukon recently put into service, offered to lead the attack, using the monster SUV as a battering ram to clear the entrance or create a new one for the rest of the troops. I had my finger on the transmit button and was ready to give the order, but something gave me pause.

I'd prepared for such a contingency; it's one of the reasons for doing an Op-Plan. The Kel car had good reception and the plane a clear, enhanced view of the scene below. Neither the UC nor Lanh had given the prearranged verbal or visual signal for help. A premature reaction might create a crisis that doesn't really exist, increasing the danger level and putting everybody's life in jeopardy.

Don't panic!

"202 to all units...sit tight until I give the word."

By then Lanh had reached the undercover car, handing off an ounce of heroin and two ounces of crack that Flaco had given to him in the garage. With daggered eyes scrutinizing his every move, Jonny got out of the car and slowly drifted to the back of the vehicle, opened the trunk, and exchanged the drugs for a brown paper bag containing $6,100 in cash. He closed the trunk with a little too much force, but there was no reaction from the three watchdogs in front of him, or the sentinel blocking the exit behind him — nor did a crazed Flaco burst from the depths of his concrete bunker with one of those AK-47's he had in stock.

Lanh strolled back to the garage with the casualness of a lazy, summer day and gave the money to Flaco — who confirmed it was all there — then returned to the undercover vehicle, which Jonny drove out of the lot after Bibi gave a signal relayed from Flaco that it was okay to move the Jeep.

Seemed DEA wasn't the only one worried about being ripped off.

The hunt was over without incident.

Now the chase.

First to leave was Lendor in his Mazda. The Jeep he used to clog the exit remained in the lot, its owner never knowing how close it came to needing additional repairs. He made a beeline to his restaurant on Harrison Street — more money to launder through the business.

Next up a yellow Toyota Tercel, taken off the lot of Locomotion Auto Repairs, arrived after its operator received a page. The nose tackle emerged and plodded inside to get a piece of the pie, staying just long enough to collect his commission before returning the borrowed car.

The parade of happy traffickers continued with the departure of Morales and his sidekick, as they walked back out to Chandler and took off in the Grand Prix. When they arrived at Santiago's Market on Main Street (ironic in that it was Morales's goal was to eliminate the name from the Brooklyn phonebook), the crack boss went inside the market/wire remittance outlet while his sidekick waited in the car. I wanted to send someone inside to make observations, but nobody on the team blended into the predominant Hispanic setting.

Coming out empty handed, Morales made a U-turn, cutting off a surveillance car in the process, then sped into downtown Worcester, where he turned right just past City Hall and again reversed direction, reigniting concerns about counter-surveillance. But the fear faded when he stopped in front of a small convenience store and again went inside by himself. Double-parked with the emergency lights flashing, Morales' sidekick drummed on the dash to loud music from the radio. I could feel the vibration of the bass as I drove by in the opposite direction.

Making a U-turn of my own further down the block, I parked the Lexus in a loading zone and hustled into the store. Immediately seeing Morales standing off to my right, I darted left and went down one of the short aisles. Peering through empty spaces on once stocked shelves, I watched as Morales filled out a form taken from a bank of slots at a workstation. Finished, the task-oriented trafficker snatched up his paperwork and got into the checkout line, which prompted me to grab a bag of chips and quickly queue behind him.

Fourth in line, I blended in with the diverse customer mix, yet still felt conspicuous. Almost a foot taller than my target, I dwarfed the crack dealer. But Morales paid no attention to the tall man behind him, whose height advantage provided a clear view of what Morales held in his hand: a utility bill with a Worcester address in the name of "Luis Ramos" and a remittance slip to pay it in cash.

While waiting in line, I considered Morales. He was in his midtwenties, about 5'6", with a slight build and an angular face framed by a light but neatly trimmed goatee and stylishly cut short hair. Contrary to the street thug fashion of the '90s, his attire was GQ-like — black shoes, dress pants, collarless white shirt, black leather jacket and an obvious but not ostentatious gold chain around his neck. Wanting to memorize every facet of his face to make a positive ID in court, which could be more than a year later, I stooped past him to grab a candy bar from the display case below the counter. When I turned back and looked up, we locked eyes. Morales's were dark and void of benevolence; sinister orbs leading to the remorseless soul of a murderer who didn't hesitate to stare me down.

Moving up and sliding his paperwork across the counter, Morales pulled out a wad of cash from his pocket, at least an inch thick, and peeled off a hundred-dollar bill and three twenties. I noticed that some jokester had scribbled "1000" on the hundred. After receiving his change and leaving the store, I absentmindedly tapped my forehead and went back to grab a drink. I watched through the storefront window as Morales got back into the Grand Prix and the duo continued their post-sale adventure. I felt a sense of comfort knowing surveillance was intact when a unit passed by in the same direction seconds later. With no other customers in the store, I returned to the counter and flashed my credentials while identifying myself as a federal agent, only I didn't specify being a DEA agent.

"The man who just left your store may have passed some money without realizing it was counterfeit. May I please see the bills he gave you?"

The cooperative attendant didn't give my request a second thought. "The twenties are already in a drop safe, but I've got the hundred right here," she said waving the doodle-emblazed bill. "I was just about to give it a test before dropping it, too. I don't have access to the safe to get the other bills, but I can call someone down who does."

"Well, actually, it's only the hundred I'm interested in." I was making this up as I went along. "The people we're looking at only do fifties and hundreds. I'd like to take that bill off your hands in exchange for good currency. Are you okay with that?"

The attendant was more than okay with my proposal, probably thinking I was just going to seize the bill as evidence and she's out a C-note.

"Would you like a copy of that man's paperwork? I have a copy machine in the back."

She must have read my mind. "I don't think it would be helpful. He has nothing to do with the investigation, but just to be on the safe side, yes, thank you."

After uttering something about confidentiality and thanking her for her cooperation, I returned to the Lexus and retrieved the money list from my black bag. Spreading out the handwritten sheets from the buy at David's Auto Repairs on the passenger seat alongside the hundred-dollar bill, I scanned the serial numbers looking for a match. Literally following the money, I hoped to find proof beyond a reasonable doubt that the relocated contributor to Brooklyn's appalling Dead Zone murder statistics was now Flaco's crack source of supply.

Halfway down the second sheet of serial numbers, I stopped searching, lifted my head, and gazed out the windshield across downtown Worcester. Holding the perfectly fitted piece of the puzzle, which when interlocked with others in the grid of a complex conspiracy would depict the picture of a safer city, I permitted myself the indulgence of a smile. The recovered bill's serial number was on the list.

Chapter 3

"Locomotion Engineers"

December 1994

Rodolfo "Rudy" Matos was the quiet one in an otherwise brazen bunch of outlaws, hanging out with the other traffickers most days while tacitly abetting their revolving door activities, but always leaving the open-air atmosphere of the garage whenever doing his own deals. Fact is, the taciturn Dominican preferred not being there at all, but did so to promote his high-end business and recruit qualified, new customers. The distribution center had become well known in the Main South neighborhood, and there was enough clientele to satisfy all the associates at the firm.

Unlike some of his bail-released, fugitive colleagues, Rudy Matos didn't need an alias. Not yet anyway. With a valid resident alien card by way of marriage to a US citizen, he was unencumbered by the anxiety of hiding behind a fictitious name, but still moved cautiously as a high-level heroin wholesaler with a financially capable customer base. Rudy earned his clients' business by offering a uniquely packaged and powerfully pure product, and their trust by not exposing them to the circus-like environment of Locomotion Auto Repairs.

Rudy watched as Rey Barnes sold ounces of crack to the Vietnamese with the Canadian connection and heard them talking about a major cocaine deal in Panama. He knew the nose tackle was surreptitiously getting Lanh heroin and crack through Flaco at David's Auto Repairs. He saw the gun-slinging owner of NV Auto Body stumble in from next door to get coke to cook at a discounted price after bringing Lanh into the fold. He even overheard the in-house marijuana distributor talking to Lanh about doing pound weight together. Enough dope and cash had passed hands without any of them being arrested or ripped off.

Matos decided the time had come to make Lanh the newest member of his exclusive drug-buying club, yet something still caused him to worry. Perhaps it wasn't really worry he felt, but fear of what the biggest heroin trafficker in the city would do to him if he recruited anybody who proved to be disingenuous. Working for an interstate kingpin with a penchant for violence will have that kind of effect on you.

Rudy made his move when nobody else was in the garage, the others outside working on cars or conducting some type of illegal activity, slipping a piece of paper with his number on it to Lanh while whispering, "call me but no say nothing to Rey," then quickly leaving the shop as though fleeing the scene of a crime, which in essence, that's exactly what he was doing.

Dealers poaching drug customers from each other seemed to be a common occurrence at Locomotion.

Matos and Lanh met the next morning at the same Dunkin' Donuts where I'd first seen Lanh crouching at the curb in a coffee klatch a few months earlier. But despite pulling the trigger to recruit the little guy, Rudy remained gun shy about selling him heroin until acquiring a little more confidence in the customer. He opted first to do one or two crack deals from a different source before going to the Big Man for his potent powder.

Rudy picked up Lanh in a blue Mazda acquired as payment from a delinquent customer in Lawrence — another old New England mill town just south of the New Hampshire border — and drove to an apartment building on Svea Street in the Vernon Hills section of Worcester. Directed by Rudy to wait in the car while he went inside the building, Lanh took advantage of the opportunity by rifling through the Mazda's glove box and transmitting his findings to me via the Kel. It wasn't something I'd instructed him to do, but the intelligence seeking informant had a propensity for impulsive behavior in places where he shouldn't be — like outside a drug stash house in a bad guy's car after being told *not* to leave the Dunkin' Donuts in the first place.

A few minutes passed before Rudy came back out with an ounce of crack and the Mazda was on the move again.

"You live here?" probed the disobedient informant.

Rudy chuckled. Apparently thinking himself clever, he disclosed paying the rent for a relative to live in one of the apartments, only to use it with a spare key to do drug deals while she was out working a legitimate job. It appeared a quick grand from a smooth transaction had boosted his trust in Lanh, which prompted the trafficker to move up his timetable.

"I can do heroin, too. Best in city."

"My people want," Lanh shot back. He, like Rudy, spoke in fragmented English, each more accustomed to a different primary language. "What price you sell per gram?"

"I gotta check, boss," Rudy replied while turning back into the Dunkin' Donuts lot. "You want a sample? I get one Colombian, one African. Let's go!"

I cursed out loud within the confines of my G-car. Traversing the city for heroin with a just purchased crack exhibit was not part of the Op-Plan. But the expletive-filled outburst ceased when my pre-buy instructions about not going anywhere apparently kicked in.

"You get! I meet you here, two hour!" Lanh shot back in his demanding style. No sooner had the Mazda left, than the little guy started barking out orders to me through the Kel.

"He go get heroin. You follow! He in blue Mazda. You follow! I walk down street. You pick me up! Hey, you hear me!? You pick me up!"

Surveillance tailed Rudy to an apartment complex in the Webster Square section of the city, a sprawling development of mixed income residential buildings sitting at the edge of a forest sanctuary known as "God's Acre." Matos entered one of the buildings with an Outlook Drive address, dialed the pager number he knew by heart, and when prompted by the *beep-beep-beep*, punched in his home number followed by his assigned ID code, hit the pound sign, heard *beep-beep-beep-beep*, hung up and waited for a return call.

Message sent.

Surveillance hunkered down for almost two hours, watching a door that didn't open and/or waiting for a car that never came, until Rudy suddenly burst out of the building and sprinted towards the Mazda. He ran right past an agent sitting in his car, who quickly ditched his portable radio beneath the seat and acted like another resident, warming up his car on the brutally cold day. Clearly a man on a mission, the oblivious drug dealer sped off.

Lanh was already waiting for his arrival outside the Dunkin' Donuts, but Rudy first had to meet someone else by Clark University, a private liberal arts school located smack dab in the middle of Main South. He pulled the

Mazda to the curb on the Florence Street side of the high-priced, beautifully maintained, campus—an urban oasis within a desert of harsh living, where non-college residents committed to its hardscrabble outskirts struggle to survive.

As the idling car spewed exhaust fumes visible in the frigid winter air, Rudy watched for his connection … while surveillance watched Rudy. Groups of students wearing goose down parkas or insulated ski jackets, some stylishly unzipped despite the weather, and big trendy scarves strategically draped around their necks, strolled by the car, but none paid any attention to the vehicle parked on the border between privileged and poor.

When Rudy saw the red Buick Electra coming from the opposite direction, he rolled down his window. A bitter blast of cold air invaded the warm cabin as the arriving vehicle sidled up to the Mazda, driver's side to driver's side. It was just like two cops meeting to share a cup of coffee, only these two were sharing something much stronger. The delivery boy reached out and stuffed the sample into Rudy's outstretched hand, then both cars drove off in different directions, neither operator uttering a word during the seemingly routine exchange.

Rudy went straight to the Dunkin' Donuts, where he gave a free sample of Colombian heroin to Lanh with the promise of Nigerian-trafficked heroin later that night. It was a tiny amount of powder in a twist-tied piece of plastic, dispensed with the same promotional logic as a toothpick speared sample of food in your supermarket aisle.

Try it and you'll buy some.

Somehow, one unit kept up with the speeding Buick, whose driver apparently felt free to do so without an arrestable substance to slow him down, following it to a large, wraparound lot in downtown Worcester, where the delivery boy parked the car and entered the ten-story Clarion Suites Hotel. Surveillance was terminated at that time, but Rudy followed through on his promise by giving a second free sample of heroin to Lanh later that night.

Below the banality of these typical surveillance observations laid the most prolific heroin organization ever seen in the City of Worcester. In a relatively short period of time, a nebulous character known only as "El Gordo" had put a stranglehold on the old mill town's heroin market. Little was known about this kingpin; even the Vice Squad's intelligence guru, Richie Burgos, who had his finger on the pulse of the Hispanic community, couldn't provide specifics. Either his reliable sources didn't have the knowledge, or self-preservation told them not to share it.

It seemed that fear of losing your life if you opened your mouth served well for Gordo. And as I would discover, that fear was not unfounded.

* * *

The College of the Holy Cross, one of nine institutions of higher learning within Worcester city limits, sits high atop a steep hill with a panoramic view of the city below. The elevated setting, with its interlacing lots and plenty of parking, had become DEA's latest "safe site" after others at a lower altitude were compromised. No drug deals were ever conducted on school grounds; DEA only sought sanctuary for a bunch of cops to meet before and after operations without curious or criminal eyes undermining its mission.

Three minutes after paging Rudy and three hours prior to meeting him for the next buy, the payphone mounted on the wall in the hallway of the Hogan Campus Center rang. I depressed the play/record button on the tape recorder, a wired listening device suction-cupped to the phone's receiver, and with my wide wingspan obscuring the view of students hustling out for morning classes or drifting in for coffee in the cafeteria, motioned Lanh to answer the call.

"What your boss say?" Lanh couldn't be bothered tendering a 'hello'.

"We good…one big one, one small one, but no can do better on big one," Rudy responded.

Lanh expressed displeasure when told the cost for an ounce of heroin would be a flat $4,300, which at more than four times the price for the equivalent weight of crack, prompted Rudy to refer to it as the bigger of the two. Rudy apologized, explaining his boss was the one who set the prices, not him, but added with a salesman's flair that their product was so pure it could be cut several times over for a greater profit margin.

Begrudgingly, Lanh accepted the inflated price tag for the heroin, but then made a new request, one I hoped was also outside Rudy's realm of control.

"I have money for another small one. Can you do?"

The uptick in the order was designed to learn more about Rudy's crack source of supply, who the diversified drug dealer said was someone other than his heroin boss. Chances were good that Rudy would act on the intelligence gathering maneuver, that he'd reach out to his supplier and try his best to be a little more customer friendly, especially after failing to come through with a better price for the heroin.

Putting another grand in his pocket didn't hurt the odds, either.

"I see what I can do."

The court order we'd gotten from a federal judge for Rudy Matos's phone didn't authorize the interception of conversations. But it did allow using a "pen register" for the recording of dial pulses, which would have identified outgoing numbers called and the time of incoming calls. Unfortunately, the DEA Tech Unit hadn't gotten out to Worcester to hook up the device. Frustratingly, the unit's lack of urgency wasn't an anomaly.

Surveillance was already set up on Rudy's apartment in anticipation of movement, but once again after hours of watching and waiting, nobody came or went. As the eleven o'clock meet time neared, Lanh, wired up and carrying cash for the deal, meandered into the Dunkin' Donuts lot and crouched at the curb. Simultaneously, Rudy came out of his Outlook Drive apartment building and took off in his Mazda — not the blue one used during the last deal, but a white one courtesy of a liberty-taking loaner policy at Locomotion — and drove directly to the double D's. Since he hadn't connected with anyone first, it appeared Rudy's crack source of supply couldn't swing the last-minute request.

"Hop in," the Dominican dealer said when he arrived at the meet location.

"Remember what I told you...don't leave that parking lot! That's a lot of money you're carrying. Tell him to go get the stuff and come back to you. Don't go anywhere!"

"Okay."

The Mazda was tailed a little tighter than I'd like but losing an off-script CI with over six-grand in government funds is how an Office of Professional Responsibility (OPR) investigation begins...or a free-spirited informant's life ends. Rudy, on the other hand, followed the Op-Plan, making a beeline straight for the Vernon Hills Neighborhood and his stash pad on Svea St.

Just shy of the intended destination, all units were told to break off and start setting up for a new takeaway. With an agent already camped out in the apartment building's parking lot, there was no need for the rest of the team to tag along with the target vehicle when it turned onto the dead-end street. No sooner had the transmission been sent, than Rudy put a wrinkle in his anticipated route by suddenly veering into a different lot and stopping the car.

I was right behind the Mazda in my G-car with Richie Burgos. Territorial tensions easing and trust taking hold, the Vice Squad detective and I found ourselves working as one more and more. We continued straight ahead while warning the other units about the counter-surveillance move. Richie knew of a back entrance into the lot, so I squared the block and snaked around the contours of a large "T" shaped apartment building until the Mazda came into sight. Squeezing the Lexus between two SUVs with its back end facing the rear of the Mazda provided good cover, as I watched through the side view mirror while Richie contorted his body to peer out the back window. Looking for surveillance cars on Vernon Street through his front windshield, Rudy paid no attention to the camouflaged one behind him.

The Mazda was parked in a section of the lot occupied by few other cars. Angled across two white-lined spaces, Rudy had an unobstructed view of the street, making it impossible for any unit to set up on Vernon without being noticed. He was "cleaning himself," a term that always made me think of my cat, looking for repetitive-appearing cars to confirm his suspicion of being followed. I made it clear that everybody should avoid the street altogether.

"What we do here?" Lanh asked Rudy, his voice cracking the transmitted silence through the bulky, hard cased Kel receiver sitting on Richie's lap.

"We wait," the crafty Dominican curtly responded while continuing to stare.

For several minutes thereafter, only the whining noise of passing car tires on the roadway surface was heard. Then Rudy spoke again.

"See that brown Thunderbird? Second time..."

Shit!

"Anybody out there driving a brown T-Bird?" I radioed.

"10-4," quickly replied one of the other units.

DEA agents are taught to exercise self-restraint in secondary surveillance roles, relying upon the eye of another to provide them with vision. Nevertheless, the urge to see what's going on with your own two eyes is strong. Sometimes well-trained agents lose focus, or law enforcement partners with little surveillance experience make rookie mistakes.

"You're burnt. The target just saw you for the second time. Find a position outside the perimeter and keep out of sight. Once we start moving again, stay at the tail end."

"Received," dejectedly replied the banished operator.

Everybody else waited in place hoping Rudy would shrug off his suspicions and shuttle on to his stash, when a red Toyota Forerunner pulled into the parking lot and stopped several car lengths in front of the Mazda. Rudy opened his door as a loud '*ding, ding, ding*' was heard through the Kel.

"There he is…you wait here," Rudy instructed Lanh, as he got out of the Mazda and started walking towards the Forerunner.

"Oh my God! Do you know whose truck that is!?" Richie rhetorically asked. "That's Julio Santana's!"

"Who's he?" I asked.

"Who's he!? He only owns the biggest money wiring business in all of Worcester! J&M Telecommunications on Main Street. He's very well-respected in the local business community, but I hear he launders drug money for some of the biggest Dominican dealers in the city. I also heard he might be in the drug business, too, but who would have thought he'd make deliveries himself! Oh man! He's a big fish!"

"Is that him in the truck?"

"I don't know…let me get a better look."

Richie slid aside the Kel receiver and climbed over the seat. Then steadying his arms on a backbench of leather, he peered through a pair of mini binoculars pulled from my black bag.

"The front windshield's too dark. I can't see if it's him or not."

While Richie continued to squint through the binoculars, Lanh's disembodied voice, freed from Rudy's presence in the Mazda, softly floated an update through the Kel.

"He give me heroin. Now he get rock from Toyota, red Toyota."

An inner sense of urgency swelled in me like a sudden tsunami.

"202 to all units…target's meeting the crack SOS," I radioed, while assigning three cars to go with the Forerunner when it leaves. "He'll probably go to a money wiring business on Main, most likely by way of Vernon to Maxwell and a right onto Millbury." My words echoed Richie's knowledge of the neighborhood as fast as the detective spat them out. "208, there's a gas station on Millbury at Maxwell. Set up there and get a good look at the driver at the stop sign." With G-car windows on a par with the illegal tint of the Forerunner's, he had the best shot of a clear view without being spotted himself. "It's critical we make a positive ID on this guy!"

By this time Rudy had reached the Forerunner, its driver's side window partially open, but at an angle that didn't allow Richie to get a glimpse of the operator's face.

The first half of the two-pronged transaction had already taken place, Rudy silently giving an ounce of heroin to Lanh at the Dunkin' Donuts. It had been fronted to Rudy the night before but he had been unable to store it at his stash on Svea due to occupancy issues. He adapted to the dilemma by hiding it in a basement bin of his apartment building. Forty-three hundred dollars cradled in the smug Dominican's pocket, further boosting his comfort level with Lanh, but in the process also creating a complacency that would turn around and bite him in the ass.

Though the half-opened window did not reveal his face, part of the driver's body was very visible. Arms extended and flailing outside the Forerunner, the contented expression on Rudy's face was wiped clean by an infuriated source of supply. Rudy was reprimanded up one side and down the other for being *so stupid* as to bring the customer to *their regular meeting spot.*

Normally, Rudy received his crack deliveries at the Vernon Street Apartments and stashed it around the corner on Svea. That's where the customer exchanges took place. It was a regimented routine between long-time, trusting associates; one that provided insulation to the source and had always been executed to perfection.

Until today.

Seemed my last-minute strategy had panned out after all.

"It too dark. I no see...I go look."

WHAT!?

As the words of the impulsive informant reverberated in my ears, Lanh got out of the Mazda and started walking towards the Forerunner. The driver saw the little guy approaching and panicked, jamming the crack into Rudy's hand, and hitting the gas. The Forerunner fishtailed out of the lot, pitching up a dusty cloud of winter debris in its wake.

"202 to surveillance...Forerunner just sped out of the lot. Careful, he's spooked!"

"He just made a left onto Maxwell," reported a stationary unit on Vernon near Fifth.

"*NOBODY* follow him down Maxwell! 202 to 208…he's heading your way. Get ready!"

The Forerunner began its descent down the steeply sloping Maxwell, which ended at a "T" intersection with the heavily trafficked Millbury. The awaiting surveillance agent was set up as instructed in the gas station on the opposite side of the busy thoroughfare, the frontend of his G-car positioned to see where the side street ends.

The Forerunner literally flew into view as it emerged from a dip in the roller coaster road, soaring through the air and landing hard with a frame-rattling thud that could rival any on the streets of San Francisco. The agent raised his binoculars and steadied his arms on the wheel preparing for its arrival, but as the SUV continued barreling down the hill, he started to worry it was going too fast to stop.

The driver slammed on the brakes, the Forerunner skidding through leftover salt and sand from the latest snowstorm, sliding to a halt just before slamming into a wall of traffic. Millbury was bumper-to-bumper, crawling in the same direction he wanted to go. The unnerved operator had no choice but to wait for a break in the procession. He slapped his hands against the wheel in frustration ready to make that right turn at the slightest gap of opportunity.

The agent across the street stared through his binoculars at the Forerunner, now slanted at a downwards angle with bright, direct sunlight penetrating its dark windshield, which negated the cloaking effect and unveiled the vehicle's sole occupant: light-skinned Hispanic male, slight mustache, close-cropped hair…and those ears! If the driver couldn't escape his phantom pursuer by land, whimsically he might just be able to fly away.

The antsy driver tired of waiting and forced his way into traffic by cutting off another car.

"208 to surveillance…Forerunner just made a right onto Millbury. I can't get out of the gas station. Who can pick it up?"

Airwave silence.

"Anybody have the target vehicle?" I inquired while watching a stunned Rudy Matos return to the Mazda.

No response.

All the units assigned to follow the Forerunner were snarled in the same traffic that delayed the SUV. The uncertainty in the agent's voice stuck at the gas station planted a seed of doubt in my mind. The Forerunner may have been registered to Worcester's money laundering king, but that didn't prove he was behind the wheel of the delivery vehicle. Only a positive identification at a fleeting moment would convince the US attorney's office to indict Santana as Rudy Matos' crack source of supply.

"202 to 205," I radioed another agent known for his lead foot. "Go directly to the business address on Main and try to get a good look at the driver before he gets out of that vehicle."

I was hoping for a second chance.

Rudy completed his transaction with Lanh but knew he'd screwed up. He was able to accommodate the customer's last-minute request, but in the process compromised his drug dealing principles and angered his supplier.

"205 to 202…I've located the Forerunner. It's parked and unoccupied in front of J&M Telecommunications."

* * *

The Cadillac turned onto Oread Street and parked opposite the flow in front of Locomotion Auto Repairs. Its out of town driver emerged from the super-sized vehicle with an attitude, moving about as if Main South were his home territory. The unseasonably warm weather, a slice of autumn in between two layers of winter fronts, prompted him to remove his jacket, thus revealing the powerful build one gets from being a workout freak. Not overly muscular, just solidly built. He and his passenger, Lanh, whose physique made it apparent he didn't know what the inside of a gym looked like, strode side by side towards the garage.

Rey Barnes donned a pair of sunglasses and pushed open the bay door to meet the Canadian. The opportunity to advance beyond the level he'd attained in his chosen profession had just arrived, and it had nothing to do with rebuilding a Mazda or Toyota engine. It was only two days earlier when Lanh shared the good news with him.

"I tell my people 'bout da powda'. They like. Maybe do big business with you. My boss want meet. No be scared…he look like cop! All white guys look same!" The two shared a laugh over the bias-based joke that typically profiles other races. *"He no want go so far and go back with nothing. Can you get quarter kilo, da powda'?"*

Rey had built up a profitable drug distribution center, but the depressed, urban environment wasn't conducive to his aspirations of being an international smuggler, an accomplishment reached by other members of his family. When Lanh told him his "boss" in Canada — someone the little guy had pumped up over the months as financially capable with an organized crime connection — wanted to discuss "big business" in Panama, Rey's eyes glazed over like that of a salivating coyote in a den of feral cats. So, when the informant proposed bringing in someone new, even somebody who looked like a cop, he bit.

The part about coming up with 250 grams of cocaine on such short notice was problematic, but he'd make it happen. "*No problem, mon,*" responded the trafficker who'd puffed himself up as an important local player with a big-time international connection. He *did* have the means to set up multi-kilo deals in Panama; he'd done them before. But in Worcester, Rey was a wannabe major leaguer playing on a minor league level.

Brian, the Boston DEA agent and former Vermont state trooper, had quickly and efficiently pieced together a nice little conspiracy case against the crew at David's Auto Repairs, but when Flaco fled for Puerto Rico a state fugitive, the nucleus of the group was gone. Bibi tried to keep it going but didn't have the smarts to maintain customer loyalty or source trust. Without Flaco in the mix, Milton Morales decided to move on, too, staying one step ahead of the Santiago brothers, whose bounty-inspired network continued to search for the family's evasive enemy. One of the investigative lines in Operation Tune-Up had reached its final point of destination, but there were still several stops ahead for the trains being operated by Rey Barnes and Rudy Matos.

When seeking an operative to play the part of "the Canadian," Brian was quick to volunteer for the dangerous assignment. Even though he now had the start of a beard and had grown out his high and tight military cut to include a little rat's tail, the young agent still had the appearance of, and carried himself like, the former trooper he was. I was confident he'd be diligent in preparing for the role, but unsure if his poster boy police looks would fly with the dirt bags at Locomotion, which was why I'd instructed Lanh to do the lube job on the garage owner in preparation for the undercover's appearance.

"Nice ride," Rey said in admiration of the Caddy after some small talk about the trip.

"It's got a hide. A really nice one. You want to see? Eh?" Brian retorted with Canadian flavor and a Cheshire grin.

Even behind the dark lens of Rey's sunglasses, Brian could see the drug dealer's eyes were wide open with interest. He told Lanh to stay with the intrigued trafficker and walked back to the Caddy. Shielding the secret of activation, he inserted the key in the ignition, turning it to engage the electrical system but not start the engine, then performed a series of automotive functions, e.g., set the cruise control, turn on the windshield wipers, unlock the doors — the combination needed to create movement. The hum of a hydraulic piston slowly pushed out a panel below the backseat, which when fully extended, exposed a sizable secret compartment.

Taking away bad guys' toys and utilizing them to catch other bad guys is ironic use of a seized and forfeited asset. The installed hide was undetectable to the naked eye and the electronic sequence to open it was exact. Like a safe, mess up the combo and you have to start all over again. The *touché finales* to the undercover Canadian prop were the Quebec license plates attached to the vehicle, courtesy of the DEA Ottawa Country Office.

Rey called out to the other resident traffickers curiously peering from the darkness of the garage. Show and tell time. The motley crew shuffled over and gawked at the professional insert designed to stymie law enforcement, looking more like children on Christmas morning than drug dealers on a crime-ridden street. The awkward silence was snapped when one of them muttered, "cool," which elicited laughter from all. Any suspicions about Brian not being the real deal were instantly wiped clean with the impressive prop.

Brian asked Rey if they could speak alone. Separating the leader from the pack stoked the wannabe's desired sense of importance, as the two treaded an international path deep within the inner-city setting. Lanh trailed them like a little puppy dog, that is until Brian sent him on a different path, telling him to stay with the awe-inspired others.

The informant's role in the investigation was changing. After successfully running the first leg of the race without falter, the time had come to pass the baton to another.

Lanh was being cut out of the case.

Although he'd continue to provide relief help whenever needed — putting out brush fires while DEA and Worcester Vice manned the hoses to extinguish a conflagration of drug trafficking in a tinderbox city, Lanh knew the drill from his RCMP days and accepted his diminished role.

Nevertheless, the little guy would claw his way back into the case in a big way.

"I understand you have a connection in Panama," Brian prodded Rey.

That's all it took. Turning on Rasta Rey's verbal faucet required no pressure whatsoever. Seemed he'd been waiting his whole life for someone worthy enough to let it flow, and thanks to Lanh's convincing act portraying the Canadian as a high roller with a big budget, that audience stood before him.

"Yeah, mon. This shit pure...dirt still on it," the streetwise trafficker noted about the product's quality, referring to a cartel storage practice of burying newly processed and packaged kilos of coke in the ground until ready for shipment.

"I set up for you. Whatever you want. You send somebody down with money. Come back with stuff, plus little extra for me. It that easy."

Rey made it sound like going to the corner store and buying a loaf of bread.

Brian said he wouldn't have traveled this far if there wasn't an interest in the proposition posed to Lanh. Now that he'd met the Panamanian garage owner and confirmed the good things he'd heard about him — a buttering that further stroked Rey's inflated ego — he'd run the idea by the money in Montreal. Then Brian moved on to a more immediate matter, asking if the quarter key Lanh ordered up was ready to go.

"Have to put together."

"*Put it together!?* You mean you don't have the stuff!?"

"No, no, I have! Just need little time, go get."

Brian lifted a dubious eyebrow. Making it clear he didn't want to hang around all day long, Rey was told to page Lanh once the quarter key was in hand and ready to be picked up.

No sooner had the rock star agent and his informant roadie left the inner-city stage, than Rey followed suit by doing the same in a customer's car taken off the lot. But as he was followed trolling from one seedy city location to the next, it became clear that his shaky declaration of readiness was nothing more than a Freudian slip.

Rey didn't have the package.

Every time the wandering Panamanian went into a new place, I instructed Lanh to page him under the guise of seeking an update, which was just a ploy to inspire a callback from a handy hardline and provide intelligence about a local supplier. But despite several well-coordinated efforts with surveillance, none of the pages were returned.

It was supposed to be a short day, at least that's what I told my supervisor when convincing him to approve the Saturday morning operation. Brian was a little nervous about his first big undercover venture, and the atypical timing was designed to lessen target suspicion and alleviated UC anxiety. Brian appreciated the consideration, although the surveillance team members called out on their day off didn't share his sentiment. But as January's daylight faded fast into winter's early dusk, so did the optimistic projection of a quick transaction.

Then Lanh's beeper chirped.

Finally, Rey's got the package.

"It a Rudy," deadpanned the informant.

Seemed that Rey Barnes wasn't the only one left drooling after the dog and pony show put on at the garage. Rudy Matos wanted to meet the Canadian to make a "big business" proposition of his own before Brian supposedly left for Montreal. Practically begging for the chance to plead his case, his only stipulation was it had to be outside the city limits. Seemed Rudy didn't want to be seen grasping for the brass ring on Locomotion's carousel of drug dealers.

Despite the dimming prospect of success with Rey, I decided the rest of the day would be dedicated to the nomadic coke seeker. There was no way I was going to set up a meet on Sunday after taking away the surveillance team's Saturday, and the entire group was slated for an all-day affair following meth-dealing members of the Hell's Angels in Lynn, Massachusetts on Monday.

"Tell him you can't meet him today," I whispered to Brian, who had his hand cupped over a payphone speaker. "Say that something unexpected popped up and you'll be staying in the area for a few days. Agree to a meet, but that it won't be any earlier than Tuesday. Tell him you'll call his apartment on Monday night about six to firm up the details, but that he better be there to take the call. Otherwise, you're gone."

Rudy agreed to the terms of engagement, Brian emphasizing he had no intention of waiting on him or anybody else. Then he hung up the phone and the wait for Rey continued. By then surveillance had been discontinued. You can only follow someone with the same cars so long before being made.

Dusk gone and a deep darkness set in, Lanh sent out a volley of "911" pages to the AWOL trafficker. Despite the writing on the wall, I clung to an unreasonable hope that the endeavors of the day — just like all the other overachieving operations preceding this one — would end in success. But when every one of Lanh's pages failed to generate a return call, I had no choice but to accept reality.

Twelve hours after it started, the failed operation was terminated.

* * *

After a Sunday with no contact from Rey despite a continued barrage of 911 calls by Lanh, followed by another long day into night chasing Harley Davidsons throughout the North Shore, surveillance was light for the Tuesday morning meet halfway across the state. It was a simple operation that didn't involve any drugs or money; just Brian and Lanh talking with Rudy at a McDonald's in Auburn, Massachusetts. Nobody was traveling anywhere; this time I had an undercover agent to control my impetuous, little informant.

Rudy arrived right on time. He was not alone. The bespectacled woman with bookish looks and rapid-fire speech introduced herself as "Sasha," a pseudonym with an exotic flavor, which when combined with her soon to be revealed double-dealing ways conjured the thought of *Mata Hari*. All four piled into the undercover Caddy and Brian wasted no time getting down to business.

"So, what's on your mind?"

"You want heroin?" Rudy anxiously blurted. "We can do big business. It good Colombian, sometime African."

Pridefully declaring his product the purest sold in the city, Rudy also set himself apart from others by saying he had a "private apartment" to do deals, a safe place "off of the main street and away from the garage." The confident but cautious Dominican only had one caveat should the Canadian he was trying to seduce decide to work with him.

Rey couldn't find out.

"How about cocaine?" Brian inquired, expressing some dismay with Rey. "Can your people handle five kilograms per month?"

"(We) can handle even more than that," Sasha replied with a dismissive pfft.

"Do you use the same source as Rey?"

"Absolutely not," Sasha emphatically replied with disgust. "Look, we'll give you a better price than what Rey charges. We know he's very expensive. People don't want to deal with him because his material is no good and his prices are too high. The place where you have to go isn't that great, either."

"When can my boss buy?" Lanh piped up.

"You tell us what you want, we'll get you a price," Sasha responded, her gaze bypassing the questioner and looking directly at the decision maker. "If it's acceptable, the material will be ready for pickup with a two-day notice. It's up to you who you want to deal with."

"Alright, let's see what you can do. Let's start off with two ounces of heroin next week."

"Hold on…how do we know you're not a cop?"

After already implicating herself in the conspiracy, Sasha picked an odd time to challenge Brian's drug-dealing credentials.

"Why? Because I'm a white guy? I'm from Canada!" the agent chuckled. "I could ask you the same thing. Are *you* a cop?" Brian asked the light-skinned, Puerto Rican woman.

"Hey, you never know," Sasha replied while ignoring the question. "We had this real smooth connection in Pittsburgh who wound up being an undercover. It's a sore subject with us. So, you're not a cop?"

Rudy was getting a little antsy with Sasha's aggressiveness. He'd already been sold on the whole Canadian sting and didn't want his wife screwing up a good thing.

"It okay," Rudy assured the DEA agent. "I trust you."

* * *

As the Mazda with its greedy, double-dealing occupants pulled out of the McDonald's lot, Lanh's beeper vibrated.

Again.

"It a Rey…three time now."

All the while Rudy and Sasha were undermining the Panamanian who'd fallen off the face of the earth, Rey was frantically paging the informant "911."

Unlike the lack of a courtesy call Rey failed to extend, I took an investigative high road and had Lanh return the page. However, the informant's greeting was anything but cordial.

"What you want, asshole!?"

There was no apology. No explanation. Incredulously, Rey informed Lanh that the package was ready and wanted to know if Brian was all set to do the deal! It was as though three hours had passed, not three days.

This guy had to be in a time warp!

The operation thought dead was suddenly resuscitated. A flurry of telephone calls followed to resurrect and tweak the previously prepared Op-Plan; get two layers of supervisory approval to do the high-level deal; arrange the retrieval and transport of the buy money from Boston; and reroute all the office bound surveillance units back out to Worcester.

It was like scrambling fighter jets for a suddenly appearing enemy aircraft.

Just like Saturday morning, Brian turned the undercover car onto Oread Street and parked in front of Locomotion Auto Repairs. Only this time there were no pleasant greetings, no show and tell exhibitions, and no air of optimism about a future large-scale transaction. Brian voiced his anger about being ignored, telling Rey if not for other business prolonging his stay in the area, he'd have been long gone and Rey would have never seen him again. The chastised trafficker hung his head in shame and feebly uttered something about his "regular guy running out," but Brian didn't want to hear it. He just wanted to get the coke and get out of town.

After two hundred and fifty grams of loose powder cocaine (and an ounce of crack) was secured in the secret compartment, Brian got behind the wheel of the Cadillac to begin his northbound trip back to Montreal.

DEA was back in the driver's seat.

The crestfallen Panamanian stood in the middle of the street pouting like a jilted lover as he watched Brian drive away.

Rey Barnes knew he'd just blown his big chance.

Chapter 4

"Family Affair"

January 1995

Enough time had passed for Rey Barnes to lament the loss of the biggest score of his life, but not too much to lose hope that he hadn't.

Brian took a seat on the folding chair in the closet-sized room and slid into place. On top of its end-to-end counter were banks of hardline telephones and wired-in tape recorders, connecting pairs designated to different cases with handwritten, sticky notes warning others never to answer an incoming call and instructions on who to contact if it rings. He flipped a switch on the wall, which activated the red light above the outside frame of the closed door. The bulb illuminated brightly, as if a bordello advertising 'open for business,' telling any other agent in the group that an undercover call was in progress.

Quiet!

"Don't talk…get to a payphone and call me back," Brian curtly instructed.

Rey Barnes flew out of his apartment building like a projectile from a slingshot. After three days of jerking around the Canadian for a quarter key of coke, he thought he'd never hear back from the hot shot with the cool car again. Swiftly reaching his urban destination, he yanked the phone off its receiver and punched in the Montreal number he'd been given. The call bounced from one country to another before Brian answered in the hushed atmosphere of DEA Boston.

"Here's the deal…my people love the idea of your Panama connection, but it's not worth it to them smuggling a small amount of merchandise over that long a distance. Can your people put together a bigger package?"

"No problem," Rey responded, his labored breath coming in gasps from running.

"Okay, we have a pilot who can transport up to two hundred kilograms in his plane. I'm looking to buy fifty kilos of cocaine for my people and fifty for an investor."

Redemption.

"I already talk my sister," Rey excitedly replied. "She go Panama. Live Brooklyn. Her paperwork straight and she speak English good as Spanish."

It was unclear if Rey was referring to an actual family member or talking in urban slang, but one thing was certain: he was hooked on the undercover story, so Brian put him in a bucket and recast his line into deeper waters hoping to catch bigger fish. The UC explained that his pilot would be paid $1,000 for every kilo flown out of Panama, a commission commensurate with his own for setting things up on the buyer's side. The more flown out, the merrier it is for everybody involved...including Rey. Since only half the cargo space was reserved, he inquired if Rey knew anybody with the money in Worcester who might want to jump onboard.

Rey expressed doubt that any of the high rollers he knew would want to risk investing in a plan with somebody they didn't know. Still, greed wouldn't allow him to completely dismiss the idea. He told Brian he'd ask around.

"How long will it take to start putting this in action?"

"These things no be rushed. Maybe two week, my sister, she go Panama."

"Does she know the business well enough to handle all this responsibility?"

Unlike the shaky ground he'd stood on when an alternate supplier pieced together a local package of loose powder coke, when it came to his sister's ability to produce a hundred kilos of pure packed in Panama, Rey declared his feet to be firmly planted on solid bedrock. Brian was assured that she was "really big" with the necessary qualifications and experience to do the job, adding if her busy importation schedule couldn't accommodate the Canadian's eager timetable, the family tree of cocaine facilitators had other strong branches.

"If she no can do, my mom can do."

At the age of thirty-two, a little too old to be toiling away his birthright on the mean streets of Worcester, it appeared as if Rey's rite of international passage into the Barnes family smuggling business had finally arrived.

They agreed to consult with their respective "people" and talk again in two weeks.

* * *

It was late in the evening when Brian again slipped into the DEA Boston UC room. He punched in the number given to him during the meeting at the Auburn McDonald's, his first contact since "Sasha" grilled him hard about being a cop. He was a little nervous; a lack of experience caused him to wonder if he'd handled the challenge properly. His anxiety abated when Rudy Matos answered the phone.

Brian said he'd be coming down to Worcester in a couple of days to talk with Rey about a major coke deal in Panama and while there, wanted to get two ounces of heroin from Rudy.

Only he didn't say it so plainly.

In a cryptic manner emblematic of traffickers' feeble attempts to create a defense — just in case somebody else was listening to their drug-related conversation — Brian said something along the lines of wanting two tires put on his Caddy while he was in Worcester to talk to the other mechanic at the shop about buying a foreign car. Brian was simply embracing his undercover role with real world authenticity, but code doesn't work unless both participants have a grasp of the language being spoken. A long, silent pause dawned a light of understanding why he'd been told during the McDonald's meet that it was "best to call at night" — that's when the Dominican dealer's English fluent, pit bull partner would be home. Reluctantly, Brian asked to speak with Sasha.

"I want to make sure he understood the order."

"What is it you want?" Sasha hissed, transforming from daytime professional in the financial field into her darker, drug-dealing persona.

"The M tire," Brian replied, referring to the Spanish slang for heroin, *Manteca.*

"The more expensive one...right?"

"Right...twenty-eight tire pressure," Brian cleverly clarified, citing the number of grams in an ounce by pounds per square inch (PSI). "What's the price?"

"Thirty-five," Sasha answered without hesitation.

"How about if I buy two. Can I get a lower price?"

"No," she firmly replied. "You're getting the best."

Her no-nonsense reply said further negotiation was out of the question.

He accepted the quote and arranged to pick up two ounces of heroin from Rudy for $7,000.

Brian then depressed the pop-up buttons on the phone, released them to a new dial tone and punched in the next number on his to-do list. Rey answered and without one incriminating word being said, arrangements were made to meet him at the garage to discuss details about Panama on the same day he'd be purchasing heroin from Rudy.

Conducting business with both traffickers from Locomotion Auto Repairs was a delicate balancing act. Rey knew nothing about Rudy working with Brian behind his back, and Rudy made it abundantly clear that he wanted to keep his relationship with the Canadian a secret. Whenever possible, rendezvouses were set up with both targets during the same supposed trip from Montreal; a logical scheduling that helped divert suspicion away from the undercover agent, who of course, also had something to hide in a drug-dealing triangle that had the feel of being a three-way love affair.

* * *

Rey Barnes needed to improve his drug trafficking skills if he wanted to play with the big boys from Central America. At least that's what his internationally successful sister told him. Discipline in speech had to be exercised; she cautioned the Worcester street-hustler to be more careful about whom he spoke to and what he said to them, especially when discussing business on the phone. The fact that Rey divulged this to a DEA undercover agent probably underscored the Panamanian's need for advanced training.

Marla Barnes was the Brooklyn-based leader of a cocaine importation network. She worked directly with her longtime Cali Cartel partner: he arranged seafaring shipments from Colombia, she found qualified clients and orchestrated bulk pickups in Panama. Holding the highest cell position on US domestic soil in a worldwide trafficking organization, she also oversaw a steady stream of courier-transported kilos into LaGuardia and JFK airports for local distribution.

Marla listened to her brother talk about the organized crime-connected Canadian who wanted to purchase a hundred kilograms of cocaine. Because her partner in Panama gave her one key for every ten in business she brought to him, that meant a ten-kilo commission would be in store for her. It would be pure profit, too; the customer would have to absorb all the associated expenses if he wanted her much sought-after smuggling services.

Every kilogram of 90-95% pure cocaine hydrochloride she brought into the US would be sold as is. But after being cut up by others several times over, it would ultimately bring profits to multiple layers of distribution. From the jungle labs of South America to the stepped-on street powder going up a nose or boiled down to base and smoked, its sheer volume would increase tenfold. Of course, Marla would have been long out of the profit chain by then, satisfied with the $17,000 to $20,000 per kilo price she'd get in New York.

* * *

Rey and Brian entered the McDonald's on Worcester's Main Street from opposite ends of the parking lot. Rey had changed the meet location last minute; the switch necessary, he told Brian, because his garage had become "too hot.". The Panamanian wasn't seeing ghosts. Despite an order to avoid Oread Street during the high-stakes undercover negotiations, a Worcester Vice detective, who apparently hadn't bought into his department's cooperation agreement, decided to do just the opposite. Brian thanked Rey for his attentiveness, telling him their business was too important to be messed up by "some stupid local cop."

Together, they ventured back out into the bitter cold and spoke about a variety of topics for the next twenty minutes in the Canadian's warm, Kel-wired car.

"Did you talk to your sister about Panama?"

Brian had tried to draw Marla into the discussions, requesting Rey bring her along so that nothing was lost in translation, but he flat out refused saying it was "too early." Apparently, his sister wasn't yet ready for exposure to criminal culpability. On the other hand, Rey couldn't wait to dive deeper into the conspiracy pool.

He babbled on about how Marla, her boyfriend in Brooklyn, and her boyfriend's brother in Panama exported kilograms of pure Colombian cocaine into the United States. They were his "people," the heart of a smuggling operation in Panama's Chiriquí Grande district. The network stored hundreds of kilograms of cocaine in an underground facility in

Panama's porous Bocas Del Toro Province. From there it was kilo-couriered to New York, bulk delivered to a cash-and-carry customer in Panama, or shipped by boat to another storage site in Costa Rica, ultimately bound for the Caribbean and then on to Miami. In an effort to impress the Canadian, Rey provided a trafficking route that only lacked a map for detail.

That would come later.

Information flowed from Rey's mouth quicker than a raft down a river's rapids. Only the jagged rocks of a serious undercover mistake could have shut him up.

God only knows how that didn't happen.

"By the way, that package you gave me two weeks ago was *excellent*."

Although an anesthesia wasn't necessary for the already loose-lipped Rey, it was an injected compliment for the extraction of more information. However, the final analysis for the purchase hadn't yet been received from an inundated lab in New York — Brian just assumed the purity was consistent with the previous buys Lanh made from Rey. Untimely, the lab report was arriving in the morning mail at DEA Boston while the undercover meeting was in progress. It would show the exhibit had a purity percentage of only 6% cocaine hydrochloride.

That's street shit.

Rey must have known what he sold to the Canadian wasn't wholesale quality. A warning sign should have brightly flashed in his mind. *Something's not right here*. Perhaps he thought Brian was playing him for a negotiation edge on a bigger load; purging the logical deduction that if this supposed major player really believed that package was 'excellent,' he's not in the game or might even be an undercover cop. Instead, aspirations of international glory blocked him from heeding the warning. Choosing to ignore rather than walk away before dragging others down with him, he continued to nervously mollify his own fragile psyche.

Had the report arrived just one day earlier, Rey wouldn't have been given the chance to talk himself into a deeper hole. I would have instructed Brian to cancel the meeting — there'd be no further dealings with the huckster who claimed to be capable of providing one hundred kilos of pure cocaine yet couldn't even come up with a quarter key of quality. Rey would have been placed on the backburner for future arrest alongside Flaco and his crew.

But fate had other plans for Rey. It allowed him to say things that would be corroborated by other sources of intelligence, which bolstered his credibility and gave me an investigative change of heart. His words would lead to the uncloaking of a previously undetected international cocaine trafficking network, and in the process, alter lives forever in the Barnes family.

Rasta Rey was having a bad day.

It would get worse.

The overly diluted quarter key of coke that Rey finally scrounged up had been stashed in a house on Oread just down the street from Locomotion. This was known because Rey told Brian when he took him there to do the deal. Watching the exchange like a Doberman on duty was the marijuana specialist at the garage. He was obviously a lookout, but mere presence isn't enough to charge someone in a drug transaction. It didn't take much to prod the talkative trafficker into implicating the whole household when Brian asked if "the kid was cool."

"All three those white boys cool! They brothers. At my garage all the time! They live upstairs. Parents live downstairs. Always let me keep my stuff there! And the lady in the house? Huh, she get *real scared* when she see me and you pick up the stuff!" Rey chuckled, apparently finding humor in disclosing the property owner allowed her home to be used in the facilitation of a significant drug transaction.

"Let me ask you something else. You have any connections for guns?" Brian's inquiry came at the request of ATF, who was investigating Rey for federal firearms violations.

"Yeah, mon. What you want? Like Derringer two shot?"

"More like a three-eighty or a nine-millimeter."

"I carry thirty-eight caliber two shot," Rey persisted, apparently trying to convince the Canadian on the merits of the easily concealed weapon that most probably settled in his pocket. "I get you nine-millimeter. You need silencer? I know someone make silencers with metal workshop machine called lathe."

Had Marla been present, she'd have strapped one of those silencers across her little brother's big mouth. Then the prattling Panamanian caught sight of the time on the Caddy's dashboard and realized he had to open up the shop.

"Shit! I'm late! Can you give me lift garage?"

Brian obliged, turning out of the McDonald's lot for the short jaunt down Main Street, while steering the conversation back to the hundred kilograms of cocaine.

"You gonna be making any phone calls to your people about Panama?"

"I call my sister tonight. You call me later at ten and I tell you."

Brian pulled to the curb on Main short of Oread, telling Rey he was avoiding any local heat that might be just around the corner. Despite his urgency, Rey hesitated before getting out, a pensive look of concern suddenly replacing his creased-on, cocky expression.

"Look, I gotta tell you…my people? Brooklyn? They leery white people, and they tell me no talk business on phone. They know conspiracy law and all that shit. They tell me, 'be careful.'"

"Don't worry so much. You do your job, I'll do mine."

* * *

According to the court ordered pen register attached to Rey's phone, he did make a call to a Brooklyn number that night, one subscribed to a "Ricardo Smith." Toll records subpoenaed by DEA New York reflected immediately following that incoming call from Worcester, several outgoing calls were made to four different numbers in Panama. Curiously, one of them was also subscribed to a "Ricardo Smith."

The Panamanian number with the carbon copy subscriber name was discovered to have a telephonic history in an intelligence database. According to DEA's Special Operations Division (SOD), which reciprocally shares information and coordinates case activities with other drug-fighting countries, the number listed to Smith in Panama had recently been intercepted on a "hot line" associated with the Cali Cartel in Colombia.

Then the same name popped up again during a US Customs records search. A Panamanian national named Ricardo Smith had been arrested a year earlier at LaGuardia Airport attempting to smuggle in two kilograms of cocaine from Panama. Released on bail but failing to show up for his next court appearance, he was a federal fugitive.

It didn't necessarily prove there was a link…that is until something else in Customs' records lessened the odds of coincidence. The fugitive's home phone number in Panama, which he provided at the time of his arrest, was the same one wedged between the Brooklyn number called by Rey in Worcester to talk with his sister about a one hundred kilo coke deal in Panama, and the

Colombian number associated with one of the biggest cocaine cartels in the world.

Ricardo Smith was a fugitive hiding in plain sight. Careful to conceal his true identity — which allowed him to continue his couriering duties between countries — yet neglectful in not changing the subscriber information for his rented Brooklyn apartment, or the Panamanian address used to facilitate the movement of Colombian cocaine into the United States.

Rey's loose lips and a gumshoe's trail of intelligence not only deduced that Smith and Marla Barnes were partners in crime.

They were also lovers living together.

* * *

Marla's tutorial about the world of international drug smuggling was beginning to resonate with Rasta Rey. He was showing signs of knowing better than to discuss criminal details on the phone. During a follow-up call with Brian, Rey assiduously kept to protocol by insisting another face-to-face was needed to provide an update. But old habits are hard to break — he ended the call by blurting out that the end of February looked good to do the 100-kilo coke deal.

During the second of what would be three meetings at the Main South McDonald's — Rey's adopted office since his garage was compromised by a renegade vice detective — Brian showed up as agreed, but he was not alone. I listened to Rey's people in Brooklyn. They didn't like doing business with "white people;" a not-so-subtle inference that it upped the odds of encountering an undercover. As a gesture of good faith meant to ease any authenticity concerns, or so Rey was told before the meet, Brian's "boss" wanted him to bring along another member of the Canadian organization — one of Puerto Rican heritage who spoke fluent Spanish.

Adding the tough talking, street smart, DEA Boston agent to the mix, whose non-Canadian, thick Bronx accent was countered by a clichéd but still effective cover story that he'd relocated north of the border after fleeing a fugitive from New York, certainly made the starry-eyed, English-challenged Rey feel more comfortable. Nevertheless, the Panamanian conduit had to follow through with the vetting instructions of his more circumspect sister.

Rey suggested they go elsewhere to discuss their high-level business, specifically a Latino restaurant on Chandler Street called El Rancho. All three hopped in the Caddy for the short trip through the thick of Main South, traversing from one bleak edge of the urban neighborhood to the other with a streaking tail of surveillance units behind them.

From his backseat interrogation pulpit, Rey peppered "Alberto" with questions about his background and drug dealing credentials; pointed inquires meant to find a chink in the undercover's armor. He'd get nothing out of the seasoned agent, although he'd report his findings of satisfaction to Marla after convincing himself that he had.

As soon as they entered El Rancho, a cluster of six men standing at the bar stopped talking and started staring. Brian thought it was simply because he stood out as the only non-Hispanic in the place, but Rey knew better, beaming with pride while strutting past the viewing committee. As if evaluating cattle at a livestock auction, all eyes focused on the two new faces.

After being seated at a table, an observant Alberto, who espied Rey acknowledge the group with a slight nod, asked how he knew the men.

"They all players," Rey boastfully declared.

These Worcester hot shots were assembled because Rey bragged to them about the major transaction *he* put together. They wanted to get an impression for a future venture after declining to invest in the present one.

It seemed the seed sown by Brian had yielded a crop.

Their pass on the project didn't matter to Rey. He was pleased just to have gotten this well-accomplished group to take him seriously, hoping it might springboard him to their status. After ordering food and drinks, more for show than satiation, Rey outlined his sister's plan.

Someone from the Canadian organization would have to travel to Panama pre-delivery of the load to negotiate the finer details of the exchange with the Colombian supplier. Rey's sister would also fly down to coordinate everything, all expenses related to her trip paid for by the buyer. They'd lodge at a hotel in Panama City, but a representation of the product would be shown in Colon, a fifteen-to-twenty-minute drive from the city, according to Rey. If satisfied with the arrangements and quality of the merchandise, options for where to land the Canadian's plane would be presented. Once a site is chosen and a delivery date set, the cocaine would be moved from storage to a nearby trailer for quick loading and a swift departure.

Both undercovers were impressed with Rey's presentation, but said they'd have to speak with their boss before committing to the plan. With a sigh of relief after apparently handling the international proposal with the aplomb of a pro, the street dealer slid back into his comfort zone by giving an update on a stolen handgun he was getting for Brian.

* * *

Rey may have bridged the gap between seller and buyer, but he was only a temporary span with limited capabilities for further advancing a transaction of this magnitude.

The time had come for the touch of a professional.

Brian arrived at 9 A.M. sharp for the third and final installment of the McDonald's sessions. Exactly two weeks since the first meet, he was a little early and a lot anxious for the introduction he'd pushed for ever since broaching the subject of Panama. He was alone this time. There was no need to bring along a lower-level associate for the high-stakes meeting with Marla.

Through the storefront window he saw the Mazda registered to Carmen Barnes pull into the parking lot. Two women were in the front seat, Rey in the back. Though he'd never seen a photo of Marla because she hadn't yet been fully identified, Brian immediately knew which of the two was Rey's sister. The tall, comely woman with the short-bobbed hair moved with poise and carried her authority well. She was clearly the one in charge.

It was awkward at first; Rey nudged Brian into the food line, excitedly asking him what his boss thought about the Panama proposition, while the two as of yet introduced women silently queued behind them. Brian muzzled Rey's indiscretion in the crowded restaurant, telling him they'd talk in the car, as the two pairs slowly crept to the counter, got their orders, and took a table.

The Barnes contingent dug into their hearty breakfasts while Brian, who was too nervous to eat anything, sipped a cup of coffee. Nothing but small talk was exchanged, mostly between Brian and Marla, as the agent and the smuggler sought out information about the other for polar opposite reasons.

Once finished with their meals, Rey, Marla, and Brian adjourned outside to discuss their business in the Mazda, an offer to use the undercover Caddy shunned. Rey's Puerto Rican wife was left behind to wait. She was good for a ride and a green card, but after just being released from prison for her second heroin distribution conviction, she was too vulnerable for being flipped and couldn't be trusted with any information about the high-stakes affair.

Despite talking for the past fifteen minutes inside the McDonald's, Brian and Marla were finally introduced by name outside in the car. They had to do it themselves. Living in a tinted world of gray where one's true identity is only revealed when the roots are exposed, Rey never considered the civility of an introduction in a more businesslike arena. Yet another stumble by someone out of his league, straining the family faith as brokers from two countries tried to put together a 100-kilogram cocaine deal in a third.

Brian said he was sold on making the initial trip after Rey's solid proposal — an attaboy that most likely lit up the go-between's glowstick — but his boss in Canada had reservations about the overall "risky venture." He wanted to know more about who they'd be sending "all this money to in a foreign place so far away" before making any commitments.

Apparently, Marla's Colombian partner had reservations, too. Which was why he wanted to meet someone from the Canadian organization in person, in Panama.

"My guy won't put together a package of that size based on phone calls alone. He wants to know you're the real thing. Do you know how many pretend to be someone they're not?"

If the too-close-for-comfort comment rattled the undercover, it didn't show.

Marla was a skilled negotiator; someone you'd want on a debate team. Parrying with the diplomatic and thrusting with a counterpoint, she lauded Brian's decision to bring along his Spanish-speaking associate (if the trip was approved by his boss), that having someone who knew the language would be in the buyer's best interest. She also said the initial trip would be beneficial because Brian not only could view and test a representative sample of the product, but also bargain face-to-face for the best price possible with her partner.

"You'll see for yourself my guy only provides quality cocaine."

"I understand Colon is where you'll take us."

"Yes, but we will stay in Panama City. Colon is not a good place (for you) to stay because strangers stick out there." Marla didn't have to spell out that meant white strangers. "We will drive to Colon in the early morning hours before the town awakes, about three or four in the morning, to conduct our business there."

That "business" entailed going to a safe house where a kilogram from another customer's order, in stock and awaiting pick-up, would be available for examination. If satisfied with the quality, a meeting would occur later in the day to further negotiate with the supplier. Marla said they had product coming and going all the time. And even though Brian's load was just a gleam in a processor's eye, each customer-tailored shipment is consistently the same.

It's all high-purity cocaine straight out of Colombia.

"Are the packages in kilogram or two hundred and fifty-gram quantities?" Brian asked, reiterating information Rey probably shouldn't have divulged.

"Kilos…sometimes I've gone down there in the past and they had the smaller units," Marla further revealed. "They're compressed into small, radio cassette-like packaging for easy concealment. Then my guy cures the cocaine by rubbing a compound on it that makes it undetectable by drug sniffing dogs."

Marla was a little confused, saying these additional precautions are taken for transportation across borders by motor vehicle. It was her understanding that the Canadian's order would be picked up and flown out of the country by private plane.

Brian vanquished any thoughts about her brother screwing up the order, confirming the mode of transport while citing his plane's capacity and touting his pilot's credentials, saying he's done other international drug running flights to and from the Caribbean.

"Really? My people have a connection in the Caribbean, too."

Marla realized her reply sounded like a buyer's option; a false impression she quickly corrected. The purchase price would not include any additional cost of transportation outside of Panama. The cocaine would have to be picked up at one of many abandoned airstrips in the country. A map and instructions on how Brian's pilot could better avoid radar would be provided once a site was selected. Regarding price, she said it was based on supply and demand but should be no more than $2500 per kilo — a ridiculously low price in North America, but one that's commensurate with proximity to its South American roots.

Marla then moved on to other financial matters. She, of course, would be paid for all her expenses related to travel and lodging in Panama, but wasn't expecting any other money from the Canadian as a fee for her services because her partner gave her one kilo for every ten sold. She did, however, want his pilot to drop off her share in New York on the way back to Canada. Brian readily agreed. The touchdown would satisfy a legal element to charge her with importing all 110 kilograms of cocaine into the United States.

Brian then produced a pen and a map of New England highlighting his trip from Montreal — a prop further supporting his cover story — and handed them to Marla, requesting she write down her full name, address, and phone number so he could FedEx a money order for her plane fare and expenses.

It was time for the undercover cop disclaimer.

"How do I know you're not setting me up?"

Brian burst out laughing. "Setting you up!? Do you know how much drugs your brother has already sold me? Why don't you ask him? You do trust your brother, don't you?"

It took a second for Brian's meaning to register before Marla joined him in laughter. The thought of Rey being an informant must have seemed preposterous to her.

"That's okay," she said while writing down the information, as Rey nervously giggled in the backseat to the joke made at his expense.

"Will the money have to be shown prior to delivery?"

Marla said it would, but that she'd soften the security concerns of flashing at least a quarter million dollars in cash by being the Canadian's "front." A trustworthy agent who'd represent the buyer's best interests by viewing the money up here, and that her partner down there would just have to take her word that she'd seen "the merchandise."

Of course, that was a misrepresentation of loyalties. She didn't care about Brian's people, their cash concerns, or their best interests. Her sole allegiance was to the importation network that without her pivotal position, couldn't move boatloads of coke from its southern hemisphere point of origin to its northern hemisphere distribution points.

Brian knew it was self-serving manipulation, but it didn't matter to him. He was satisfied with his undercover performance and the conspiratorial evidence he'd elicited.

Marla also seemed pleased with the outcome. It was a good initial meeting with a qualified client who'd put $200,000 in profit in her pocket.

Rey? Well, he was happy, too. He had finally made his mark in the international world of drug-smuggling; a limited role that should have ended there, only Marla insisted the Canadian continue communicating with her through him.

Keeping her brother in the loop to carry on the Barnes family tradition was the right thing to do. After all, if it wasn't for Rey introducing the well-heeled client to his highly successful sister, none of this would have ever happened.

Chapter 5

"Thin Chance" San Juan, Puerto Rico

April 1995

The Lexus entered the mouth of the Callahan Tunnel from the North End and descended deep beneath Boston Harbor. The aged structure with its dim fluorescent lighting and grimy ceramic tiles—some missing to leave gaps like lost teeth—spat out the car on the Eastie side into the drizzly remnants of a pesky nor'easter. A quick shift into the right lane and I took the exit for Logan Airport.

Once above the turbulent airspace clinging to the eastern seaboard of New England, it was an easy, nonstop flight that landed smoothly on the tarmac of Munoz-Marin International Airport in San Juan, Puerto Rico. Within hours, I went from the slush of filthy streets to the splash of pristine waves. A rented car took me to my hotel on the outskirts of the city, where a ninth-floor room presented a spectacular, panoramic view. Hugging the white, sandy shore of the Caribbean Sea, it stretched from a gleaming downtown skyline to the popular Condado Beach with its chic resorts and glitzy casinos.

I gazed down at the oil-glistened guests on the hotel's private beach or extended in lounge chairs by the pool. Others chose shelter from the sun, enmeshing themselves in hammocks strung between palm trees with overhanging, shady fronds.

They all looked relaxed, peaceful.

Just as I began picturing myself in the placid scene below, the shrill ring of the telephone shattered my reverie. Reaching to silence it, I espied the folder on the bureau that reminded me I wasn't there on vacation.

I was tracking a fugitive.

"Hey, bro! You ready for some dinner?" It was Richie. "I know the best Cuban restaurant on the island!"

Richie Burgos's familiarity with the local cuisine came as no surprise. Born and raised in Puerto Rico before moving to the central Mass city that eventually employed him, his career in public service began with the fire department before realizing he'd rather be extinguishing crime. It wasn't long before his communication skills were recognized as an asset on the street, and he was assigned to the intelligence-driven Vice & Narcotics Unit.

Over the years Richie had built up an extensive database of intelligence — all of it filed in his head. He had many sources of information — some developed working off a beef as informants, others law abiding citizens who knew he truly cared and wanted to make a difference in their troubled neighborhoods. The affable detective with the wispily layered, perfectly combed hair, and oversized glasses that framed a mustachioed face full of kindness, brought a smile to the faces of others. His easygoing and unthreatening manner made people feel at ease. Everybody talked to Richie because everybody liked him. His amiable nature was sincere, too; not a façade meant to elicit information.

"Man, this is too good to be true! It's like a dream!"

Richie's simplistic, retro-sixties way of speaking uttered when he first realized the benefits of working with DEA. Awe-struck while viewing over a hundred surveillance photos taken from a surreptitious site high above David's Auto Repairs, he immediately recognized many of the faces as drug dealers his department couldn't effectively target due to a lack of money and other resources. His eidetic memory not only knew their names, but their aliases, addresses (including girlfriends' where one might put his head down for the night), criminal associates, vehicles, and other background information.

I wasn't there to witness his childlike exuberance as he viewed the photos, self-exiled behind the scenes while Brian led the early-on cooperative charge in the field. But listening to the story, the image of a youngster sitting crossed legged on the floor while chewing a piece of bubble gum and finding superstars in newly opened packs of baseball cards came to mind.

Richie shared his overload of intelligence and informants with other detectives in his unit, which enabled them to generate search warrants and make arrests before mechanically moving on to the next target in a seemingly endless parade of drug dealers, most occupying a lower level on the city's totem pole of traffickers. Passing along a steady stream of leads for others to follow-up on had its benefits for Richie. It lessened the need for him to write reports and testify in court; not exactly fortes of the detective, he'd readily admit.

But Richie was capable of so much more. He was a treasure chest of investigative valuables collaborating with others satisfied to take whatever spilled over his brimming edges. Nobody knew how to extract the information he'd accumulated and take it to the next level. Even Richie was unaware of his potential. Not having the opportunity to conduct bigger cases due to years of petty political turf tussles didn't help in his development.

Richie and I became inseparable partners. Together, we showed others that a mutual effort between agencies can produce better results for those needing drug enforcement the most — the people of an inner city. Combining my aggressive investigative style with Richie's superior intelligence-gathering ability, we'd construct a case unlike any ever seen before in Worcester by bringing out the best in each other.

Although Richie had returned to his country of birth many times over the years, this trip was different from the rest because he didn't come back as Puerto Rico's favorite son, but in an official capacity as a deputized DEA task force officer (TFO). He was still a local cop, but now he also wore another hat with expanded jurisdictional powers throughout the United States and its territories, albeit on a temporary basis until completion of the case.

So, while Brian stayed back in Boston to catch up on paperwork related to his undercover work with Rey Barnes and Rudy Matos, Richie and I traveled to Puerto Rico to track down Jose "Flaco" Garcia, the third automotive root target in the case, who fled a state fugitive and if not arrested before additional criminal exposure was revealed, would also become a federal fugitive.

* * *

Richie and I met in the hotel lobby and drove to a downtown restaurant he couldn't stop raving about, an opinion apparently shared by others as we waited for a table on the weekday evening. While waiting, I absorbed the atmosphere best described as sophisticated *Casablanca*. Colorful artwork graced white walls splashed with swirls of lime green and Capri blue. Lethargic ceiling fans gently swayed leafy potted plants strategically placed throughout the expansive, open dining area. Neon signs for Havana Club rum and Cristal beer pulsated above an elegantly carved, dark mahogany bar. There was even a piano player filling the air with smoky tunes from a bygone era, the ethereal space shared with the promising aroma of a delectable meal.

Once we were seated, I ordered a mojito while my teetotaler friend was satisfied with a glass of water. When the waitress set off on the first leg of her assignment, I began discussing our business.

"Okay, here's the agenda for tomorrow. First, we have to show our faces at the DEA office to let them know we've arrived. They might free up an agent to give us a hand, but I doubt it. They've got too much shit of their own down here to help us find a state fugitive."

"But didn't you tell me...what was it you called them? 'ASACs? GSs?' Man, you guys got initials for everything! Didn't you say your boss called the boss down here and got the okay for us to be here? And that you sent some kind of 'teletype' confirming you and me were coming down to look for Flaco? How many times do you guys have to do the same thing?"

The astute detective raised a valid point about bureaucratic redundancy.

I responded with some lame analogy to TV westerns from the 1950s; how when a good guy rides into town looking for an outlaw, the first place he always goes is straight to the sheriff's office.

"I mean, you don't want to piss off the locals. You never know *what* they'll do."

Richie pushed up his glasses and stared back with an amused look. The tongue-in-cheek retort was an obvious reference to the shotgun reception I'd received in Worcester.

"So, we'll check in at the DEA office down here," I continued, "then shoot on over to the PD. You said we're all set with your guy, right?"

"All set...Lt. Santiago is expecting us. He said he'd give us his best investigator."

Lieutenant Miguel Santiago oversaw the Extradition Division of the Policia de Puerto Rico, an expansive state-police-like law enforcement agency with over eighteen thousand officers and island-wide jurisdiction. Apparently, enough stateside fugitives flee to the US territory to justify the unit's existence. Because Richie had the collateral duty of being his department's Spanish-speaking liaison, he and the lieutenant had spoken about other Worcester fugitives in the past. Not surprisingly, the genial detective befriended the veteran squad leader.

"Are you ready to order?" interjected the waitress while placing the drinks on the table.

Richie was ready a week ago, quickly ordering a house specialty he couldn't stop talking about. I selected a chicken and plantain dish and the waitress left to put in the order.

"His best investigator, huh? You know what that means? It means whoever's got nothin' to do."

"No, no, bro! He said this guy's a 'killer worker!' Arrested some of the biggest drug dealers on the island! Every time I've asked the lieutenant for help, he's always come through for us!"

"Okay, okay," I replied with a chuckle, brushing aside my cynicism while acquiescing the ringing endorsement. "After the lieutenant gives us his 'shining star,' let's head on over to the port and see what we can dig up."

"Sounds good to me!"

The Port of San Juan in the historic Old San Juan section of the city is the seaport facility that handles cargo/freight and the many cruise ships destined for this popular port of call. Its sixteen piers are equally divided between goods and passengers. From past life experience, I was familiar with the passenger side of the port. Tomorrow I'd see the other half, as our interest lay in the importation of motor vehicles.

One of Richie's reliable sources revealed that Flaco had shipped several cars from New York to San Juan over the past year, some with a secret compartment containing large amounts of cash. Analyses of subpoenaed telephone toll records, review of court-ordered pen register data, and a little old-fashioned human intelligence provided several leads to where these vehicles might have ended up in Puerto Rico. Volumes of importation manifests would have to be pored through at the port to refine the intelligence, but confidence was high about pinpointing a good address for the fugitive.

Naturally, it was Richie who uncovered the thin man's chicanery at David's Auto Repairs. Flaco's state arrest for cocaine trafficking under his true name was verified by a mugshot. There was time to prevent him from fleeing as a fugitive; a certainty considering the alternative of sticking around for a guaranteed conviction and a lengthy jail sentence. But preventing his flight from justice wasn't only fleeting, it was complicated.

What Richie also learned was that Flaco's long-delayed trial was on the court calendar that week. He could have been picked up for violating his conditions of release. Surely distributing heroin and crack under an alias while out on bail qualified. Or he could have been arrested on a fresh federal charge as the leader of a trafficking group. However, the affidavit showing probable cause for either option would have exposed Lanh as an informant — not by name, but by obvious deduction — and divulged the existence of the ongoing investigation, thus tipping off other defendants and inspiring *them* to become fugitives. Prematurely taking down the entire case with a two-day lead was out of the question. It was logistically impossible, nor was it desirable.

Complicating matters further, Flaco's live-in girlfriend was in a position to warn him about the issuance of any arrest warrant. She worked at the Worcester County Courthouse — the same building where her lover's trial was scheduled to take place.

Despite dead ends at every turn, Richie and I had no intention of just letting Flaco walk away. A stakeout of the fugitive-in-waiting's residence was set up the night before his trial. On standby was a state police cruiser, ready to make a motor vehicle stop just short of the state line or at the threshold of Logan Airport. So close to the start of his trial, yet far enough away from its place of occurrence, Flaco would be placed under arrest based upon the reasonable belief that he was *attempting* to become a fugitive from justice. It would be independent probable cause to revoke his bail without disclosure of the federal case, at least according to the Worcester County Probation Office when presented the no-name "hypothetical" scenario.

It wasn't until the following morning when Flaco made his move, but instead of heading to the highway, he drove straight to the courthouse. Richie ran into the building thinking the clever criminal was trying to slip surveillance by walking in the front door and sneaking out the back, but to his surprise found him seated with counsel at the defense table.

With Flaco in the confines of the courthouse, surveillance was discontinued after the all-night affair. However, a fresh unit resumed the watch at the end of the court's day when the trial was continued until the next morning. But despite another opportunity to beat feet, Flaco perplexingly retraced his path to prison, as the trial proceeded towards a certain conviction.

Richie and I wondered if Flaco was dumber than we thought.

He was smarter than we thought.

Both the prosecution and defense wrapped up their cases by noon, as the judge broke the jury for lunch before beginning their deliberations. Flaco broke, too ... out the front door nobody was watching in the middle of the court's day for Puerto Rico.

"Man, I hope we get this knucklehead," Richie distastefully lamented while savoring his meal that evening. "You know how many times we arrest somebody and the state lets them go? Happens all the time, bro. Then we get lucky and catch a big guy like Flaco in the middle of a deal with good weight. Poof! He's gone. You never see these guys again."

"Don't worry, Richie, we'll get him. I seem to recall you've had some pretty good luck finding fugitives out of state."

"You mean New York? Oh man, that was unbelievable!"

"How'd that go again?"

In truth, I remembered. But hard-fought victories in the name of justice are badges of professional pride that other like-minded cops never tire of hearing about.

While Richie was on vacation in Rochester, he saw a face that looked familiar in his hotel's parking lot. He got a little closer until his steel-trap mind confirmed who he thought it was — a fugitive the state had released on bail four years earlier after Richie's unit arrested him for cocaine trafficking and gun possession. He got into a car and Richie followed suit in his rental, sticking with the fugitive until coming across a cruiser on patrol. He waved it down and showed his ID, the car was stopped, and the fugitive arrested. The guy swore up and down that the warrant wasn't for him — he had a New York driver's license in a different name, but fingerprints don't lie. His were faxed to the FBI and they matched those on file for the Worcester arrest.

"Afterwards, this guy apologized to me for not telling the truth," Richie chuckled. "Told me he was 'just scared'. Yeah, right...scared of being caught!"

"Would you care for some dessert?" the waitress politely asked while clearing away the empty plates on the table.

I was too full and said so, but Richie protested.

"Come on, bro! You've *got* to have some desert!"

"Richie, I can't eat another bite!"

The detective's insistence had nothing to do with hunger. Vicariously, I was a guest in Richie's home. The proud Puerto Rican had taken me to a thoroughly enjoyable restaurant in his country of birth. Richie just wasn't ready to end the dining experience with his good friend.

The caramelized flan was delicious.

* * *

After a hearty breakfast and a strong cup of Puerto Rican coffee at the hotel, Richie and I made a cameo appearance at the DEA San Juan office before heading crosstown to Policia de Puerto Rico Headquarters. Escorted to the Extradition Division, we were cheerfully greeted by Lt. Santiago. This was the first time Richie and the lieutenant had met in person, and although I didn't speak Spanish, I could see these two knew and liked each other.

Santiago ushered us into his private office, a typically drab, governmental room but for a generous supply of Caribbean sunshine streaming through a large, square window, where I briefed the bilingual squad leader about our mission. As far as anybody else should know, our visit was strictly a state matter. (The Worcester County DA's Office agreed to extradition *only* because the feds were footing the bill.) Nobody should be told I was a DEA agent. In fact, up until then, the extent of the operation's compromise-conscious measures also applied to the lieutenant, who wasn't aware of DEA's involvement. The goal was to "wall-off" the multi-tentacled, active investigation in Worcester, putting one of its primary targets on state ice without him or his co-conspirators learning of the federal connection. I couldn't have stressed more that confidentiality regarding DEA's interest was paramount.

"I understand this is a sensitive matter. Any shared information will be on a need-to-know basis. Only my most trusted agent and I will know about the federal government's involvement. I've assigned him to work with you the entire day. He's very good, makes the most arrests in the unit. If anybody else asks questions about who you are and why you're here, they'll only get a shrug of the shoulders with 'just a couple of state shepherds looking for their lost sheep.' Don't worry, I'll take care of you."

I had a visceral reaction to that phrase: 'I'll take care of you.' In past experience, it too often translated to, *you're screwed.*

Cynicism is a quickly learned trait in police work; mistrust imbued by the constant flow of lies and double-dealings from bad guys, informants, and even some of the good guys. It's a hard edge that teaches you not to take anything for granted and understandably rubs some people the wrong way. But when you assume everything you hear is truthful, cases can be compromised, and in the dangerous world of drugs, it may even get someone killed. There were times when I deeply resented the acquired characteristic. Sitting there listening to the lieutenant's kind offer of assistance, yet doubting his sincerity, was one of them.

Lt. Santiago picked up the phone and said something in Spanish. Moments later, a casually attired, physically fit looking agent with an olive-skinned complexion that sported a five o'clock shadow at ten in the morning knocked on the glass paned door. The lieutenant waved in our guide for a day. Neither Richie nor I caught his name, if it was thrown at all, only hearing the lieutenant glowingly refer to him as his "best man."

The non-English speaking guide was briefed by his supervisor while silently absorbing and thoughtfully acknowledging his marching orders with an almost constant nod of the head. Richie translated for my benefit; the lieutenant sharing every bit of confidential information he, himself, had just learned, before continuing the effusive praise of his second-in-command's investigative prowess and noteworthy achievements.

I turned towards the guide, his head bowed in what appeared to be genuine humility, making me feel even more ashamed for doubting the lieutenant's sincerity. Skepticism assuaged, but my resentment of it still piqued, we set off for the Port of San Juan.

The guide picked up some gear before meeting us at our rental. As he came down a long-descending set of concrete steps in front of police headquarters, I was taken aback by his change of appearance. He now donned a black jumpsuit with a sewn-on Policia de Puerto Rico patch; slung over one shoulder, a large black duffel bag, over the other, a submachine gun. He tossed the oversized satchel onto the backseat and jumping in next to it, we began our quest.

The route to the port was filled with depressing sights of poverty, suffering, and fear. Mangy horses roamed untethered through dusty vacant lots; a pack of emaciated dogs sought out scraps of food from an overturned, strewn can of garbage; metal bars filled windows of decrepit tenement buildings as though barriers to prevent jailbreaks. In reality, those bars imprisoned a crime-permeated community trying to protect itself from the human animals of the street.

I caught a glimpse of the guide in the rearview mirror; his slicked back, dark hair and mirrored sunglasses accentuating an already intimidating appearance. The guy looked like he was ready for war.

"Something you know we don't?"

Richie translated.

A slight grin of understanding cracked the guide's otherwise serious face.

He explained that the Puerto Rican Police Department believes a strong public presence deters crime. It's why they're call *La Uniformada* ("the Uniformed", Richie further translated). Many in his unit choose to wear their jumpsuit in public, and none ever go anywhere without their equipment. At any given moment, they could be called upon to participate in the arrest of a violent felon.

"And the SMG?" I more pointedly asked.

"What can I say? Puerto Rico's dangerous."

Puerto Rico's dangerous.

Richie said the same thing last night. And the beefed-up police presence the guide spoke of was obvious, although somewhat deceptive. Marked units routinely patrol city streets with their overheads in constant rotation, even during non-emergency situations, as brightly colored lights bounce off buildings and ricochet blocks away to give the impression of omnipresence.

I got a firsthand taste of this practice on the way back to the hotel after dinner, pulling to the curb at the sight of emergency lights in the side view mirror. Diligently waiting for the cruiser to pass, I cursed other drivers who failed to yield, as one by one they remained in lane and drove by our idling rental. But when all I could see was the unobstructed view of the approaching police vehicle, I redirected my annoyance at the cop in the car, impatiently mumbling out loud, *'come on, come on, what's the problem?'* When it finally drove by at a nonchalant 25 MPH, I bafflingly turned to a muted Richie in the passenger seat, the prankster's body bouncing up and down from suppressed laughter.

He knew.

The trip to the port transitioned from pitted pavement to bumpy cobblestone, as the urban corrosion we'd just driven through was replaced by tree-shaded plazas and aesthetic period buildings emblematic of Old San Juan. As we veered left and away from the centuries old fortress up ahead known as El Morro, the sight of mammoth cruise ships rose like leviathans out of the sea to announce our destination was near.

I parked the rental in a gravelly area near the edge of San Juan Bay, a short walk to a massive lot with hundreds of vehicles on the other side of a guarded gate manned by a police officer in a small shack. The officer came out and cordially greeted the guide. Based on the gregarious exchange between the two, it was obvious they knew one another.

The three Spanish speakers huddled in conversation, which once again left me out of the loop; a frustrating exclusion I had had no choice but to accept. I bided my time by gazing out over the water just beyond the rows of newly arrived vehicles, all of them lined up alongside a warehouse big enough to qualify as an airplane hangar. It wasn't long before raised and excited voices caused me to turn back, where I saw Richie holding a photo of Flaco.

"He recognizes him!" Richie announced in English before jumping back into the lively Spanish exchange.

The officer said about a month earlier, he made a $30,000 offer to buy a dump truck from a frequent importer of motor vehicles. It was rejected. Ten minutes later, he saw the thin man in the photo talking to the importer and surmised it was about the truck. His assumption was confirmed a few days later when he made a second offer but was told the truck had been sold. Flaco bought it for $55,000…cash. The importer then nervously blurted out that the buyer was one of the biggest money launderers on the entire island. I figured he failed to file a currency transaction report for the cash exchange and was trying to divert attention away from himself.

Like a swimmer coming up for air, Richie broke for sidebars of English to update me before diving back into the fluid conversation. I furiously took notes. Then with the crackle of a radio transmission, the tide changed. The flushness of victory drained from the guide's face; Richie's too, as both assumed the same ashen look of concern.

It was clear something was wrong.

"They've got Flaco holed up in a house with some of the most wanted criminals in all of Puerto Rico! The lieutenant's unit has the house surrounded, but these guys aren't coming out…and they're all armed! It's a bad situation, bro! A SWAT team is on the way and the lieutenant wants us to get back to the station as fast as possible."

The three of us sprinted to the car. The guide pulled out a portable emergency light from his duffel bag and handed it to me. I wedged the bubble between the dashboard and windshield and plugged the power cord into the cigarette lighter. Immediately, the cabin filled with a whirring sound of motion that dizzily dispersed the rotating blue light. An adrenaline-fused foot hit the gas pedal a little too hard, causing the back tires to kick up a dusty cloud of gravel and dirt before grabbing solid ground and sending the car in motion.

The spinning blue bubble brightly announced our rapid approach. Other drivers knew the unmarked car wasn't on routine patrol and immediately got out of the way. Strolling cruise ship passengers, souvenir shop tourists and patrons at open air cafés all gawked at the speeding car as it passed by, their heads swiveling like spectators following the serve of a tennis ball.

The sunny day filled with optimism suddenly turned dark with doubt, as an ominous black cloud avalanched off the bay and engulfed Old San Juan. Gripping the wheel and pulling forward to where my nose almost touched the windshield, I squinted to see through the deluge as wiper blades valiantly battled the torrential onslaught. My focus remained steadfast, but other thoughts tried to hijack my racing mind.

Can I shoot another human being?

I came close a few times as a local cop in New Jersey, the closest when I stumbled upon a teenaged boy holding a gun to a girl's head. I repeatedly ordered him to drop the gun, but the boy didn't react — a moment frozen in time for both the kid and the cop, neither privy to what's going on in the other's mind. I had to make a split-second decision. The legal justification was there, the threat present. If I hesitated too long, the girl or some other innocent person might be killed because of my inaction. But if I pulled the trigger, my conscience, even though the action was warranted, might punish me for the rest of my life, or public opinion might unfairly label me the bad guy. Intuition and training rather than fear and an inability to decide told me not to shoot. Thank God because it turned out to be horseplay with a replica.

The car began to hydroplane on PR-1, its backend fishtailing on the slick asphalt surface. I eased off the gas and avoided the urge to hit the brakes, as the vehicle straightened out.

Concentrate! Be calm! Don't kill yourself before someone else has the chance to!

Directions in one language; translated into another; registered; executed.

As we approached the front of police headquarters, the storm stopped as quickly as it came. Water dripping off everything and the sun blazing again, the three of us jumped out of the car and bounded up the stairs, taking two steps at a time; hearts pulsating, bodies soaked in sweat from anxiety and a steep climb's physical exertion.

When we entered the Extradition Division's squad room, Lt. Santiago was standing outside his office. The door was open and other investigators could be seen inside. We rushed over to join the briefing session, but the lieutenant stopped Richie and me, explaining he first wanted to go over the situation with his own unit. As the shaded door to his office closed behind them, we were left standing outside, crestfallen.

I understood the lieutenant's rationale; we were outsiders, unknowns. You first want to consult and strategize with the people you know best. The people you trust. But as the minutes ticked by, the wait became downright agonizing.

I thought about everything *I* needed to do: notify the DEA offices in San Juan and Boston along with DEA Headquarters; consult with the US attorney's office in both districts about legal considerations; review criminal histories and make a risk assessment; arrange for sufficient manpower and equipment for the operation; coordinate efforts between federal and local agencies; write up the Op-Plan…all of this and more had to be done and approved in a nail-bitingly short period of time.

My mind was reeling.

When can I get started? Why are they taking so long? Damn it! Why did I bring my five-shot Smith & Wesson instead of my sixteen-shot Sig Sauer!?

Comfort and better concealment of the smaller gun at the expense of greater firepower now seemed foolish.

Finally, the door opened and one of the lieutenant's investigators came out. He said something in Spanish to Richie, and then went back inside the office, again closing the door behind him.

"Richie, what's going on!?"

"They arrested him!"

"They got Flaco!?"

"No, they arrested the guy who was helping us find Flaco!"

* * *

The jump-suited, SMG slinging guide, the lieutenant's second in command

and most trusted agent in his unit, had just been arrested by a special unit attached to the Governor's Office in San Juan. The story about Flaco was nothing more than a ruse to get him back to the station ASAP before word leaked of his indictment.

Richie and I were used as pawns.

The yearlong investigation — the second secret divulged to Lt. Santiago that day — ensnared ten corrupt cops in total. The guide was the alleged ringleader of the group that provided protection for the Cali Cartel to move cocaine and marijuana through Puerto Rico into the United States. He was also suspected of being responsible for several drug-related murders.

Lt. Santiago's praise of his "best man" was chillingly prophetic.

He *was* a 'killer worker.'

The hunt for Flaco ended as abruptly as the screeching halt in front of police headquarters that day. The anxiety of encountering a barrage of bullets from a band of thugs in a fortified house burst like a balloon meeting the tip of a hot pin. It was replaced by a nebulous feeling of emptiness, until reality swept away the wispy void to reveal the clarity of a new anxiety.

Was Flaco associated with this group? Had he been warned that DEA was in town to arrest him? Did the police officer at the port — the guide's buddy — feed us a bunch of bullshit that went nowhere? Was the federal case in Worcester compromised?

I stood there with a blank stare camouflaging the whirlwind of thoughts in my mind before Richie's voice registered midsentence.

"...something a little stronger than a glass of water."

We found a nearby bar and spent the afternoon washing down the shock, Richie foregoing his normally non-alcoholic ways, albeit on the sweet side with a swizzle stick. There was nothing more we could do. The fugitive arrest operation was dead. The only thing we'd be catching in Puerto Rico would be the next morning's first flight back to Boston.

Chapter 6

"El Gordo"

1986-1995

"If we look at the 1980s crack cocaine epidemic in the United States, we can appreciate what might happen now that Colombia is involved in the heroin trade. There have been reports of ever-increasing purity levels of street heroin... [making it] now possible for individuals to become addicted without using a needle."

—Humberto Fernandez, *Heroin*, 1998

Esperanza is a municipality of the Valverde Province in the Dominican Republic. Located twenty miles northeast of Santiago — the DR's second largest city — it has a population of some seventy thousand with an urban center and four municipal districts — rural areas that are further divided into neighborhoods, or as some call them, villages. Much like Main Street through the Main South neighborhood of Worcester, Esperanza's central thoroughfare bisects the community. Travel is often brisk on Ave. Maria Trinidad Sanchez, at times seemingly a racetrack, as swarms of noisy motorbikes dart in and out of traffic like angry hornets, zipping around other motor vehicles as they spew noxious fumes into the Cibao Valley.

Spread out beyond the business district into the barrios and severe poverty clearly comes into focus. The Cordillera Septentrional mountain range is a majestic backdrop for ramshackle houses seemingly patched together with nothing but spit. The warm Caribbean climate graces these homes with sunshine, but it does not bring cheer to those living inside, a cruel twist of fate in a municipality whose name, Esperanza, *means hope.*

Roberto Portes was born in Esperanza. The village he grew up in was small and everybody knew each other, but the enduring indigence loomed large and befriended no one. He was smarter than the rest, getting an education and becoming a prosecutor in the DR, a position of trust working with police officers to ensure that justice was served for all. But instead of following his oath of allegiance, Portes swore out a different kind of vow — one that he and his family would never experience poverty again.

No matter what it took.

Portes filled out his large frame sufficiently enough to earn his well-deserved nickname, El Gordo, which in Spanish means the big or fat one. He was the first of a generation to leave the slums of Esperanza and pursue his dream in America. Many others from his village would follow his path to prosperity or be recruited by the Big Man, but Gordo was the leader.

There'd come a time when I'd get to know many of the Esperanzans who went to America to deal drugs. Through multiple and extensive debriefing sessions, I absorbed both their collective mindset and their individual feelings. They were all considered overseas achievers in their poor neighborhood — idolized by the youth as role models and admired by the adults too afraid to try to change their lives. I felt empathy listening to their stories, even sympathy for some, as they described the desperation of being trapped in a socioeconomic environment conducive to nothing more than an empty future. In their village, illegal entry for the specific purpose of distributing massive amounts of drugs in the United States was not only considered acceptable behavior — it was a rite of passage. They all knew their actions were criminal but truly felt justified in committing them. In their minds, drug-dealing was the only way to escape an abject life filled with poverty and despair, selfishly choosing to ignore the pain and suffering it created for others.

Several of these Esperanzans would tell me they were sent off with much fanfare. Two even said it was "like a soldier going to war for your country." If you returned home with money — drug money — you were considered a success and lauded as a hero, but if you came back as poor as when you left, you were a failure, a label that stuck with you forever.

The criminal acts of these interlopers and others like them represent but a sliver of the overall Dominican population, a proud people with strong moral principles and deep love for their country. Their illegal entry for the sole purpose of distributing drugs is an insult to those who legally immigrate and ethically integrate into American society. They mock the toils of immigrants who strive to realize the true American Dream in an honest and honorable way.

Of course, Dominican traffickers aren't alone in satisfying the drug-gluttonous appetite that exists in America. Other foreign nationals and US born predators also nourish the feeding frenzy that's anything but victimless, as users ranging from the so-called "recreational" to the stone-cold addicted bankroll the human suffering they play a part in sustaining by padding the pockets of the distribution chain.

America's drug problem is the creation of a melting pot of poison; one that if not curbed by a steady stream of demand reduction education starting at an early age will continue to produce new generations of users, along with the aftereffects of lost productive lives, premature deaths and the purgatory of pain endured by family and friends, thus enabling drug distribution and its damage to society to continue in perpetuity.

* * *

Roberto "El Gordo" Portes illegally entered the United States in 1986 to begin his new career working for a brutal Dominican organization in New York known as "the Company." Its leader, Maximo Reyes, perhaps the biggest trafficker in the city at the time, oversaw a vast network that distributed 100-125 kilograms of cocaine and crack per week. Using cold-blooded violence to eliminate competitors and maintain internal order during the "Crack Wars" period, this group is known to be responsible for committing at least seven murders and four attempted homicides, which included the shooting of a police officer lured out by a 911 call where a sniper lay in wait. Considering its savage nature in a city averaging more than six murders per day, the body count attributable to this organization is likely much greater.

Gordo, who was known then by his Americanized name "Ricky," quickly rose through the ranks to become a star player for the Company, designated the leader of a Brooklyn crew that terrorized the same "Dead Zone" precinct patrolled by Milton Morales. He was responsible for the distribution of 4-5 kilos of coke and crack per week. But despite the organization's violent reputation, he wasn't immune to a little competitive pushback. It didn't take long before a rival tried to muscle in on Gordo's territory, but a warning shot to the leg thwarted the takeover attempt — an incident that empowered Roberto Portes to set his ambitious sights higher.

With more than three years of experience under his broad belt, Gordo left the Company to establish his own drug business and began recruiting some of the homeboys from Esperanza. One of the first to come over was Luis "Luichi" Pena, a childhood friend of the Big Man's, who started working as a bagger in Gordo's "plant" — a staging area in Brooklyn used to process and package crack and powder cocaine for street distribution. The neophyte Luichi, who'd ultimately play a pivotal role in the dark history of drug trafficking in Worcester, quickly learned the trade, making invaluable connections that would serve him well in the future.

It wasn't long after his friend's arrival that Gordo had his first encounter with the law. The drug boss was forced to flee New York because the NYPD had issued an arrest warrant for him, or at least the alias he was using at the time, one of many he'd adopt. Esperanza's prodigal son returned home after acquiring more than enough money to be hailed a "hero," but soon realized he'd also acquired a taste for something else ... power. After a cool-down period and the acquisition of a new name, he reentered the States, but felt it was still too hot to go back to Brooklyn, so he started fresh in a different city.

Lawrence, Massachusetts, a city with a population of about eighty thousand but thought to be much greater due its large number of undocumented immigrants, was chosen by Gordo as his landing point for two reasons: he blended into the predominantly Hispanic landscape and at about two hundred miles from New York, it was relatively close to the heartbeat of his Brooklyn business.

And it was still *his* business.

Even though Gordo had designated others to execute the day-to-day affairs of the New York operation during his hiatus, the Big Man continued to oversee it from Esperanza. There was enough loyalty and fear amassed amongst the minions to assure respect and compliance with his wishes.

His buddy, Luichi, took on another role in the organization as an interstate courier. Every week or so he'd hop on one of the ubiquitous transportation vans that ran between New York and Lawrence with at least half a key of coke and three ounces of heroin, start-up amounts that would dramatically increase. Heroin was a new addition to Gordo's product line; there was a strong market for the drug in Massachusetts and the higher profit margin intrigued the businessman.

Lawrence presented Gordo with a golden opportunity for expanded power, although he'd still have to overcome the typical issues associated with establishing a business in a new location. There'd be opposition from the overcrowded drug-dealing base, who resented this big city hotshot muscling in on their territory, and the hands-on work with the product itself increased the risk of arrest. Gordo's training and experience with the Company addressed the former, and once a steady clientele was built up, he'd insulate himself from the latter by transferring employees from Brooklyn or importing new ones from Esperanza.

Roberto Portes was building an empire.

Had the New York arrest warrant not been issued, Gordo would have been content remaining in Brooklyn, running his well-established and lucrative cocaine and crack distribution business, but fate inspired the adaptable Dominican to broaden his criminal horizons. He'd eventually establish a second major cocaine distributorship in Camden, New Jersey, flooding the Philadelphia metropolitan region with hundreds of kilos of coke, but it would be heroin that dictated the future of Gordo's growing power and great wealth.

It was the dawn of a new addiction in America, one that would evolve into a twenty-first century crisis that continues today. Heroin processed in South America—until then not a major heroin-producing region of the world — was introduced to the United States. It was smuggled into the country by Colombian cartels, but Dominican organizations led the domestic distribution charge, particularly along the densely populated Northeast corridor. The Dominican traffickers employed a marketing strategy that increased user appeal with a purer, yet cheaper priced street heroin, which at the same time reduced the stigma associated with the drug by ushering in previously unheard-of needle-less methods of intake. This created a perfect storm of salability that lured in a new generation of junkies.

One of the vanguards of this deadly movement was El Gordo.

The Dominican trafficker from Esperanza would ultimately go on to establish or supply distributorships for his Colombian heroin in seven different states, spreading out and seeping into communities from the Northeast, Mid-Atlantic and Great Lakes regions of the country. But before the budding multi-regional drug crime boss could leap half a dozen states forward, he'd first have to take one step back.

Gordo got arrested in Lawrence.

Luichi would tell others that he witnessed his boss being arrested on S. Union St, and how he loyally started collecting money for his bail from local customers with outstanding balances. But when one of them gave him nothing but attitude, the quick-tempered collector overpowered the disobliging debtor, tying him to a chair in a first-floor apartment and promising that's where he'd stay until someone came up with the money he owed. Apparently, it got worse from there, because the police found the jettisoned customer in an alleyway amid the shattered glass and splintered wood from a broken window above him, still bound to the chair. Also discovered in the debris was a photo of Luichi and his wife, which inadvertently sailed out the window with the deadbeat dealer. Asked to identify the couple in the photo and whether they were connected to what happened, the criminal turned crime victim refused to answer. The cops thought him uncooperative, something Luichi would have corroborated had he stuck around.

Gordo, who was charged under a fictitious identity, never returned for his court appearance, forfeiting $10,000 in bail money; a write-off of doing business as he again fled back to his sanctuary in the Dominican Republic. An arrest warrant was issued in Lawrence for the fugitive with the fake name, who was also wanted in New York on drug charges without fingerprints on file under another alias.

Gordo was a ghost — a dual state fugitive under two different identities, neither one real.

Luichi decided it best to skip town before he was scooped up, too. He wanted to return to New York, but his wife had grown accustomed to living in the Bay State and persuaded him to remain in Massachusetts. They moved to the Jamaica Plain section of Boston, where Luichi launched his own cocaine distribution business using the connections he'd made working for Gordo in Brooklyn. The apprentice had blossomed into a master himself, no longer needing the teacher to show him the way.

Luichi's independent success grew as he hired others to work the profitable point developed on Huntington Ave, yet he yearned for something he'd left behind in the central part of the state. Dangling the proposition of high-rise city living in a luxury condo, he cajoled his wife into moving again, this time not far from a little town on the Connecticut border with a clustered Hispanic population that included his paramour. Then with the experience he'd gleaned in Brooklyn, Lawrence and Jamaica Plain, Luichi dipped his toes into the warm drug waters of his new home in Worcester, Massachusetts.

He found the city and county by the same name rife with opportunity; a welcoming region already occupied by other high-level Dominican traffickers, none of whom seemed bothered by the newcomer's arrival because there was more than enough business for everybody. No deep concerns about the consequences of arrest, either; it was generally known if the cops got lucky, bail money allowed them to walk away from a community without ties and an identity without validity. It was jokingly referred to as their "get out of jail free card."

But foreign national traffickers throughout the commonwealth knowingly took advantage of lenient court practices and porous state laws every day.

What made Worcester more appealing?

With the unwitting help of the district attorney's office, who for years prevented DEA from opening its own office in the city, several of these higher-level dealers would independently tell me that they set up shop in Worcester specifically because it was the only high-density, urban area in the state without a strong federal presence.

These savvy criminals all feared federal law and its stronger conspiracy statutes; enhanced enforcement resources; greater chance of a no-bail detention; comprehensive investigations likely to end in conviction; and ultimate deportation following a lengthy "truth in sentencing" incarceration.

Breaking bad doesn't mean being dumb.

While Luichi was busy setting the table in Worcester, Gordo began dining on his drug profits in the Dominican Republic. He lavishly spent his money on luxury vehicles for everyone in the family; bought an incredible amount of valued real estate, which included a custom-built mansion in Santiago and a huge tract of farmland in Esperanza; and he purchased La Gioconda Discoteca, a prodigious palace bursting with frenzied dancers and free flowing liquor.

Meanwhile, Luichi would become influential not only in Worcester's underworld of drugs, but also in its aboveboard business community. He established a clothing shop on Water Street called Santo Domingo Fashions—a front to launder his drug profits—and sponsored fundraisers to support one of the primary political parties in the DR. These monthly events geographically rotated from city to city up and down the Northeast corridor. A secret society of Dominican drug dealers conducted meetings at the same time, many of whom, like Luichi, were also business owners in their respective communities. Matters of importance such as voting on new admittances and setting agreed upon prices to maintain control of the regional drug market were discussed.

It smacked of being a Dominican mafia.

On the way to establishing himself as Worcester County's king of coke, Luichi also saw another golden opportunity to make money — heroin. The product was in great demand and the area ripe for expansion, but he hadn't built up the kind of capital required to venture into the big cost, high yield field to make it worth his while, and he didn't have a major New York supplier who was willing to extend him credit. He needed a well-financed investor with a capable source of supply willing to front the expensive, illicit commodity.

So, Luichi reached out to his mentor, who by this time had again scratched his recurring itch for power by returning to the States and was temporarily staying at a family house in the Washington Heights section of Manhattan. He made a proposal: if Gordo advanced him heroin bought from his Colombian connection in Queens and had it delivered to Worcester, Luichi would process, package, and sell it to an established customer base and split the profits fifty/fifty.

Gordo saw a little of his ambitious self in the go-getter he'd recruited from Esperanza. He agreed to the partnership, but with the caveat that someone from his current crew in New York would be transferred to Worcester to work the product with Luichi.

Homeboy or not, trust only goes so far.

The partnership was a prosperous one but after the better part of a year and at the height of its success, Luichi announced he wanted it dissolved. Seemed that while Gordo's money and fronted heroin were being used to build up the business, Luichi was developing a relationship with a Nigerian heroin smuggler in New York. Now that he had sufficient funds for larger loads and come to terms with his own source of supply, Luichi was ready to cut the cord, along with his partner's percentage of the profits.

The breakup didn't upset Gordo. Not in the least. He, too, was ready to move on after using his friend to achieve his own secret objective. With Luichi discovering new, fertile territory and Gordo's latest Esperanzan protégé dispatched to till the soil, the Big Man had insulated himself from the risks associated with exposure and expansion, something he was unable to accomplish in both Brooklyn and Lawrence. The partnership's assets, wholesalers that included Rudy Matos — significant distributors in their own right — were divvied up, as two separate organizations emerged in Worcester, one selling high-purity Colombian heroin and the other a Nigerian-trafficked product originating in the Golden Crescent region of Afghanistan, Iran, and Pakistan..

Gordo then made his next move. Relocating his family from Manhattan to the Main South neighborhood of Worcester, he rented a second-floor apartment on Florence Street behind Clark University. Not far from the shuttered manufacturing plants of the Industrial Revolution, he then leased a downtown suite at the Clarion Suites Hotel and established a new kind of mill, one that had nothing to do with textiles or machinery, as Worcester became the corporate headquarters for everything heroin in the Roberto Portes organization.

He stocked the mill with all the wares necessary to process and package a wide array of products. Pestles, bowls, strainers, food processors, metal molds, a heavy cast iron vise, scales, identification stamps and other paraphernalia were brought in to mix, shape, compact, weigh, wrap and label his popular one ounce "tablets," and the thousands upon thousands of glassine bags filled with one-time hits.

Gordo quickly and forcefully established himself as the top dog in Worcester's heroin market by offering a more potent, yet better priced product than anything previously seen in the city. He was a crafty businessman with a uniquely identifiable line of merchandise, developing a variety of heroin products meant to satisfy everyone from the high-end wholesaler looking to maximize profits, right down to the street user flirting with nirvana and death.

His tablets were compressed, shaped, and wrapped to look like small bars of hotel soap; a clever disguise designed to blend into the mill's setting and minimize suspicion. He priced these "tabs" by the gram, which varied from client to client depending upon the number of ounces ordered, frequency of purchase, and the customer's nationality (non-Dominicans paid more), generally selling in the $3,000 to $3,500 per ounce range. Custom amounts of loose powder in lesser weights were also available at a higher rate.

El Gordo aimed to please.

His mass-produced bags of personal use heroin were sold in "packets" (one hundred bags, each bag containing a miniscule, one-time use amount), appealing to distributors who couldn't be bothered with the mixing, weighing, and packaging process. Each tiny bag was meticulously measured for immediate use and not to be "stepped on" with additional cut, which increased the weight but reduced the formulated purity level each bag was known for on the street.

Mess with Gordo's reputation and a price was paid ... and it wasn't monetary.

He produced six brands of bagged product, all with varying but consistently applied purity levels recognizable by a unique and quirky logo stamp: "No Fear," with a headshot image of a high-haired *Kramer*-like character; "Exellent," [sic] with a blazing sun wearing a frown; "Black Magic," words floated above the iconic faces of comedy and tragedy; "Popular Demand," the name vertically printed between a pair of slithering snakes; "Magic," with a winged Pegasus taking flight; and the most powerful and correspondingly expensive "Energizer," with its bass-drumming "Energizer Bunny," which sold for $800 per packet.

Expansion was rapid and Gordo needed employees. Processors, baggers, distributors, couriers, money counters, and enforcers were some of the positions that opened in the burgeoning heroin facet of the organization, so he went to the well in Esperanza. After illegally entering the country in New York, false identities were established through a corrupt connection at the New Jersey Department of Motor Vehicles, and the workforce was sent up to Worcester.

Though Gordo had a Dominican-only hire rule, there was one exception. He wanted his primary interstate courier to be a natural born citizen who spoke fluent English and had a clean criminal history and driving record.

The least amount of suspicion raised during a motor vehicle stop, the better the odds your shipment will meet its destination. A Worcester local of Puerto Rican heritage with a spotless resume was employed.

Gordo amassed a fleet of cars for his workers to use and had them all installed with secret compartments. The two primary interstate vehicles were equipped with sophisticated hydraulic hides — one in the dashboard behind the radio and the other installed between the backseat and the gas tank — while the day-to-day local cars had a container inserted behind the glove box for easier access during deliveries and money pick-ups.

Tens of thousands of dollars were collected every day and Gordo wanted the money stored separate from the drugs, so he acquired a small Main South bodega to stash the cash until it was either transported by car to New York, body carried to the Dominican Republic, or wired through Julio Santana's money laundering business or the remittance service at Santiago Market. The store was a nice little pickup from one of Gordo's bigger heroin wholesalers, a Dominican known as "the Philosopher," who hastily fled the state after being arrested and released on bail, leaving behind an almost $30,000 debt that somehow had to be satisfied.

In the beginning, Gordo had about a pound of heroin and two kilos of coke transported from New York every seven to ten days. He'd phase out the coke part of his business in Worcester, though the powder continued to flow through his Brooklyn plant and Camden, New Jersey distributorship under the leadership of his Manhattan based underboss, Juan "Cuqui" Madera.

His reasoning for stopping the distribution of cocaine in Worcester was simple: Gordo and Luichi continued to be friends after the breakup, even acting as alternate sources of supply for each other whenever the need arose. Out of respect for his buddy's established territory, he chose not to further expand and infringe upon Luichi's continually growing cocaine enterprise. But that didn't mean the Big Man had gone sentimental ... there was just no time to concentrate on coke in Worcester with the skyrocketing demand for his way more profitable heroin.

The frequency and weight of his courier's trips increased as more and more high purity Colombian heroin was brought up from Queens and parlayed into an even greater amount through the mill at the Clarion Suites Hotel. Gordo would eventually reach the point of putting out more than *six kilograms of heroin per month*, which when combined with the two kilos of Nigerian trafficked dope distributed by Luichi every month — a huge amount that still paled in comparison to Gordo's output — these two kingpins were responsible for just about all the heroin that flowed through the veins of an addicted city in crisis.

Though deciding to suspend his cocaine operation in Worcester, Gordo prudently continued to supply the drug in a limited amount to one of his heroin wholesalers. When one guy generates more than a million dollars in business over the course of a year, you go out of your way to keep him happy.

Gordo's biggest distributor of bagged heroin, a gun-toting, bicycle-riding thug known as "Baty," who controlled the market in Worcester's most violent and crime-plagued housing projects—Great Brook Valley—received two hundred grams of pure cocaine and a big jar of inositol every month, along with personalized instructions on how to properly cut the drug. It was a consideration given to the youthful, inexperienced mixer, who also received three pre-measured packets of El Gordo's highest purity "Energizer" brand heroin once a day, sometimes twice a day, every day. That's *at least* three hundred tiny bags of addiction in just one section of the city, *every day for a year.*

Gordo's Energizer bags were consistently prepared using a 2:1 ratio of heroin to cut. Working an ounce at a time, his processors turned 28 grams of high-purity Colombian powder into 42 grams of what was still a very potent mix, certainly one capable of killing an overindulging customer. Accurately weighing and filling each glassine envelope with a tiny amount of the diluted drug, the enhanced weight always filled five hundred bags. At $15 a bag on the street, Baty raked in a minimum $1.6 million dollars in sales over the course of a year.

In the drug business, the mathematically challenged need not apply.

Learning through his missteps of the past how to better insulate himself from detection in the future, the comfort level Gordo felt in a virtually fed-free Worcester not only empowered him to grow bigger — it inspired him to expand further.

Defying traditional trafficking patterns by making the old mill town an unlikely source city for heroin sent to other areas of the country—with distributorships in the states of Rhode Island, New Jersey, New York, Pennsylvania, Virginia, and Michigan—and with plans for the grand opening of a multi-drug superstore in Houston, Texas, the once poor Dominican prosecutor from Esperanza had found his seat of power in Worcester, Massachusetts.

Chapter 7

"Anatomy of a Drug Deal"

February 1995

A month had passed since the first McDonald's meet in January between Rey Barnes and Brian, kicking off earnest conversation about a 100-kilogram brokered purchase of pure cocaine from Rey's sister in Panama. Concomitantly—and while giving the impression that "the Canadian" was consolidating business trips—Brian also made his first heroin buy from Rudy Matos.

The heroin buy's surveillance was a solid one that saw Rudy descend the back stairs at 46 Florence Street just before delivering two ounces of heroin to the undercover agent. Prior to this observation, there was no reason to connect the address with the heroin sample received by Rudy and destined for Lanh directly across the street two months earlier. Now it seemed the pass-off point from the delivery boy in the red Buick Electra was not serendipitously selected.

In appearance, the house itself struck me as nothing but vanilla. A modest, two-story structure on a tree-lined street, it blended into the urban neighborhood with the hopeful feel of suburbia. A chain-link fence enclosed a small front yard; perfect for a dog's unleashed freedom of movement while watching the steady flow of students across the street at Clark University.

Straddling one side of the house was a broad, blacktop driveway that could accommodate two rows of four, or maybe six cars. Perpendicularly rising from that driveway's back edge stood a wooden staircase. Only the first eight steps could be seen from any angle on the street before the rest of the stairs vanished behind the building. It logically led up to a second-floor entrance, but with a background of wide-open sky, the flight surrealistically appeared to be dangling in space. This baby boomer's sci-fi imagination might even have it leading to a monster created by special effects master Ray Harryhausen.

Utility records indicated the house was a single-family residence, but telephone records reflected two services at the address, one for a "second floor unit" under the name of "Roberto Diaz." The pen register on Rudy's Outlook Drive home phone showed that prior to the deal, an outgoing call had been made to that second-floor number immediately after Brian ordered the heroin; an important piece of evidence not shared by the DEA Tech Unit until after the deal was done. The Northeast Lab analyzed the purchased exhibit and determined it to be a very high 68% pure heroin hydrochloride.

Stick that in some junkie's arm and he or she'll be dead before the needle comes out.

Maybe the fantastical thought of a monster at the top of the stairs wasn't so far-fetched.

* * *

February 21, 1995

When Brian reached out to order three more ounces of Colombian heroin, Rudy said to call back the next night after he checked on availability and price. The Dominican distributor then dialed a local hardline number he knew by heart and spoke with the underboss, who told him the merchandise was in stock, but that he couldn't say how much it would cost until speaking with the Big Man.

Rudy started his workday the next morning in usual fashion at Locomotion Auto Repairs, hanging out with the other drug dealers like taxi drivers awaiting their first fare. It didn't take long before Rudy was dispatched, as he pressed the tiny button on his beeper once to calm it down and then again to view the display screen. Recognizing the number he'd been paged to call, Rudy bolted from the garage and headed in his Mazda for the nearest Main South payphone that accepted incoming calls.

The boss didn't like to be kept waiting.

The pager on the kitchen table at 46 Florence did a jig from the vibration of the incoming call. Pushing aside his drug ledger and putting the meeting with his workers on hold, El Gordo terminated the device's dance and reached for his latest clone phone. The cell phone had SIM numbers that were illegally intercepted and replicated. It had a limited life use, typically until the true owner received his or her next monthly bill and freaked out seeing the outrageous amount of money owed for the calls they'd never made. Gordo punched in the payphone number and a clipped Spanish speaking exchange ensued.

Rudy cringed when given a price of thirty-six hundred an ounce. Brian had been none too pleased about the cost during the last exchange, telling the Worcester trafficker, 'you better do better on price next time!' Well, this was next time, and despite an increase in the weight, after tacking on his standard $200 per ounce sales commission, he'd have to charge the Canadian a hundred dollars more per ounce.

He built up the courage to plead his case for a lower price, but the Big Man cut him off. Even though Gordo's structured telephone use minimized the likelihood of being intercepted, he still didn't like discussing details over the phone. The distributor was told to come to the house if he wanted to talk business and the line went dead.

Rudy's knees buckled a little as he climbed that back staircase. His efforts would prove futile, and the heroin dealer knew better than to press the issue. If the Canadian decided to walk because of price, then so be it. His wellbeing was more important than a healthy bank balance. Satisfied he'd exercised due diligence on his client's behalf, he descended those stairs much steadier afoot than going up.

* * *

"It no mine...I no make price."

Rudy's sheepish response to Brian's outrage after telling him the price for the three ounces of heroin was delivered with humbling embarrassment to the point of being overly apologetic. He clearly had no control over pricing and no doubt worried about losing the business he'd worked so hard to steal.

Begrudgingly, the Canadian accepted the inflated price and set up the deal for the next day.

* * *

February 23, 1995

Early in the morning, a surveillance team watched as Rudy and his wife came out of their apartment building on Outlook Drive. He was carrying a basket of clothes while she cradled their small child. They got into separate cars and were followed in tandem to the Great Brook Valley housing projects, where the infant and their dirty laundry were dropped off with a family member for tending. Then just like any other couple trying to make ends meet, they kissed each other goodbye and headed to work in their respective vehicles; Sasha to the financial company on Lincoln Street, Rudy to Plumley Village for his first drug deal of the day.

Once finished with his business at the high-rise, low-income housing development, Rudy proceeded to his next appointment at 46 Florence. Eight steps up and he was out of sight.

* * *

Maria opened the door for Rudy as her young son sat at the kitchen table doodling in a notebook. On another page of the spiral-bound binder was the child's tracing of a handgun. He shuffled into the living room, where Gordo and two of his workers, Ruben and Elso, were discussing the day's busy agenda. The Spanish-speaking conversation was placed on hold to take care of the immediate business at hand.

Rudy announced the Canadian was all set to do the deal. Once it was completed, he'd return to the house with all the money.

Gordo was pleased with the cash and carry declaration; he was in the midst of amassing as much money as possible before dispatching Eduardo back down to New York for more heroin from the Colombian. He dialed a number on the house hardline and said to whoever answered, "someone will be there in a few minutes...be ready," then brusquely hung up the phone. Turning to Elso, the boss instructed him to take the rental and pick up Nelson. "Tell him I want five tablets," he further ordered. Normally the worker would have used the Buick with a hide behind the glove box, but it was being utilized by someone else on another assignment.

The Big Man then yelled for Maria to bring in "yesterday's." His wife came into the living room with a white plastic bag. It contained the previous day's drug proceeds that she'd collected and bundled in various amounts. The package was triple-bag-wrapped to prevent others from seeing its contents.

"Drop this off at the store after you pick him up," Gordo told Elso. "Fello will be expecting you." The slick subordinate with the Don Juan looks acknowledged his marching orders, slipped on the faux leather "Oakland Raiders" jacket, and set out to begin his tasks.

He weaved his way through the back streets of Main South in the white Dodge Caravan until arriving at an apartment complex on Jacques Avenue. Nelson was standing outside waiting for him, shivering in the cold New England weather he hadn't gotten used to more than a year after arriving from Esperanza. The pudgy-faced Dominican quickly got into the warm rental and the two workers buzzed off to their next destination.

Once they arrived at the little bodega on Main Street now called Sandra's Market, both went inside. Elso talked to Fello and Marvin out front, while Nelson slipped into the backroom behind the counter. The elder of the shopkeepers, a leftover from the Philosopher's ownership, was retained at Maria's request because she felt sorry for the old man. Marvin was Gordo's hire — he thought that working at the drug proceeds depository would be a good experience for his stepson. The safe already opened, Nelson put the bag of money Elso took with him from Florence Street alongside two similar deposits and a loaded semi-automatic handgun.

* * *

The scraggly bearded, gaunt-looking DEA agent, who could easily pass as a junkie, droopily entered Sandra's Market after "Raiders" — the identifier given to the then unknown Elso because of the jacket he wore—and Nelson, the also as then unknown Hispanic male from Jacques Avenue went into the bodega. Elso was talking to an elderly Hispanic man and a teenaged Hispanic boy, but there was no sign of Nelson. Deducing the second target from the Caravan had gone into the backroom, the agent bought a piece of fruit and left.

* * *

After dropping off the money and returning to the Caravan, the workers drove to the Clarion Suites Hotel in downtown Worcester. Nelson went inside while Elso chilled out in the warmth of the rental.

"202 to surveillance…is there anybody in the hotel lot who can quickly go inside and see where this guy is going?"

I sent the transmission from my stationary position two miles away, monitoring the moving surveillance with Richie in the Lexus while watching Brian wait for Rudy in the undercover car.

"221 to 202…I'm in the lot right now! I can go in!"

The voice that responded to my transmission made me cringe. It was the MDC detective whose unbridled enthusiasm and lack of discretion led to my encounter with a shaky shotgun. I preferred someone else go inside, but since there were no other takers, I reluctantly gave the go ahead, although it was one dripping with Jersey sarcasm.

"Okay…but be careful not to expose yourself."

Swiftly entering the hotel, the detective headed straight for the elevator and stuck his arm out just as the doors were closing. They reopened and he stepped into the transporter to join the only other person inside. The third-floor button was lit, so he pushed the fourth. As the slow-moving elevator ascended to its first scheduled stop, Nelson got out and turned right in the hallway, gazing back as the doors were closing to make sure he wasn't being followed.

The coast clear, Nelson inserted the key entrusted in his care and entered the hotel suite being used as a heroin mill. He removed five tablets from the batch processed and packaged the night before, three ounces for Rudy and two for another Dominican wholesaler. Stuffing the tablets shaped and wrapped to look like little bars of hotel soap in his pocket, he secured the rest of the stash in its hiding place and left the mill, slamming the door shut behind him.

Meanwhile, the elevator completed its lethargic climb, and the MDC detective followed the exit signs to a stairwell. He descended four flights and pushed the horizontal bar on the self-locking door, exiting the hotel into the parking lot on the Madison Street side. Elso sat in the Caravan around the corner in front of the building, oblivious to his side door egress. Retrieving the portable DEA radio stuffed beneath the seat of his car, the detective then discreetly reported his critically important observations.

Atonement.

* * *

After picking up the five tablets, Nelson and Elso then headed back to 46 Florence Street, careful not to violate any motor vehicle laws on the way. In possession of 140 grams of heroin without the buffer zone of a secret compartment, they didn't want to get stopped with something that could put them behind bars for ten years. Uninterruptedly, they arrived at their destination and scurried up the back staircase.

When the two workers entered the second-floor apartment, Gordo nodded to Nelson, who reached into his pocket and pulled out three of the five tablets. An antsy Rudy Matos, who was late for his appointment with the Canadian sprung off the couch like a Jack-in-the-Box, grabbed the three ounces of heroin, and scooted out the door.

Gordo told Nelson to put the other two tablets for "Flaco" in the kitchen closet. It was a short-term storage site for the soon-to-arrive distributor, who was not the fugitive still on the run in Puerto Rico, but another skinny drug dealer (Hector Bisono) with the same nickname, a Dominican who was one of Gordo's most prolific heroin wholesalers.

Flaco, the Dominican, would be delivering $6,000 when he picked up the two ounces, which would reduce his $15,000+ tab in Gordo's drug ledger of choice at the time, a thick bound, Spanish language comic book. Buried among the cartoon caricatures were handwritten pages with the names and running tallies of his wholesalers' debits and credits. With the sheer volume of heroin put out on the streets of Worcester and beyond, Gordo had to keep track of what his non-COD distributors owed him, but he wanted those records to be as unobtrusive as possible — just in case the police paid him an unannounced visit.

There were nearly two dozen names in the ledger, including a virtual who's who of Worcester's biggest heroin suppliers; wholesalers removed from retail level dealers, each with their own area of distribution that saturated an addicted city.

* * *

Rudy bounded down the stairs like a rubber ball and sped off in his Mazda. He was forty minutes late for his scheduled meet with Brian, and when he finally arrived, had no intention of staying there, sticking his arm out the window and motioning for the Canadian to follow him. The undercover Cadillac latched onto the heroin dealer's car, and they took off in series.

Just like he'd done during previous transactions, Rudy started looping blocks and making sudden U-turns to see if he was being followed, so the ground units backed off and the DEA plane took over. Brian understood that measures had to be taken to offset the obvious counter-surveillance moves, but without the security blanket of a familiar car in his rearview mirror, the undercover agent relayed their route through the Kel to ensure that wherever they wound up, he wouldn't be there alone.

Once again anticipating he'd go to his safe house on Svea Street, I had a unit set up there awaiting his arrival. But Rudy's circuitous course instead meandered in a different direction, surprisingly one that ended up at his apartment building on Outlook Drive.

"I don't like all this driving around! Where are we going!?" Brian protested to the cautious trafficker, who'd jumped out of his car and ran over to the Caddy.

"No worry, we here. I make sure no cop follow. Be right back."

Rudy scampered towards the back of the building, disappearing from Brian's view as the trafficker turned a bricked corner. None of the surveillance units could see where he went, either, but high in the sky the plane's spotter watched with magnified vision, as the drug dealer used a key to enter the building via a rear door.

Reemerging a few minutes later, Rudy poked his head around the corner and waved for the Canadian to join him. Money for the buy remaining in the Caddy's hidden compartment, Brian followed a trail of footsteps in the snow-covered landscape until reaching the backside of the building. By then Rudy had ducked back inside, peering from darkness through a crack in the pushed open door. With a whispered invitation, he urged the UC to come inside. When Brian did so, the self-locking door slammed shut, and the Kel went dead.

They descended downstairs, deeper into the dank of a poured concrete basement, further thickening the barrier blocking any Kel transmissions, and passed through a laundry room until reaching a binned storage area. The wily Dominican then dipped into his pocket and pulled out three neatly wrapped, rectangular shaped objects that looked like little bars of hotel soap.

"You got money?"

"It's in the car."

"Go get," Rudy snapped while pulling back the heroin, clearly expecting the Canadian to be prepared to do the exchange.

As soon as Brian exited the building, the Kel kicked in again. He walked back to the Caddy, executed the sequence to access the secret compartment, and removed $11,400 in cash, a bulky amount of money mostly in tens and twenties inside a shirt box, each half of the box separately gift wrapped allowing its contents to be viewed without disturbing the paper.

Rudy again was peeking through a cracked opening when Brian returned, the wedge inserted between the door and its frame by the UC to re-gain access kicked aside. The careful Dominican was taking no chances; he was ready to seal himself inside had anybody but the Canadian turned the corner. When Brian was allowed readmittance and the door closed behind him, the Kel again went silent.

"That's a lot of cash to carry around," Brian said after Rudy lifted the top section and started counting the money. He then manipulatively suggested Rudy keep it in the box; a smart move that'll not only deter someone from ripping him off in the high-crime city, but a thoughtful safety measure that'll impress his boss when the money is delivered to him.

Discreetly hidden on a cardboard flap beneath each half of the gift-wrapped box were my initials. Rudy would take his cut and pass the boxed balance onto his supplier. The bold, easily seen colors of the wrapping paper around a box too big not to be carried, would make it easier for surveillance to literally follow the money.

Then during the wee hours of the morning before the next scheduled day of pick-up, a trash pull operation would take place. Agents would sift through garbage later while wearing disposable gloves and enduring the smell of rotting food and worse, but the box would be found, soiled, but still displaying my initials. An important piece of evidence; strong probable cause supporting the issuance of future arrest and search warrants. I'd identify the exhibit during a hearing in federal district court; the connective proof needed to convict multiple defendants in a long-term, complex conspiracy case.

At least, that's how I envisioned it.

"It okay," Rudy replied, as he stuffed the money into his pants pockets, then crumpled up both sections of the box and jammed the cardboard mass into a nearby trash can.

The exchange completed and participants parted, Rudy returned to 46 Florence with bulging pockets like giant tumors. He stayed about five minutes before coming back down the well-worn set of stairs, slimmer at the hips than he appeared going up.

* * *

Ruben counted the money on the kitchen table and confirmed it was all there, freeing Rudy to leave the apartment and pick up an ounce of crack from Julio Santana for his next drug deal. Gordo was in another room getting ready for his trip to New York. It was the reason why he'd rented the Caravan. He and Elso would be in the trailer car behind the Lincoln Continental driven by Eduardo, the organization's interstate courier. More than $50,000 in cash would be transported in the Lincoln's secret compartment.

The plan? When both vehicles arrived at the family house on West 178th Street in Washington Heights, an automotive version of musical chairs would occur. Eduardo would switch to the Honda Accord with the bigger hide, which will already be filled with three kilograms of cocaine from Gordo's plant in Brooklyn. He'd then transport the weekly allotment to the Big Man's distributorship in Camden, New Jersey, while Gordo and Elso took the Lincoln and delivered the money to the Colombian in Queens.

The power brokers would then throw their substantial weight around, as Gordo and his heroin supplier finalized the details for the next fronted load. After staying the night in Washington Heights, Gordo would be chauffeured back to Worcester in the Caravan. There'd be no drugs, money, or weapons in the rental vehicle. The handgun Elso carried — a security measure in case someone tried to take the money during the trip to Manhattan or rob them on the way to Queens, would be left behind.

After delivering the three keys of coke to an auto parts store in Camden and staying the night at a motel in Philadelphia, Eduardo would return to New York, switch back to the Lincoln, and retrieve 600 grams of heroin from the Colombian's flunky in the Bronx. He'd then transport the fresh stock to the Clarion Suites Hotel in Worcester, where other organizational members would continue the cycle of packaging and distribution.

* * *

The number of "unknown Hispanic males" — a factual identifier for report writing that's descriptively enhanced by a worn piece of clothing, a noticeable physical feature, or an initial location of observation — had piled up on the trail that ended with Rudy delivering three ounces of heroin to Brian. What their specific role in the transaction was, if any, was also unknown, but since two of them were currently inside 46 Florence Street, I thought this might be a good time to put a name on a face or two.

"Richie, can we get a marked unit on standby to do a stop and ID some of these guys once that minivan starts moving again?"

"Let me ask my sergeant."

"But it's got to be *a worker.*"

Richie knew what I meant. There are cops who care about the job and doing things the right way. And then there are those who wear a uniform and a badge, but don't really give a shit so long as they get paid.

"All set...we got a good guy," Richie reported after conferring with his supervisor on a Worcester PD portable. "He'll lay low on Main Street until we need him. Sarge will coordinate the stop with him on a private channel when we're ready to go."

* * *

El Gordo and his two workers descended the back staircase and piled into the Caravan, the boss putting the money Rudy dropped off at the house in the glove box; a last-minute addition to the cache collected over the past few days. Eduardo had been called and instructed to meet them at Sandra's Market, where all the drug proceeds would be squirreled away in the electronic hide behind the radio for the trip to New York. That's also when Elso would grab the gun from the safe to ensure its protection. After Nelson was dropped off at his apartment on Jacques Ave to tend to local matters, the interstate adventure would begin. But first, there was one more piece of local business to take care of in Webster Square.

Gordo was driving on Park Avenue when he noticed the police car in the rearview mirror. He calmly shifted lanes to let it pass, but the cruiser stayed behind him. Then its bright overhead lights started rotating.

He told his workers not to panic then quickly laid out their cover story: all three were from New Jersey, but Gordo had moved to Worcester (he had a real Mass license with a fake name and an address other than 46 Florence) and his friends had come up for a visit. If the cop found the money, they were to keep their mouths shut. He'd do all the talking.

Elso and Nelson nervously nodded, as Gordo turned off the busy Park Ave into a parking lot alongside Minute Carwash.

* * *

"Three unknown Hispanic males down the backstairs and heading towards the Caravan."

Richie relayed the eye on Florence Street's broadcast to his sergeant, who in turn notified the marked unit on a different frequency, and the cruiser started creeping into position. The plan was simple: once the Caravan was far enough away from the house to be a disassociation, the uniformed officer would develop independent probable cause to stop the rental, identify at least the driver, and then let them go on their merry way with a verbal warning. It should appear to be a routine stop without raising any suspicion of being something other than that.

The cruiser came from the back of the pack, swiftly passing a line of surveillance cars that yielded to its approach. A signal-less lane change and the overheads were activated. The rental's driver complied, turning into a carwash lot, and stopping next to the building. The cruiser pulled up right behind it to complete a perfectly executed, low profile motor vehicle stop.

Then seemingly out of nowhere another car sped into the lot and abruptly skidded to a halt, nearly crashing into the cruiser as it kicked up a maelstrom of sand and salt. Two Worcester Vice detectives — including Richie's sergeant — flung open their doors and ordered all three occupants out of the Caravan. One of them threw his arms on top of the minivan after exiting as if he was preparing to be arrested.

Suddenly, the routine stop had the appearance of being a buy/bust.

Richie and I watched in horror from the opposite side of the four-lane roadway, stunned at what appeared to be another betrayal of trust by the

Worcester P.D.

"Richie, what the hell are they doing!?"

"I don't know, bro…"

* * *

The sergeant lagged well behind the DEA surveillance cars with good reason. His Crown-Vic-like car might as well be equipped with a light bar and Worcester PD decals; all the bad guys in the city knew it was a narc's. After radioing the officer in the cruiser to start moving up, the patrol car passed one DEA unit after another until latching onto the target vehicle. Overheads activated, instead of pulling to the curb like most people would, the Caravan took a left into a parking area. Closely followed by the cruiser, both vehicles disappeared behind a carwash.

The sergeant had never been part of an undercover buy operation that in itself would qualify as a major seizure in his budget restricted squad. He was impressed by what the feds could do, but with the investigative rewards came the increased risk of danger. He worried about the uniformed officer's safety. A high-level organization capable of selling this much heroin meant retention precautions to protect the proceeds it generated had to be taken.

Out of sight behind a building with three suspected traffickers mostly likely in possession of a large sum of money, the sergeant had a bad feeling as he instinctively hit the gas to back-up the one-man unit. Flying past the DEA cars with his emergency bubble whirring as fast as his mind, he cleared the corner of the carwash and immediately slammed on the brakes, sliding to a stop just before hitting the backend of the cruiser.

The cop he'd worried about had everything under control.

Hoping to minimize the damage caused by his overreaction, the sergeant ordered everybody out of the Caravan and the emerging passengers were patted down. Then in a voice loud enough for the suspects to hear, he turned to the uniformed officer and said they were right around the corner when the call came in and decided to back him up.

"Sounded like you needed help. Is everything okay?"

The startled officer didn't expect another car to come barreling into the lot, especially one driven by the supervisor who'd told him the operation was supposed to be low-key. Then he saw the look on the sergeant's face and understood.

I fucked up.

"Everything's fine, sarge. Just a motor vehicle violation."

The Caravan's driver intently listened to every word being spoken. Standing about six-foot two and closing in on three hundred pounds, he was an imposing figure who could pass as a lineman for the Patriots. His thick neck rose to meet a full Hispanic face with a sloping mustache that converged upon cherubic cheeks, and a pair of dark, probing eyes that had a bit of a squint to them. You could tell there was a lot going on behind those eyes.

The sergeant apologized to the Caravan's occupants and said he's going to have to write a report, politely asking all three for identification.

"It okay, officer...I understand," the driver responded in halting English.

The driver then said something in Spanish to his passengers while pulling out his wallet and producing a Massachusetts license with the name, "Junior Diaz-Pena." The unknown Hispanic male from Jacques Ave showed a New Jersey license, but Raiders said he didn't have an identification on him, so the sergeant verbally took his information.

"Again, I'm sorry for the misunderstanding. Have a nice day."

* * *

Gordo and Elso calmly exited the Caravan when told to do so, but a guilt-conscious Nelson got out and reflexively flung himself spread eagle against the side of the rental.

Enough was overheard by the boss to know what happened. One of the detectives thought the uniformed cop needed backup, but when told it was nothing more than a motor vehicle stop, he apologized to the kingpin and his people. Gordo would later tell his workers, "I'm the biggest heroin dealer in the city and this stupid cop is apologizing to me!"

Identifications were requested to document the incident, prompting Gordo to tell his workers to turn over their fictitious New Jersey driver's licenses. Nelson relaxed enough to comply, but a defiant Elso, whose license was in his back pocket, claimed not to have an ID. The recently arrived Esperanzan had just paid $500 of his own money for the alias and wasn't about to put miles on it already. Foolishly, he made up another name and address on the spot and risked being caught in a lie. But the detective just wrote down his information and the police cars drove away.

"A slight inconvenience," the boss declared to his underlings.

The Caravan was exchanged for a different rental and Gordo proceeded forward with his planned trip to New York.

Chapter 8

"A Room with a View"

March 1995

Something was going on inside the Clarion Suites Hotel that had nothing to do with weary travelers or business conferences. Twice now it had popped up during surveillances, the last in the middle of a three-ounce dope deal when a detective found redemption by discreetly following an "unknown Hispanic male" — who now had a name after a rash-acting sergeant recovered his own fumble — to the third floor of the ten-story hotel.

It was time to push aside my concern about compromise and trust somebody outside of law enforcement.

Ten days after the eventful heroin buy, Richie and I steadfastly walked through the front door of the Clarion Suites' main entrance. Veering left along a wall in front of us that ended at a sharp edge before turning at a forty-five-degree angle, a sizeable lobby and the front desk came into view. In a city where it seemed like a drug dealer lurked around every corner, this time one did, as Richie grabbed my arm and persuasively guided me back behind the wall.

"That guy at the front desk? I arrested him for cocaine distribution."

Not a good start for public trust.

"Okay, then it's probably not a good idea showing my face and telling him I'm a cop, too. Let's do it this way: You go up to the desk by yourself and ask to see the manager. I'll wait back here. When he or she comes out, ask if the two of you can speak somewhere in private. Make up some reason…a robbery near the hotel, car break-ins in the lot, anything but drugs. Just make sure your friend behind the desk hears you."

"And what do you want me to say after that?"

"Don't worry about that. I'll catch up with you by then."

As I peeked around the corner, Richie stood on one side of the front desk and a sour faced clerk with telephone in hand on the other. Moments later, the fast-paced click of heels echoed down a hallway until the source of the sound appeared in the lobby. A nattily attired, stiff backed man with wiry hair and a pencil thin mustache confidently strolled up and extended a greeting to the Worcester detective.

"I'm the general manager of the hotel," he said while introducing himself by name. "How may I help you?" The nametag pinned to his copper-colored blazer corroborated the pompous-sounding pronouncement.

"Yes, is there someplace we can talk in private?" Richie asked after flashing his badge and making up an impromptu story for the clerk's benefit.

The GM obliged without question, retracing his steps with the slow-footed Richie in tow. Exhibiting my own air of belonging, I briskly followed suit, joining up with my lagging partner well beyond any curious eyes at the front desk. The manager looked back after catching sight of my sudden appearance, probably thinking I was a Worcester detective, too, until the three of us slipped into his office and I closed the door while displaying my DEA credentials.

"I'm sorry to have to tell you this, but we believe somebody is using your hotel to distribute large amounts of heroin. The good news is we can help you with your problem." I then handed the GM an Administrative Subpoena requesting the name of every suite holder on the third floor. "This should satisfy your hotel's requirements."

The GM silently reviewed the legal document, and apparently convinced of his obligation to produce, opened a desk drawer and took out a blank Clarion Suites standard floor plan. He numbered each unit as it corresponded to those suites on the third floor and then began pecking at a clunky computer on his desk. On a separate sheet of paper, he wrote down the name of every occupant on file, then handed over his quickly completed assignment.

"Our occupancy rate isn't what it used to be, so a few years back corporate decided to convert some of the suites into condos. What you have are the names of all the current third-floor residents, by deed if owned, registered name if leased. Unfortunately, not all the units are occupied at this time," he lamented. "Keep in mind that some of the owners sub-lease their condos without telling us."

I was pleasantly surprised at the speed of his responsiveness. Not everybody receiving a subpoena is this cooperative. But as I continued listening to the GM wax nostalgic about the heyday of the hotel's inhabitancy — its fall commensurate with the rise of downtown drugs and associated violent crime — I sensed his feelings went beyond that of someone whose livelihood had been deleteriously affected. This man cared about the city, itself; a chord that resonated with me, as a deep down, foreign feeling of trust emerged from its dormant hiding place.

"I'll do that. After we go over this list, we may have some additional questions about a specific suite. If so, can I contact you directly?"

"Of course," the GM replied with a dismissive wave. Grabbing a business card from a silver tray on his desk, he jotted down a number. "This is my private line. If there are any drugs being dealt out of this hotel, I want it stopped as soon as possible."

"On that, we are in agreement. There's one other area of concern ... somebody in your hotel, perhaps even an employee, may not share your concerns about drug dealing. This is a sensitive investigation and I trust you'll keep everything we've discussed here today in total confidence."

A thoughtful pause was followed by a dawning expression of comprehension.

"This subpoena will go directly into my safe and I'm the only one with the combination. Only corporate will be told who you are and the reason for your visit. Nobody in the hotel will know," he assured me while rising to seal the pact with a handshake. "Now, if there's nothing else, I do have a hotel to manage."

Richie and I left via a side door to avoid the front desk, returning to the Lexus in the parking lot where we anxiously scanned the paperwork. There were sixteen suites on the third floor, but only ten were currently occupied. Stepping out of the elevator and turning right in the hallway, just as the trailed target did during the three-ounce heroin buy, the number of occupied units dropped to seven — five condos and two monthly rentals. The registered name on one of the rentals, suite 315, rang a bell.

"Junior Pena...Richie, wasn't that the name of the big guy driving the Caravan?"

* * *

I accepted the general manager's offer of additional assistance, arranging to meet him again at the hotel to find out more about the occupant in suite 315. After slipping in through a side door to bypass the front desk, I took a seat in his office.

"Okay, the gentleman in 315 has been a guest of ours for quite a while now, but only for a few months in that particular unit," the GM shared after waiting for the requested information to pop up on his slow computer. "Prior to that, he leased 201 and then 302 for almost a year. Payments are timely, always made in cash, and housekeeping has a standing order not to clean the suite unless notified to do so. He has one car registered with us."

When the GM read out the plate of the red Buick Electra used to deliver the heroin sample to Rudy earlier in the case, I knew we had the right suite.

"I noticed on the floor plan that the suite across the hall from 315 is currently unoccupied." There was no need for the GM to consult his computer; he was painfully aware of every vacancy in the hotel.

"Yes, it is."

"Does it have the same layout as 315?"

"It's similar in design but with a slight modification." The GM then proceeded to get lost in his element explaining the difference between the two suites. The vacant unit had a counter with stools that separated the kitchen from the dining area, he said, elaborating that it was for those wishing "a more casual eating atmosphere and greater living space". He expounded that suite 315 did not have this partitioning, but that the difference created "an airy openness allowing for the inclusion of a formal dining room."

The panache of his descriptive manner reflected that of an experienced salesman.

"Is it possible to see this unit?"

"Of course," the GM replied while opening a drawer and removing a set of keys on a giant O-ring better suited for a dungeon master. "Follow me."

I trailed his quick, upright stride to the elevator and up two flights, where the GM got off, turned right, and walked the almost full length of the hallway until reaching a door on the right. As he sorted through the jangled mass of metal, I furtively glanced across the hall at the door marked "315," which I estimated to be another fifteen feet further down the corridor. My glance turned into a stare as I wondered what evil lurked on the other side of that door. Feeling exposed while waiting, I hoped it wouldn't suddenly open to catch me in all my vulnerability.

Click…

The GM found the right key as my 1950s sci-fi movie imagination vaporized and we entered suite 316.

The unit was fully furnished with a view of the parking lot once your line of sight bypassed an industrial sized air conditioner on the adjoining flat roof. Bad timing or a regular occurrence brought the lengthy rumble of a nearby Worcester & Providence railroad train, which shook the floor as the GM described the comforts and conveniences of the suite along with all the amenities offered by the hotel. I half expected his spiel to include the cultural and sporting events going on in the city, but mercifully, I was spared.

Pacing approximately fifteen feet along an interior hallway that ran parallel to the third-floor corridor, I mentally noted where it stopped before returning to the kitchen. From my black bag, I removed the Clarion Suites floor plan and placed the document on the counter.

"Is this schematic to scale?"

"Yes, it is."

"Good, I'll take it…that is, DEA will take it. On a month-to-month basis."

The GM appeared to be surprised by the announcement that incrementally improved his vacancy rate.

"Like our neighbor across the hall, I'll pay you in cash and won't need housekeeping unless requested. The suite will have to be registered under a fictitious name, though, and we only want to deal with you … nobody else in the hotel must know that DEA is here."

"That can all be arranged. When do you want to start?"

"How about today?" I said while dipping into my bag and pulling out a stack of bills for the preauthorized investigative expense. "Oh, there's one other thing … we'd like your permission to drill a small hole through the bathroom wall to insert a thin wire with an attached micro-lens. It'll be professionally installed and undetectable to anybody outside the suite. Once we vacate the unit, I promise it'll be patched up and painted to your satisfaction."

The US attorney's office had already been consulted about the need for a court order and determined that as long as a person in authority gave permission to install a camera with a view of the semi-public area, a judge's authorization was not necessary. The lens would line up with an unobstructed view of the door to suite 315, thus allowing DEA to covertly watch and videotape all the moving parts of a suspected heroin mill.

The GM's expression of surprise turned to one of awe by the surreptitiousness of it all, but there was no hesitation in his response.

"If there are any drugs being distributed from this hotel, I want it stopped. You have my permission."

* * *

An agent settled into the stationary post in suite 316 and peered through the peephole at the door across the hall. Mobile teams were set up outside the hotel and at 46 Florence Street; one unit splintered off the pack, racing to the Westborough District Court ten miles east of Worcester. Rudy had just paged Brian from a payphone inside the courthouse to say he'd be delayed until his case was called. "Just a motor vehicle violation," he downplayed, but the responding unit would determine he'd been charged with possession of a clone phone. Immediately after the hearing, Rudy said he'd pick up the heroin—the first buy after covert surveillance of the suspected heroin mill had been established—and meet the Canadian to do the deal.

Despite the early morning start to the operation, the bad guys' workday had already begun. Half an hour into his clandestine shift, the agent in 316 saw the door of suite 315 swing open, and two workers came out. One, a recent arrival from Esperanza known as "Pole" by his peers, but with chilling implications called "Loco" on the streets, stuffed something into the pocket of his denim jacket before securing suite 315 with a yank.

The two targets left the hotel lot in a rental car and drove directly to 46 Florence Street, where the underboss, Ruben Madera-Perez, went up the back staircase, while Loco ran across the street to a white Buick LeSabre parked in front of Clark University. He unlocked the front passenger door with a key, removed something from the pocket of his jacket, put it in the glove box, then slammed the door shut and relocked the car. Re-crossing the street at a more leisurely pace, as though no longer carrying a heavy burden, he went eight steps up and out of sight.

Typical of the cattle drive process in the state court system, over three hours elapsed before Rudy's case was called. After receiving a "continued without a finding" judgment — not a conviction, but an abeyance under which the charge would be dismissed if after six months he didn't commit another criminal offense — Rudy dashed out of the courthouse with the intention of distributing heroin.

As the court-inconvenienced trafficker sped west on Route 9 bound for 46 Florence, four shadowy figures came down the tread-worn staircase at the back of the house. El Gordo and three of his workers (one up from the Bronx to pick up a cell phone cloning device known as a Kingfisher, a courtesy item he'd deliver to a regional distributor in Michigan, who also wanted half a pound of heroin) piled into the rental and drove to a car dealership next to where the day's surveillance started — the Clarion Suites Hotel.

While Gordo and his gang were on an organizational outing to purchase a new car for the fleet, Rudy arrived at 46 Florence and scampered up the back staircase. Almost immediately thereafter, he bounced back down the stairs and made a beeline for the white LeSabre. Now possessing the key to unlock the car, he opened the front passenger door and reached into the glove box, but after several minutes of fumbling frustration, he gave up and sprinted back to the second-floor apartment across the street.

Two miles away, the three workers stood and waited in the dealership lot while Gordo took a test drive. A surveillance agent with binoculars, slouched catty-corner in his car, watched as underboss Madera-Perez lifted his jacket to retrieve the vibrating beeper on his belt. He then went inside the dealership — if you could call a little white shack in the middle of the lot a dealership — to use the office phone. After a brief conversation, he came back out and hopped into the rental to answer the call for help.

Back on Florence, Rudy sat and waited behind the wheel of his Mazda, dejected, hood up, engine dead. He was having a bad automotive day. First, he couldn't access the hide to retrieve the heroin left for him in the LeSabre, then when he tried to start his own car, it wouldn't turn over. His spirits were lifted when the underboss arrived and not only showed him how to open the secret compartment, but also said he could take the LeSabre to do the deal.

Watching through the zoom lens of a camera from a van parked three car lengths behind the LeSabre, an agent captured the moment and shared it with surveillance, as one team followed the underboss back to the car dealership and another trailed Rudy to the Auburn Mall.

"You going to jail or what?" Brian jocularly remarked after Rudy arrived and took a seat in the undercover Cadillac.

"It nothing," Rudy dismissively replied, the court's compassion clearly not changing his criminal intentions.

"That's a relief, because I need you around to buy more drugs," Brian joked as the two shared a laugh. "Let's do this and then talk for a few minutes."

"Okay, follow me."

Inside the LeSabre, Rudy stretched from the driver's side and opened the glove box. He disengaged the locking mechanism, but still encountered a little difficulty that elicited a grunt or two, before Brian heard *snap* and saw the rear wall panel fall forward to reveal a secret compartment. Rudy delved deeper into the black hole and removed two compressed rectangles of heroin, each wrapped to look like a little bar of hotel soap. After the exchange was made, Rudy stuffed the money into the abyss and clasped the rear panel back in place. Brian then secured the heroin in his own hide, and it was time to talk.

Five successful heroin transactions bought more than drug exhibits; they also bought trust, enough of an investment to seek out even more value for the government buck. Instead of tripping from Montreal for two to three ounces of heroin every two to three weeks, Brian proposed coming down once a month to purchase at least half a pound of the potent product. His people now felt comfortable with a greater cash outlay, for Rudy had also earned *their* trust, so he was told, but the increased weight would have to come commensurate with a reduction in cost. Since Rudy said he didn't set the prices, the Canadian wanted to meet and negotiate a better one with whoever did. Brian quickly assuring the wholesaler that he and his profit margin wouldn't be cut out; after an agreement was struck with Rudy's boss, Rudy and Brian would continue their good working relationship.

Rudy didn't need convincing. He'd been hooked on the Canadian's authenticity ever since the dog and pony show put on at Locomotion Auto Repairs. Greed was now his guide. Very receptive to the idea of doing bigger business and thinking his boss would be, too, he agreed to pass on the proposal and get back to Brian.

* * *

From the room with a view to the car with a hide, a link had been established between suite 315 and the heroin distributed by Rudy Matos. There'd be other covert surveillances conducted at the Clarion Suites that weren't in conjunction with a controlled buy, mostly stationary ones solo manned by me without a supporting cast. Whenever possible after a day in the office or doing surveillance on the streets of another drug-infested city, I'd trek out to Worcester for a second shift at the post. In an occupation inundated with work and staffed by a disproportionate few, making the effort to reap the benefits of proactivity fell squarely upon the shoulders of every case agent.

Sometimes I'd stay overnight, catching a few hours of sleep before resuming the watch early the next morning. Nobody ever stayed in suite 315; the new day's first sighting was always an arrival, an entrusted worker using a key to open the suspected mill for business before others reported for duty. When I left the hotel bound for Boston, I'd always depart at the same time, giving the impression to anyone who cared to pay attention that the tall man with the black bag slung over his shoulder was just another guest with a mundane job and regular office hours.

The embedded lens saw, and its companion recorder taped, many faces coming and going, as the inner circle of an active criminal network defined itself. These recordings gave clues to position and power within the organization; indelible images not only on the tapes, but also in my mind from reviewing them over and over again. Each unvarnished face — at times pausing in the doorway as if posing for the camera — failed to hide its owner's guilt. But circumstantial evidence and an agent's intuition wouldn't be enough to convince federal prosecutors to indict any of those faces.

El Gordo outright rejected a meet with the Canadian. Brian would go no higher than Rudy. Still, strong probable cause existed to believe suite 315 was being used as nothing but a heroin processing and distribution center. With a little freshening up when the time was right, there'd be enough probable cause to get a federal search warrant. The US attorney's office agreed, telling me if I could produce unequivocal proof that suite 315 was being used solely as a heroin mill, this evidence combined with the cumulative amount of drug and non-drug evidence already on the table would make a compelling case for arresting *all* the faces captured on tape.

Then in a flash, the optimistic option that seemed so solid evaporated, as I watched three workers drag a large duffel bag and a suitcase on wheels out of suite 315. After that, the only people seen coming and going from the unit were housekeeping.

The mill had been moved.

Chapter 9

"A Change of Plans"

April/May 1995

"I no can tell my sister come to Worcester all the time!"

Rasta Rey Barnes was livid. All Brian asked him to do was set up another meet with Marla to introduce his pilot and go over the logistics of flying in and out of Panama. The undercover agent did his best to calm him down, immediately withdrawing the request and assuring the angered trafficker that everything was okay.

But everything wasn't okay.

Not only did Rey refuse to set up a meeting, but his unexplained outburst manifested into the garage owner going incommunicado — again. For a week afterwards, he wouldn't answer Brian's calls or return any of his pages. But when Rey took the next step of avoidance by disconnecting the number at Locomotion Auto Repairs, his silence spoke volumes.

He was washing his hands clean of the Canadian.

There was nothing more to be gained by exposing Lanh to the sordid activity going on at Locomotion, so he'd been instructed to stop hanging out there. However, the informant was still locally available as a pinch-hitter for the Canadian whenever the need arose.

Tracking down Rey in the bowels of Main South, the little guy learned that his diminished status as a go-between in the Panama affair, combined with the discovery of Rudy's drug affair with Brian behind his back, had bruised his fragile ego. Rey's pride went so far as to say he no longer wanted to have any further business dealings with Brian.

Jealousy on two fronts had prompted Rasta Rey to close the door on the biggest drug deal of his life, but in cause-and-effect fashion, it allowed the

UC to open another.

"I just heard some disturbing news," Brian told Marla after contacting her at the Brooklyn number she'd provided during their meet at the McDonald's.

"What happened?"

"Can you call me back from a payphone, collect, I'll pay, so we can talk freely?"

Marla agreed, taking the Montreal number along with the assurance it was a "good phone," thereby, putting the onus of precaution against interception on the smuggler's end.

The red light outside the UC room in Boston aglow, and the green button on the recorder inside depressed, the incoming call came in ten minutes later. Brian started out by apologizing for contacting her directly, but he was left with no other choice after hitting a barrier with her brother. All he asked him to do was set up another meeting with her in Worcester, explaining that his pilot needed answers to technical flight questions too detailed to be discussed over the phone, but for some reason, Rey denied the request.

"Just have your pilot write down his questions and when we go to Panama, I'll get them answered in person. My people won't talk anything flight-wise on the phone."

"I don't understand what's going on here," Brian responded with true confusion. "Rey told my little friend that he doesn't trust me anymore and now he doesn't want to do the deal."

Marla was nonplussed. "I don't know what he's talking about!" There's no problem with me! In fact, I spoke with my guy yesterday and he asked when we're coming down."

Brian sighed with relief, telling Marla he was glad to hear everything is still a go.

"Hey, I know your brother was the one who put us together, but how about I deal directly with you from this point on?"

"That's fine with me," Marla replied, no doubt coming to the same conclusion that Rey's rough and tumble street style had no place in such a high-stakes, international matter. "Look, I'll be heading up to Worcester in a few days to visit Rey. Why don't the three of us get together and sort things out."

Brian said it was no longer necessary. Now that he knew his pilot's questions would be answered and he'd established an open line of communications with Marla, there was no need for another meeting involving her brother.

Marla was content, too. So long as the Canadian and his money were mollified, she probably couldn't care less knowing Rey had just been cut out.

* * *

With the impediment of Rey's rash behavior brushed aside, the initial trip to Panama and the ultimate pick-up of 110 kilograms of cocaine (including Marla's ten-key commission) began to take a more solid shape. From mid-March to the beginning of April, Brian and Marla frequently spoke with one another; each conversation strengthening an infrastructure of trust that built the foundation of a solid conspiracy.

Marla did meet with Rey in Worcester shortly after Brian first called her. He admitted to being angry with the Canadian but told his sister it was because Brian hadn't yet agreed on his cut — an explanation that ran contrary to the truth extracted by Lanh and confirmed by Rudy. His alternative facts version was understandably given, though. How would his internationally accomplished sister react if she lost this substantial sale and hefty commission due to her brother's temper tantrum of jealousy?

"Here's a new number for the garage," Marla told Brian, clearly irritated that she had to get involved in such a petty dispute. "He's expecting your call." Grateful to be rid of the distasteful mediation matter, she then moved on to more pertinent issues.

Marla's partner in Panama was anxious to meet the Canadian and get things rolling. After consulting their respective calendars, they agreed on a travel date. Brian said he'd purchase a round trip ticket and FedEx it to her address in Brooklyn. He'd also make a reservation under her name at her hotel of choosing in Panama City, Brian adding he'd pay her lodging and expense money in person when they met down there.

Marla had a different agenda in mind. The experienced negotiator insisted on making her own hotel reservation (which hotel she would not reveal), saying she'd "save" the Canadian money by only lodging there one or two nights. Then she'd stay at her sister's house after Brian left for however long it took to get things done, ensuring everything for a smooth in and out trip would be set up for his pilot when he arrived. They agreed on a $1,500 cash fee to cover all her incidental expenses in both Panama and New York, which included a portion of the rent for her Brooklyn apartment while she was out of town biding Brian's business.

Because she didn't know how long the prep would take, Marla wanted the return date on her airline ticket to be left open-ended. She also wanted to fly out of New York via Lacsa Airlines to San Jose, Costa Rica, and from there catch a connecting flight to Panama City; an itinerary she always took when "dealing with this stuff." Whether the request was meant to boost her frequent flier miles or minimize entry scrutiny on a direct flight from the United States, she didn't say.

Brian agreed to her terms and then confirmed the address she'd previously given him. Upon further reflection, Marla decided to make a slight adjustment.

"Change the apartment number to 729 (from 723). I don't want (it) to get mixed up with the others."

Overseeing a busy multi-kilogram distribution business in New York, Marla wanted any financial consideration related to this customer transported, bulk transaction separated from the day-to-day dealings associated with her regularly smuggled shipments via courier. Anything connected with her brokering service should be sent to the apartment leased in her own name down the hall, not the one she lived in with her fugitive partner.

Apparently, not everything was shared between lovers.

* * *

"I've got some great news!"

A buoyed Brian uttered the announcement as he strolled from one end of the expansive DEA group to the other. I looked up from the pile of paperwork on my desk and gave him my full attention, expecting to hear the latest update about his undercover trip to Panama, or maybe he'd heard something enlightening from Rudy Matos about why El Gordo had suddenly shuttered the suspected heroin mill at the Clarion Suites Hotel. However, Brian's declaration of "great news" had nothing to do with either.

"I've been named the division's polygrapher!"

"Oh...congratulations. I didn't even know you were interested in the position."

DEA had just initiated the Polygraph Program as another aspect of its recruitment process, a tool that would later be expanded for use in criminal investigations. Each of the twenty divisions (at the time) nominated one agent of the highest integrity for the position. Brian was selected to be the New England Field Division's representative.

"Yeah, it's a good move for me and my family. You know, regular hours. I'll be home at night, not much travel." To the young agent's chagrin, there'd be a lot more traveling involved than he originally thought.

Brian went on to say he'd be in the next class once DEA Training set a date for the school; a lengthy one for a program being prioritized by the agency, which would either be held at the academy in Quantico, or if a classroom wasn't available, some other suitable site in Virginia. What concerned me was he said it could possibly start in two weeks.

"Two weeks?! But you'll be able to come back for undercover operations … right?"

"They tell me it's a really demanding school with lots of homework and long study hours. If you fail just one test, you're out. I'll have to stay there the whole time and once I return, it's a full-time position that prohibits me from doing anything else. I'm sorry to tell you this, but I won't be able to do any more undercover work."

The firmly entrenched conduit to reaching the goal line, the one person on a multi-pronged, complex conspiracy field who'd carried the ball to *two* critical crossroads, was being taken out of the game midstride by his own team. I would soon be overseeing an undercover investigation that no longer had its primary undercover agent.

Brian had made a career choice. I was stunned at the turn of events but didn't blame him. A bureaucracy waits for no one. He'd had to seize the opportunity or DEA would have taken it away and given it to another.

In every long-term federal drug investigation, there comes a seminal moment when every case agent says to themself, *'this is as far as I go.'*

My time had just arrived.

* * *

"There's been a change in plans," Brian told Marla after confirming she'd finally received her airline tickets, a twice delayed delivery because she seldom occupied her own apartment to sign for the FedEx package. "My people now want a gallon of paint as a sample."

"How much?" the code-confused smuggler asked.

"One gallon of the one-hundred-gallon order."

"Why do you want a sample now when it could be different from the larger supply of paint you'll receive?"

"Let's just say it's what my people want."

Marla had never entertained such a request but didn't think it'd be a problem. She'd contact the supplier and get back to Brian, ending the flash-coded conversation by saying the quality of the shipment he received later may be even "smoother" than the sample he'd get now.

It was less than a week before the scheduled trip to Panama. Brian's imminent departure for polygraph school necessitated the "change in plans." A strong circumstantial case had been made against Marla and other co-conspirators, both identified and unidentified, but it was still a dry conspiracy. The Canadian's "people" — the US Attorney's Office in the District of Massachusetts — refused to prosecute her unless DEA put some "dope on the table." Not just any drug exhibit, either, but one with all the elements undeniably proving beyond a reasonable doubt that Marla was on the highest domestic level of an international smuggling organization.

If a kilogram "sample" of *pure cocaine*—a significant weight in itself that underscored the magnitude of the entire transaction—was purchased *in Panama,* the nearest point of transit in the pipeline of processed Colombian coke destined for North America, the US attorney's office would be convinced of Marla's ability to deliver the agreed upon amount. They would indict her as the leader of a conspiracy to import 110 kilograms, *even if the full shipment was never seized*, which now seemed inevitable without the primary undercover to make it happen.

Intercepting a big shipment would certainly be impactful. However, taking out of circulation the organizer who facilitated a steady stream of them would create a network vacuum that had a more wide-ranging impact. Getting the required evidence to arrest and convict Marla was now the primary focus. It was an adapted goal caused by a bureaucratic decision — and it all hinged on satisfying the parameters of a one-shot undercover buy.

* * *

"My guy doesn't normally do a gallon of paint as a sample. Maybe something smaller when we are down there. Maybe a pint," Marla told Brian two days later. It was a compromise to conciliate the client's last-minute addendum. Then she dropped a bomb that obliterated a crucial paragraph from the original contract.

A complication had arisen that now prevented her partner from meeting the Canadian.

"I don't want to say (why) on the phone, but it has something to do with a secret business, a base," Marla quasi-explained. She went on to say that her partner's unavailability wouldn't affect their transaction. The broker had been authorized to move cocaine from Colombia and make all the arrangements in Panama, which, of course, put her on an even higher plateau. But striking an operational objective of identifying her supplier didn't bode well with Brian.

"Let me remind you — it was you and your brother that said this trip was necessary so your guy could see I was 'the real deal'," Brian bristled. "Now he's not even going to be there?!"

"You must understand we have been partners for a long time. Things will get done. Now is not the time for him to be meeting anybody new."

Marla obviously didn't want to share any details about this "secret business" stuff, but when Brian started asking questions about her partner's susceptibility to arrest, without an explanation, she ran the risk of losing the customer.

"Look, the reason he doesn't want to meet anybody new is because of something that's going on with Interpol. They have a base in Panama City and there's a lot going on with some German people in the countryside." She assured the Canadian it couldn't be traced back to her partner, but to be on the safe side, he was heading back to Colombia until things calmed down.

It was meant to be a comfort, that she had everything under control and there was nothing to worry about, but Brian reacted like a cautious buyer should when told the police might have an interest in someone who's about to deliver 110 kilograms of cocaine to you. He said it was a problem that would have to be discussed with his boss before proceeding forward. They agreed to talk again later that night.

The DEA Panama Country Office did some digging and learned that Interpol — which did have a base in Panama City — had just the day before confiscated 140 kilograms of cocaine off a yacht in international waters between Colombia and Panama, a significant seizure that resulted from a wiretap investigation in Germany.

* * *

When Marla informed her Colombian partner that the Canadian had to be told about the German seizure or they risked losing his business, it intensified the source's anxiety. Panama was just too hot right now to do anything drug-related with another foreigner. Not even a sample of any size would be available. Realizing this could be a deal breaker, she was prepared with a back-up proposal to assuage Brian's anticipated anger.

"I have some fresh merchandise coming into the airport (New York) tonight and can put one aside for you. They're the gallon cans. If you like the quality, our trip will not be necessary."

"You'll sell it to me at Panama price?"

Marla laughed. "No, my friend…New York price." She wasn't about to take a hit on a brick that goes for at least $17,000 in New York and give it to him for three-grand.

The cavalier rejection irritated Brian. Already making the financial arrangements for them to meet in Panama, buying a kilo down there at market rate — not a price he could pay anybody in New York — would offset the business expense, or so she was led to believe.

"Plus, I need the answers to my pilot's questions from your people," Brian added, reminding Marla that she told him it would have to be done in person, in Panama.

She was prepared for this problem, too.

"We have someone who works for us in the control tower at Tocumen. He can coordinate with your pilot on which runway to use when landing and then direct him to a specific hangar. That way your pilot can safely pick up the stuff there and (immediately) depart."

By having the shipment ready and waiting to be loaded at Panama's primary international airport, it eliminated the need to circumvent detection while landing at a private airstrip, along with all the dangers associated with a clandestine in-and-out flight.

"Or we could transport the load to Miami for pick-up, but that would substantially increase your final price," Marla offered as another option. She was pulling all the stops to appease the Canadian and save the sale. But at a price of nine-to-ten-thousand-dollars per kilo — an outlay of a million dollars in cash — that option was outright rejected.

"How about this...we go to Panama as planned and if I can't meet your guy, have him send someone in his place." Brian explained he wanted the chance to negotiate price directly with the Colombian or his in-country representative; bitingly making the point it'll boost his waning confidence that her partner was the "real deal." But the sample was non-negotiable. Without it, Marla was told she could just forget about the whole thing.

Chapter 10

"Colombian Exchange" Panama City, Panama / Queens, New York

April/June 1995

The two Boston-based undercover agents waited in the lobby of the Caesar Park Hotel in Panama City. Nearby, another DEA agent, who was permanently assigned to the Panama Country Office, kept a close eye on them from the comfort of a leather chair, peering out over the cover of a fanned out, bilingual newspaper. His full beard, tweed jacket, and reading glasses perched at the tip of his nose gave him the look of a college professor on holiday.

Outside the swanky hotel was the rest of the surveillance team — both of us. I was in the Kel car alongside the building and a detective with the Panamanian Technical Judicial Police (PTJ) was set up at the front entrance. The Op-Plan called for more units than were made available, but the underwhelming show of support in the host country dashed that aspiration. Instead, the lone PTJ unit would tail the target vehicle when it left, while the professor and I remained behind to protect the undercovers. Although, with Panama law prohibiting DEA agents from carrying a firearm, I wondered how we were going to do that if the shit did hit the fan.

DEA prevailed in the standoff with Marla's apprehensive partner. He gave in to Brian's demands, agreeing to send a representative in his stead to meet the Canadian *and* provide him with a kilogram sample of pure cocaine, thus allowing all the North American pieces to be put in motion on their respective southbound flights.

Marla was fashionably late for the noontime meet, entering the five-star hotel without detection by the unit out front and confidently strolling towards the waiting undercover agents. The stylishly attired, attractive smuggler warmly greeted Brian as if an old friend. Then she was introduced to Alberto, the Spanish speaking UC her brother met in Worcester while Marla watched in anonymity from inside the McDonald's. The trio then adjourned to a more private setting, going downstairs to discuss their business in the hotel's lounge/restaurant.

Marla started out by relaying her partner's apologies for not meeting Brian in person. She had no reservations about referring to him by name, doing so several times. It was probably a smoke screen to shield his true identity, or perhaps it was a personalization meant to make the Canadian's unaccommodating service of the last few days feel more customer friendly.

"Hernando has directed one of his people, a Colombian woman, to work with me in making sure you're satisfied with the quality of his product."

"How well do you know this woman?" a skeptical Al inquired with his thick, transplanted Bronx accent.

"I know her very well. She's nervous about meeting you, *too*."

Brian skipped the undercover foreplay and went straight into logistical matters.

"Does she know we want to buy a kilogram of cocaine and not just look at it?"

"She knows. The cost will be $2,900. We were going to do the exchange at her place, but now that is not possible because she has family staying with her for Holy Week."

Brian suggested they keep it simple. That the Colombian woman meet them there at the restaurant with the kilo in a shopping bag and after discussing details about the final price and delivery terms of the shipment, leave the bag under the table in exchange for the money, which he'd slide across the table in an envelope. Marla was good with this arrangement.

Then he slid a different envelope across the table. It contained his pilot's questions, written in Spanish for her people's convenience. Brian said they needed to be answered whether or not he decided to use her connection at the airport, a service that came with an implied fee. Marla nodded and put the multi-page list of technical aviation questions in her pocketbook.

"I'll be meeting with my guy from the control tower at Tocumen later this week. He can answer these questions. I also have someone who can help us out, if needed, at the military airbase." (Marcos A. Gelabert Airport, the former Albrook Air Force Station that now operates in the public domain, was still often referred to by its previous military designation.)

Marla then jotted down two phone numbers and handed the piece of paper to Brian.

"I'll page her when I get back to my hotel about the sample. Call me at the top number at 1:30. You can reach me at the second after you leave (the country)," adding that she'd be staying at her sister's place for the next two weeks while arranging everything in Colombia and Panama.

Brian acknowledged his marching orders and gave one of his own, telling her to "make sure the cocaine's quality is of high purity."

"It'll be fish-scale. Very shiny when broken up. The woman has access to the big stash and the kilogram would only be of the highest quality." Marla then shifted a little uneasily in her seat before broaching the next subject. "Hernando wants to be very careful when doing the 100-kilogram load because recently a bunch of his cocaine was seized by the police on the open sea between Colombia and Panama. He wants to do it in increments of ten to lessen the potential loss or damage if any of the cocaine is seized by the police."

Both Brian and Al protested. There was no way their people were going to send down a plane with hundreds of thousands of dollars to pick up the shipment in piecemeal packages; a reaction based upon Marla's calm acceptance that she'd anticipated. Nevertheless, she'd satisfied her obligation to present the proposal and said she'd pass on their feelings to Hernando.

Finished with their business for the time being, Marla said she'd give Brian an update after speaking with the Colombian woman, then left the hotel, departing the same way she arrived by getting into an idling taxi sitting at the curb. The PTJ unit latched onto the cab and began the one-car surveillance; a brief one that ended immediately after leaving the hotel grounds, when the detective either lost sight of the target vehicle or interest in the whole affair.

* * *

I camped out with the two undercovers in my hotel room; an impromptu Op-Post, which for security reasons, was someplace other than the meeting place chosen by Marla. Though the PTJ unit failed to identify where she was staying, a subscriber check of the number provided didn't. Surveillance would be set up at her hotel as she waited for the Colombian woman with access to the "big stash." This perfect wall-off opportunity just might lead to the seizure of a shipment of cocaine without compromising the case in Worcester. But fancies of finding the mother lode would only be a pipe dream when the country attaché told me *nobody* was available to assist us.

Frustratingly, without an eye on her identified hotel during a tortuous four-hour wait — Marla thrice-telling Brian during hourly updates that the Colombian woman hadn't yet contacted her — he finally received an update of substance.

It was one none of us liked.

"I don't know how to tell you this," Marla reported. "The paint is ready, but the Colombian woman wants to send a salesman to deliver it. She wants me to pick up the papers (money) first and the salesman will deliver the stuff to you later tonight, at about eleven someplace away from the hotel. But she insists you must be alone."

Hot off the heels of the 140-kilogram Interpol seizure destined for a German customer, the Colombian woman, like Hernando, apparently got cold feet about delivering any quantity of coke to another foreigner.

"COD is the only way this is going to happen," Brian irritatingly responded. "And not later tonight by myself — at the hotel, *now*."

"I understand. Hold on," Marla replied and put down the phone.

Clicking heels were heard through the receiver, each step fading with every receding stride until ceasing altogether. Then an indiscernible conversation began that said Marla was not alone in the room. When the talking ceased, the clicking resumed, each approaching step growing louder until the phone was again picked up.

"COD is acceptable, but the salesman is not available until later tonight."

"Then *you* deliver it yourself!"

"*Me?!* Why don't you want the salesman to make the delivery?!"

Brian said he'd waited long enough. Too long. If the package was ready now, he wanted it now. Not during a midnight run from some flunky in a dark alley.

The ultimatum caught Marla off-guard. The unpalatable thought of handling drugs herself was an affront to her polished, professional image

— not to mention risky business that exposed her to arrest, something she worked hard to avoid. But if the customer wasn't placated, *now*, she ran the risk of losing her substantial commission on the entire transaction.

"Okay, I'll meet you in the lobby at six-thirty."

* * *

Spiked pumps echoed on the marble floor of the Caesar Park Hotel, as Marla adjusted the shoulder strap of her oversized bag and glided towards the undercovers. A cordial greeting and the three of them retraced their steps downstairs to a corner table in the restaurant.

"So, how we doing?" Brian prodded, espying a package protruding from the top of Marla's brown, leather pocketbook.

"Not too good. I don't have the stuff."

"You're a bad liar," he said with a smile.

Marla laughed as she removed the package from her pocketbook. It was a stringed bag that festively proclaimed, "On Your Birthday" and "Especially for You." Inside the bag was a gift, at least in appearance, which was wrapped in blue paper with colorful balloons and a celebratory declaration, "Let's Party!," the smuggler tacitly displaying a little drug-related sense of humor. Brian took the package and nodded to Al, prompting him to pass the envelope with the money to her in exchange for a kilogram of pure Colombian cocaine.

"You'll find it to be 93% pure," Marla boasted with knowledgeable product pride.

Processed cocaine is never really 100% pure. This would be as good as it gets. Traces of impurities from soaking the coca leaves in sulfuric acid or a gasoline solvent, combined with other chemicals used to extract the coca base at an unsanitary jungle lab, are always residual in the final product that goes up a nose or permeates a pair of lungs.

Not only did the purity percentage prove that the sample came directly from Colombia, but outside the tightly taped, fully encased kilo was a layer of moist, caked dirt, meaning it had just been removed from an underground storage site that mostly probably housed hundreds of kilos more. As further evidence of Marla's high-ranking status in a worldwide distribution network, written on the sample's wrappings was a brand name associated with the Cali Cartel — identical to those on 498 kilograms of cocaine previously seized off the coast of Jamaica.

"The price of your shipment will be $2,900 each because it's coming straight out of Cali at twenty-six (to us)." She added that it will be of similar quality and with a reasonable markup of only $300 per kilo, $2,900 was still an excellent price to pay. Nevertheless, it was substantially higher than the $2,300 to $2,500 estimate Brian was given.

Whenever a seizure or theft causes a drug organization to take a hit on their profit margin, it somehow has to recoup lost income. Marla's network opted for the gradual recovery method after the high-seas interdiction by Interpol, jacking up the price and passing on the cost of doing business to their customers. Others might choose a more expedient approach. They wipe the slate clean with one fell swoop.

* * *

El Gordo and the underboss of his Worcester operations left the Queens address in the white Ford parked in front of the building. The Colombian, Orlando Sanchez, had given them permission to take the car, along with instructions on how to access the secret compartment containing 500 grams of heroin, so long as it was returned later that day with all the money from the transaction.

The short trip between boroughs ended in the Bronx, where four other members of the Dominican organization awaited their arrival at Gordo's safe house, an apartment rented for the purpose of doing deals with trusted clients, which included the man who put together the one about to happen, Guillermo "Tony" Minier.

Gordo and Tony were two of the more ambitious fortune seekers from Esperanza. Both started their careers with "the Company," the notoriously violent Dominican organization in New York, before splintering off to establish their own respective distribution businesses. Taking divergent drug paths, each supplied the other with significant amounts of their chosen specialty; Gordo's heroin streamed through Tony's Bronx distribution center, while Tony's coke flowed through the Big Man's Brooklyn plant.

Tony helped spread Gordo's poison beyond the borders of the Bay State, especially after he began outsourcing it to a distributorship in Virginia. But as the amount of heroin supplied by Gordo continually increased, the

Big Man's dependency upon Tony's coke lessened. Most of it now came from a different source in Manhattan, and soon Tony's coke-line would be completely severed because Gordo had recently come to terms with a Cuban smuggler in Miami.

When Gordo and his underboss arrived at the safe house, they went straight up to the fifth-floor apartment, where the kingpin ordered one of his flunkies to go down and retrieve the heroin from the hide. The half-key of dope was put in a closet next to a kilogram of cocaine, which was slated to be picked up by a New York customer later that afternoon. It was one of two dropped off by Gordo's old pal, Luichi, who'd transported them from Worcester while traveling south on vacation with his family. Luichi acted as an alternate source of supply for his friend whenever the need arose, which was the case here because Gordo's primary supplier in Manhattan, and his backup source in the Bronx, Tony, were both out of stock awaiting deliveries of their own.

A good customer of Tony's was soon to arrive with one of his (the customer's) buyers, who'd be carrying $50,000 in cash for the heroin. It was a short window of opportunity to make a quick profit; a fast turnover foregoing the normal processing and packaging procedure at the Worcester mill. Once the deal was done, Sanchez would be paid his money and Gordo's courier, Eduardo, would be dispatched to pick up another half key of heroin and transport it to Worcester, thus replenishing a nearly depleted inventory.

There was a knock on the door and three Dominicans were admitted: Tony's customer, his cash-carrying buyer and the moneyman's muscle. Tony proffered a warm welcome and started some small talk, but Gordo wasn't interested in social banter.

"Do you have the money?"

The buyer glanced around the crowded room and added up the six to three odds.

"Does everybody have to be here?"

Gordo understood. Nobody likes a lopsided chance of getting ripped off. Addressing the buyer's concern, he told Tony and Eduardo to remain in the apartment with him and ordered the other three workers to go downstairs and wait.

Once the playing field was leveled, the buyer said he had all the money, but first wanted to see the merchandise before doing the deal.

Gordo nodded to Eduardo, who retrieved the heroin from the closet and placed the package on a table in the sparsely furnished apartment. The buyer examined it and evidently satisfied, reached into his jacket to complete the exchange, but instead of producing the money, he pulled out a handgun.

Eduardo saw it coming and lunged for the weapon. As the two struggled, the buyer's muscleman brandished his own gun, pistol-whipping the spunky little courier. Gordo gang-tackled them all, his substantial weight of nearly three-hundred pounds sending a mass of bodies flying to the floor.

Then a gunshot pierced the air.

"I've been shot!" Gordo cried out, as blood began to seep from the tiny entry wound in the Big Man's torso. "No more struggling…let them take what they want!"

The boss and his battling courier were bound, gagged, and laid out on the floor like a pair of rolled-up carpets. For his audacity to fight back, one of the invaders viciously kicked Eduardo in the balls. The employee jackknifed in searing agony, trying in vain to deflect the repetitive, oncoming strikes.

A stunned Tony, who apparently didn't anticipate the fierce resistance, slumped to the floor, never drawing the handgun he always carried. Mouth taped shut and hands tied behind his back, loosely, he feigned restraint while playing the part of the victim. Then the robbers grabbed the half-kilo of heroin, the kilogram of cocaine, and $17,000 in cash from the morning's sale of the other key of coke and bolted out the door.

When the sequestered workers downstairs saw the three bandits running out of the building, two gave chase while the other scurried upstairs to find out what happened. The foot pursuit was short lived, though, as the robbers jumped into a waiting getaway car and sped away.

Gordo was bleeding badly and needed immediate medical assistance. Calling the police to the scene of a drug-related shooting was out of the question. Somebody in his crew had to take him to a hospital, but nobody volunteered because all but one feared revelation about their illegal immigration status. So, despite the brutal beating he'd taken, Eduardo, the lone Puerto Rican in an otherwise all Dominican organization, transported Gordo to the nearby Bronx-Lebanon Hospital. A deposit was made outside the emergency room and before anybody took notice, the courier slipped back into the anonymity of city traffic.

* * *

Gordo had dodged a bullet, or at least his vital organs and spinal cord did, but avoiding the deadly crosshairs of the Colombian would prove to be more difficult. Sanchez wanted his money. Even before the convalescing kingpin was discharged from the hospital, Sanchez began applying pressure for payment, flexing his cartel-connected muscles by threatening to abduct and hold hostage one of Gordo's employees until the debt was satisfied. With the Worcester mill's inventory low because the replenishing pick-up had never been made, and a wave of fear among his minions fretting about who'd be targeted for kidnapping further stifling productivity, Gordo's deepest pain was felt in his pocket.

Once well enough to be questioned about the shooting by the NYPD, the victim known by one of his many aliases said he was an out-of-town visitor randomly accosted on the street by a strung-out junkie. There was a twisted irony to the heroin trafficker's lie, but part of his bogus story was corroborated by the New Jersey driver's license with the Passaic address. The desensitized detective, who had no clue he was interviewing a fugitive wanted in two states, including his own, wrote a report and moved on to the next violent crime in the 44th precinct.

* * *

"Look! See for yourself!" Gordo exclaimed while lifting his shirt. "You cannot hold me responsible for this!"

Gordo stood in the parking lot of a Queens Burger King pleading his case shortly after being released from the hospital. It was a neutral, public location for the meeting between the Dominican boss and his Colombian supplier. Members of both groups — strength in numbers to either address or discourage an impulsive action — stared at the raw, stitched-up surgery site.

"Tony is your problem, not mine," Sanchez unsympathetically responded. "Nobody but you should be held responsible for paying my money."

"Then why do you want to kidnap one of us?" intrepidly asked Eduardo, the battling courier who was also seriously injured during the rip. "We are only the workers."

Sanchez chuckled at the Puerto Rican's pluck as he stood up not only for himself, but for all of Gordo's worried workers. The Colombian had gotten to know Eduardo from the many money deliveries he'd made to the house in Queens and liked him. So much so, he wanted him to marry his wife. Of course, it would be nothing more than a paper arrangement, one that allowed her to secure a resident alien card and legally reside in the United States.

"You have nothing to fear, my friend. If anybody should be worried, it's him!"

Sanchez's mocking chortle and pointed finger made Gordo seethe with anger. It was a blatantly disrespectful act meant to belittle the Big Man.

"Alright, alright, I will pay," Gordo acquiesced, "but it will have to be made in installments. And if you want your money, I will need more product to work."

The proposition made good business sense for both. After all, the Dominican's thriving distribution enterprise couldn't produce revenue without the Colombian's destructive dope. Sanchez agreed, but with a caveat of his own.

"Only after the first payment is made," he replied while continuing to thrust a taunting finger, "will I authorize the release of more product."

Sanchez made it abundantly clear who ranked higher on the totem pole of trafficking.

* * *

Whether swaggering at his favorite Latino restaurant in the Bronx or hanging out with other nefarious characters at the telephone center known as La Familia, Tony Minier felt comfortable in his criminal environment and wouldn't be hard to find. Gordo had every intention of confronting his once trusted associate, but first he had to get his heroin business up and running again.

Putting the squeeze on wholesalers with outstanding balances, his troops quickly amassed $30,000 for the first installment of his debt and the Worcester mill was restocked. However, Sanchez took advantage of Gordo's exigency by raising his usual $80 per gram price — another slap in the face that further intensified a deepening ill will between titans.

Organizational adjustments had to be made, too. Gordo established a new safe house in the Bronx with tighter security measures and named a new liaison to interact with the Colombian. His nephew, "Jonny," would take over on an interim basis until a permanent replacement arrived from Esperanza. The change wasn't because Eduardo had been placed on disability for his work-related injury; Gordo just didn't like the fact that his primary interstate courier, who continued to perform other transportation duties for him, had developed such a chummy relationship with the man he now despised.

While Gordo was busy making personnel changes and modifying infrastructure, Tony was actively pleading his case to a street jury, telling anybody within earshot that he was the real victim of duplicity. He shored up his defense by conspicuously cruising his Bronx neighborhood with two other thugs, supposedly on the lookout for the three Dominican bandits who committed the robbery, ready to avenge what they'd done to Gordo. Whenever given the opportunity, he was quick to flash a .380 caliber handgun as proof of his righteous intent.

But just below the surface of his façade, Tony knew the consequences for the botched rip would ultimately come looking for him. He was prepared if Gordo got too pushy for payment, which was why he hired the two goons who always seemed to be in his company as added protection, making it clear to trusted others that there'd be no hesitation, nor would there be any remorse, in having his friend killed. Then the debt from the robbery would drift off into thin air along with the gun smoke of an assassin's bullet.

What the Bronx trafficker hadn't considered was Sanchez had a change of heart about responsibility, adding Tony's name as co-payer on Gordo's account. When he learned that "people from the office" would be paying him a visit unless the tab was promptly paid in full, a figure that then totaled $59,000, Tony deduced the Colombian wasn't referring to auditors in his accounting department.

Gordo and Tony were entwined as one, leading to an unlikely alliance with the shared belief that the best defense is a good offense.

* * *

The humidity slapped Gordo in the face as he lowered his head and exited the plane at Miami International Airport. Catching a ride on the carousel of shuttles, he picked up a rental and drove to the motel on Okeechobee Road in Hialeah. The inn wasn't far from the Cuban's farm, where Gordo would work out the details for the purchase of thirteen kilos of coke, the beginning of a new northbound pipeline of powder.

After staying a few days in Florida, he'd then travel to Houston for the second leg of his business trip. If the quality of two kilograms of heroin from a Dominican known as "the Consul" met his high standards, Gordo would have also found a new supplier for the drug that had become his cash crop.

While the boss was busy making arrangements down south, Eduardo was en route to Michigan with eleven tablets of heroin in the organization's Honda Accord with the big hide under the backseat. His multi-state mission was to convey all the money he'd collect in Massachusetts, New York, New Jersey, and Michigan to either Florida or Texas, which one he'd be advised, and then transport the new source purchases to the coke processing plant in Brooklyn and the heroin mill in Worcester.

The Michigan transaction, alone, would tack on almost thirty thousand to the total, although an even greater profit could have been realized had inventory met the customer's half-kilogram order. The mill at the Clarion Suites Hotel was only able to produce 300+ grams without compromising the Big Man's quality control standards.

It was all that was left from Sanchez's final delivery.

* * *

The two cars set out in tandem towards their destination on 38th Avenue in the Murray Hill section of Flushing, Queens. The final briefing at a seedy pool hall was rote for those who'd participated in the first two failed attempts; scrubs caused by the presence of a Colombian protection detail and Tony's car breaking down. The meeting was mostly for the benefit of the two new guys on the team, but when the reconfigured squad left the Bronx, each co-conspirator was clear about his role in the offense:

"The Ruse" — Jonny's sole responsibility was to get the action team into the alarmed apartment. He'd gained the trust of the Colombian after making his first money delivery; greed allowing Sanchez to brush aside his affinity for the little Puerto Rican he'd replaced. Fee: $4,000

"The Designated Hitter" — Felo's youthful appearance belied the cold-blooded nature of a professional killer. Armed with a 9 MM handgun and a well-honed knife, he was also known to the Colombian, previously introduced as Gordo's nephew (false) during the first aborted stab at Sanchez's life. Fee: $10,000

"The Lookout" — Tony's long-time associate and interstate courier, Miguel, would stay outside the building and take action if the Colombian's cavalry arrived on the scene again. He and Tony were suspects in another drug-related homicide, giving reason to believe the Puerto Rican underling wouldn't hesitate to use the .38 caliber revolver he carried. Fee: $3,000

"The Grunt"— Poto was a recent arrival from the DR recruited from the bowels of the Bronx. He'd carry a black bag containing duct tape and rope to immobilize anybody else found inside the apartment. His late model, red Honda Accord would also provide a reliable backup should Tony's cranky Olds break down again. Fee: $3,000

"The Mastermind"— A criminal covenant had been struck — eliminate Sanchez and there'd be reparation for the robbery. Tony did all the planning, provided the weapons, incurred the operational expenses, and ponied up the blood money for his cadre of mercenaries. Though denying complicity in the rip, he showed a guilty conscience that a hefty profit margin from his pilfered share could absorb. Gordo's readiness to forgive also had an avarice edge: he never had any intention of paying for the last load of fronted heroin cajoled out of the Colombian.

After sliding into parking spaces on the one-way street, four figures emerged from the cars and strode in pairs along the tree-lined neighborhood towards the six-story, red brick building. Jonny and Felo swung open one of the double doors and entered the vestibule, a buffer zone lined with doorbells and mailboxes, while Tony and Poto waited outside lurking in the shadows. Sanchez answered through the intercom, Jonny responding that Gordo had sent him with another payment. A buzz and the duo entered, Tony and Poto stealthily sneaking in behind them, as Miguel slowly moved the Olds up to the front of the building.

Jonny and Felo used the elevator while Tony and Poto took the stairs. A knock on the door of the third-floor apartment, a flash of money through the peephole, and Sanchez turned off the security system and opened the door. It wasn't a lot of money. Tony provided Jonny with just enough to get the ruse team inside. Jonny had been instructed to tell the Colombian there's more out in the car, that after being shot and ripped off at the Bronx safe house, Gordo told him not to carry the full amount until verifying nobody else was in the apartment. It was an understandable precaution that Sanchez apparently bought.

When Jonny opened the door to go out, Tony and Poto, who'd slunk into position on the other side, burst in. Sanchez screamed as the money he was counting flew into the air and twirled like confetti at a parade. Felo silenced his wailing by putting a bullet in his head. Blood sprayed everywhere, as the drug lord's body collapsed near his collection of books about the life and death of famous Colombian cartel figures. Though Sanchez was already dead, the psychopath in Felo wasn't satisfied. He unsheathed his knife and stabbed the lifeless body multiple times before slashing its throat. Then he ripped the gold chain off Sanchez's neck and pocketed the bloody trophy.

While Felo was desecrating Sanchez's body, Poto was taping the mouth and binding the hands of his wife, Rosa, who ran into the bathroom and unsuccessfully tried to lock the door behind her. As she was being restrained, a crazed Felo rushed in and pushed Poto aside to continue the carnage. With a handful of hair and a swipe of his knife, he slit her throat. She was left to die on the bathroom floor and the murderers fled the scene, leaving behind two bodies and a strewn pile of blood-soaked money.

* * *

Eduardo paged the boss from his Michigan motel for further instructions after completing the eleven-ounce heroin delivery. The callback was swift.

Gordo instructed him to head to Houston with all the money he'd collected. The Big Man would catch a flight from Miami and meet him there — he wanted to negotiate a deal for the heroin before it was no longer available. Afterwards, Eduardo would drive him back to Miami, where Gordo would finish his coke business with the Cuban and fly home alone. The courier would remain behind to do the dirty work, retrieving the drugs from both cities and transporting them north for processing and distribution.

The document-producing trip put Gordo a long way away from what happened in Queens. Its timing was not by chance as he declared the big news of the day.

He no longer owed the Colombian anything.

Unfortunately, the Consul's heroin offer failed to meet Gordo's high-quality standards and had to be rejected. However, the unencumbered kingpin hadn't put all his eggs in one basket. Concomitant with finding disappointment in Houston, his underboss was also meeting a possible successor to the departed Orlando Sanchez in New York — another Colombian living in Queens who owned a cigarette wholesale company in Manhattan.

Like a phoenix rising from the ashes of death, Gordo's heroin business was reborn, as one Colombian source of supply was exchanged for another. The mill reopened, but with production increasing more than fourfold, a bigger location with more privacy than what the Clarion Suites had to offer was established elsewhere in Worcester, as an expanding enterprise spread its wings wide and soared to an even greater height.

Chapter 11

"An Honorable Tenacity"

June/July 1995

Brian received his travel orders and would soon be departing for polygraph school. His final performance in a leading role was at New York's LaGuardia Airport, where he and his pilot — another DEA Boston undercover agent who supposedly flew down from Canada to showcase the plane that would transport 110 kilograms of cocaine out of Panama — met Marla Barnes at an airport restaurant to discuss the logistics of a pick-up that would never happen.

The pilot's aviation questionnaire was returned at that time, fully answered, and further supplemented by thirteen additional pages of data on Panamanian air installations, radio frequencies and flight coordinates, courtesy of Marla's corrupt connection at Tocumen Airport. The damning piece of evidence had been shuttled back by her frequent-flying, fugitive boyfriend, Ricardo Smith, the courier's prints all over the paperwork.

Marla rescinded her offer to transfer the shipment inside an airport hangar, saying things at Tocumen continued to be "too hot," adopting the paranoiac mantra of her Colombian connection, then taking it a step further by not wanting to chance doing the deal on the mainland. She said the safest place was offshore on one of the islands of Bocas del Toro, offering the services of a speedboat to transport the coke from a storage facility (at Brian's expense) and guarantying the pilot he'd be issued permits authorizing the private plane's entry into the country, and domestic air flight from Panama City to the popular resort locale.

Losing the trusted operative was a critical factor in abandoning plans to set up the seizure. Once Brian left Boston, DEA Training wouldn't even allow him to make undercover calls, so whatever communications needed to occur had to be done before his UC expiration date. But other factors also came into play in making the decision.

A seizure's timing had to coordinate with Tune-Up's takedown; both major undertakings that needed extensive preparation through the court and in the field. Otherwise, it would expose the undercover's identity too early and jeopardize a year's worth of work in Worcester. Then there was the lack of support in Panama. If the manpower made available to find the mother lode from a good starting point was a harbinger of support to come, executing a safe and successful operation of a lesser load from scratch wasn't in the cards. I revisited Marla's option of picking up the coke on US soil in Miami, but the Panamanian government wouldn't authorize DEA to arrange shipment beyond its borders; a diplomatic dilemma that meant if the seizure was going to happen, it would have to be in Panama.

With Marla now indictable for the full amount of the conspiracy, it was decided the cocaine itself would be a sacrifice on the investigative altar of justice.

Failing to introduce her partner or a representative to Brian to negotiate a better price — a pivotal part of the agreement — created an out to put off the deal while making Marla believe she'd made the decision. Withholding her expense money because she hadn't satisfied all the terms of their contract, the infuriated smuggler told him the shipment's delivery would be put in abeyance until she was reimbursed. Livid, but with no red flags raised about the undercover's manipulative motive, knowing where to find the high flight-risk, foreign national when time came to arrest her vanquished one of my case-ending anxieties.

Compensating for Brian's premature departure while seeking the evidence needed to dismantle Gordo's heroin operation proved trickier. The Canadian ordered a pound of heroin from Rudy Matos before leaving for training. The hope was that Gordo would dismiss any suspicion about his neighbor across the hall (which is what I thought) and reopen the mill at the Clarion Suites, thereby freshening up probable cause for a search warrant so I could shut it down again.

Gordo thought the big jump in weight sounded like a cop's attempt to set him up, which of course, it was, and rejected the proposal. However, he accepted a more reasonable counter of a half-pound now, half pound later, but it would have to wait until Rudy returned from a business trip. On the day Brian was boarding a plane in Boston bound for Virginia, Rudy was boarding another in New York for, of all places, Panama. I'd later learn he was being sent on an exploratory mission by Gordo to scout out potential heroin suppliers — just in case things didn't pan out with his new Colombian partner in New York. It appeared the trusted wholesaler was moving up in the organization, but because his task would take a month or longer to complete, it put one of the primary targets of the case in the wind, which when combined with other unstable variables left me no choice but postpone the planned takedown.

Time heals all wounds, including those caused by stripping away the primary undercover in an undercover investigation. Never could I have imagined it would also give me a rare chance to help so many others to heal from the wounds caused by heroin.

* * *

The investigation that humbly began almost a year earlier with an informant crack buy from a strung-out, gun slinging dealer in the heart of Main South, had developed into a wide-ranging, complex conspiracy involving a multitude of the highest-level traffickers in Worcester and their interstate or overseas sources of supply. Preparations for the endgame were in full swing; a process that involved grand jury testimony, composition of arrest and search warrant affidavits, coordination with multiple federal, state, and local agencies, defendants' placement, and all the other machinations in planning a massive federal round-up.

None of it was possible without the little engine that could. During the course of the case, I'd come to know Lanh. The former RCMP asset had many admirable characteristics, integrity, courage, and perseverance to name a few. I tried to uncover those self-serving motives inherent in most CIs, but they just weren't there. Sure, he disobeyed my directions at times, violations for which he was always reprimanded. But his noble-minded reasoning for committing them couldn't be criticized. He was someone with a deep inner drive and high moral fiber; qualities rarely associated with the maligned title he'd assumed.

Lanh not only met the glowing reputation that preceded him; he far exceeded it. He knew his job in Worcester was done, that his place was on the sidelines while DEA played out the rest of the game with an undercover agent. Nevertheless, his tenacious nature didn't deter him from pestering me about going after another trafficker; someone he'd been grooming ever since Lanh arrived in the old mill town.

Like an annoying gnat, Lanh refused to fly away, repeatedly trying to get me to target some Vietnamese guy he said was "really big" — an often-exaggerated descriptor heard by agents. I told him there was no time to take on anything new, that the last thing I needed was *more work*. But no matter how many times I swatted him away, Lanh kept buzzing back.

He met this supposed major heroin trafficker known as "Ah Sinh" at a Main South pool hall shortly after arriving from Canada. They would often shoot pool together and talk about topics of interest to both — travel, their home country, a shared passion for fishing — anything but drugs, a subject he purposely avoided.

Lanh heard through others that Ah Sinh held the loftiest position in the region's Asian underworld. He decided to bide his time with the target, make a name for himself in the city and nurture their relationship until Sinh broached the topic of drugs. It wasn't until the little guy built up a reputation of his own (through DEA) as a player with an organized crime connection in Canada that his patience paid off; a recent development while I busily prepared the takedown of Operation Tune-Up.

I wondered why someone who supposedly sold units of pure Southeast Asian heroin (approximately 700 grams) for $90,000 apiece would propose doing a hand-to-hand crack deal. Lanh said it was a test of trustworthiness, but I was skeptical, several times rejecting the pesky informant's requests to make a buy until the little guy finally wore me down. I agreed to let him purchase two ounces of crack and have it prosecuted by the Worcester County DA's Office, who by then realized the political value of the newsworthy investigation and committed to taking the case after the US attorney's office declined prosecution.

Lanh viewed the buy as a means to a much bigger end, but all I wanted to do was appease my nagging informant and continue with the case ending preparations. By doing a one and done from an unsubstantiated heroin trafficker, whom I viewed as a notable crack dealer significant enough to be taken off the streets, I could then refocus my attention on making the case against Gordo — a *confirmed* major heroin trafficker.

But Lanh hadn't befriended a credential embellished crack dealer. Ah Sinh was the New England cell leader of an international heroin network. Relocating from the law-enforcement-saturated Chinatown section of Boston to a near non-existent one in Worcester, I would come to learn that the regional crime boss was one layer removed from the biggest importer of Southeast Asian (SEA) heroin smuggled into the United States *and* Canada.

* * *

DEA's Mobile Enforcement Team (MET) Program had been established just a few months earlier; a mid-fiscal year initiative authorized and directly funded by Congress. The program's purpose was to combat the surging problem of drug-related violent crime in America, which was mostly attributable to the increased street-level purity of heroin and the highly addictive nature of crack, by deploying specialized teams on short, intense missions with the goal of disrupting or dismantling identified organizations. It was designed to be a cooperative effort rather than a unilateral one, where DEA worked with resource-strapped police departments that otherwise couldn't efficiently target these violent groups.

Each DEA domestic field division designated one of their groups (eight to ten agents and a supervisor) to become its MET. All future cases initiated in the group were required to be an approved MET investigation; its sole mission was to weed out the targeted organization quickly, but effectively, then ride off into the sunset for its next deployment, hopefully leaving behind a trail of goodwill for the local police to walk hand-in-hand with its healing community.

DEA wanted the program to hit the ground running. However, the necessary elements to determine what constitutes a qualified MET deployment was a time-consuming process, so headquarters allowed each division to convert at least one ongoing investigation that already satisfied the prescribed parameters. Tune-Up was one of two selected in the six-state New England Field Division (the other the Hell's Angels case in Lynn, Massachusetts).

At a time in the fiscal year when divisional funds were either exhausted or appropriated, while most agents went without the resources needed to advance their cases, I was instructed to buy ungodly amounts of heroin with MET monies — purchase of evidence funding I'd otherwise never even have the audacity to *think* about requesting.

For years, both DEA and the FBI compiled databases on one of the biggest and most violent Asian crime groups in the United States, each agency taking separate paths that often crossed in more ways than one. An organization based in northern California calling itself "the Company" (same name, but different than the Dominican crew Gordo started his career with in New York) regularly imported hundreds of units of heroin from Thailand into Vancouver BC, which were then routed to strategically located distribution points throughout the United States and Canada. Infiltrating the upper echelon of this extensive criminal network was a difficult task. Law enforcement often turned to wiretaps, which produced some seizures, a few arrests, and a broader organizational overview. But the number one target and many of his regional cell leaders remained untouched, as the enterprise continued to expand.

A perfect storm of investigative opportunity had formed in Worcester: a low-pressure system brewing for the past year with a patient Vietnamese informant had simultaneously joined forces with a high-pressure spending front of newfound funding. Concomitantly, an FBI investigation in Sacramento, California would soon begin tracking the conversational jet stream on the latest clone phone used by John That Luong, the international organization's overall leader who was better known as the notorious "Ah Sing."

The similar sounding attributes initially made identification confusing. It was thought that "Ah Sinh" and "Ah Sing" might be the same person, especially since the Worcester target often traveled to California and bore a striking resemblance to Luong, who frequently flew in the opposite direction to the Bay State. Both were round-faced, clean-shaven Vietnamese males with broad muscular builds and thick black hair styled in similarly combed back, high pomp fashion, tapered down to the ears. But concurrent sightings on opposite ends of the country confirmed they were indeed two different people.

Sinh Van Ta (herein called "Sinh") had the title of "Ah" bestowed upon him when chosen to be the New England cell leader. He wasn't the only "Ah" in the organization; there were other powerful, regional leaders throughout the two countries also given the title of respect. All possessed a tendency towards violence that generated a wave of fear; each was personally chosen for the highest-ranking geographical position by Luong.

Unlike his cell leaders, Luong's attribute didn't include his given name. His was a sign of supremacy, most probably derived from a Victorian opium den proprietor named Ah Sing. The real-life person was also the inspiration for the same named fictional character in *The Mystery of Edwin Drood*, Charles Dickens' final, unfinished novel, as the man and the myth evolved into somewhat of a heroin forefather in the Asian underworld.

Lanh easily passed his test of trust by purchasing two ounces of crack from Sinh, the exchange occurring atop a grassy knoll playground on Ripley Street. Down below one of Sinh's workers, transferred to the East Coast a year earlier after the murder he'd committed in Los Angeles County, provided protection on the outer rim of the inner-city school zone.

The crack came out of an Asian pool hall sitting at the crossroads of Vietnamese and Dominican drug trafficking in the city. The Queen Bida on Main Street was a place where young members of Sinh's organization with aspirations of advancing in the drug world learned the trade while distributing crack and powder cocaine. It was a training ground where only the most capable and deeply loyal were promoted to the heroin side of the business.

Though the pool parlor was new to the investigation, its origin of supply across the street wasn't. A cooperative of Dominican businesses — including the money wiring one owned by Julio Santana, Rudy Matos's crack source of supply — was a distribution outlet to many in the city. This Dominican strip that spanned a city block in the heart of Main South was stocked by Worcester County's king of coke, "Luichi" Pena, Gordo's recruit from Esperanza, who opened the floodgates of Colombian heroin by introducing his mentor to the old mill town — all of which swelled an interlocking conspiracy already stretching the boundaries of complex.

After the crack test, Sinh wasted no time proving his professed heroin prowess, offering up a unit of "China White" he currently had in stock. Lanh told him his people in Canada wanted to start out with something smaller, perhaps a quarter unit (175 grams), to first assess the quality. Putting this into perspective, it was a quantity that would qualify as a significant *seizure* in most DEA domestic offices. Sinh expressed a preference not to "break up" the vacuum-packed SEA unit. Nevertheless, he agreed to accommodate his new client's request.

The two met to do the late-afternoon deal at a Vietnamese restaurant on Park Ave called DaLat. The site was selected by Sinh as they took a table in the otherwise empty dining room. In the apartment above them, a sentry looked out an opened window, screen removed, maybe hoping to catch a cool breeze on the hot, early July day, but definitely scanning for signs of surveillance in the commercial area's busy thoroughfare below.

Sinh wanted to count the cash in a backroom, but Lanh rejected the idea, telling him he wasn't comfortable doing their first big transaction behind closed doors, that it would have to be a swap at the table with a certain amount of trust exhibited on both parts. The cell leader again bent to the wishes of the man with the money, which the informant went outside to get.

The little guy calmly ambled to a car left at the curb by a DEA agent, who'd walked away from the vehicle and melded into the pedestrian atmosphere before being picked up around the corner, while another agent, who was already camped out in the KFC lot across the street, picked up the eye on the car and more importantly, its cargo. Using a spare key given to him during the pre-op briefing, Lanh opened the trunk, removed a shopping bag, then casually returned to the DaLat, as two interested parties on opposite ends of the criminal justice spectrum followed his every move through pairs of binoculars.

Sinh pushed aside the bowl of pho he'd been served during Lanh's absence, more a prop to legitimize his presence than a meal to satisfy his hunger. As a watchful waiter stood off to the side, the informant rejoined the cell leader, placing the small bag on the floor between them. Sinh gave its tissue paper covered contents a cursory examination before nodding to the waiter, who went into the kitchen and returned with a bag of his own, this one having all the markings of a takeout order. At a negotiated price of $21,250, it had to be the most expensive item on the menu, but when analyzed by the Northeast Lab to be 90% pure heroin hydrochloride, it was worth every penny.

* * *

"The quality was as you said it would be, but the package was short...seven grams short," an upset-feigned informant told Sinh outside the Main South

Dunkin' Donuts, apparently the meeting place of choice for all local drug dealers, big or small, ten days after the quarter unit exchange. "What are you going to do about this?"

"Are you sure? My boy's very careful when he weighs this stuff. Did you include the loose powder inside the bag? Whenever you break up a whole piece, some of it's bound to fall off."

"Of course, I did! Do you think I'm new at this!?"

"Tell you what, when you're ready for the next delivery, I'll give you a better price to make up for the shortage," Sinh diplomatically responded.

"Well, I'm ready now: give me two days and I'll have the money to buy half a unit (350 grams) this time. If the weight is right and the quality's the same, my people will probably want a whole one, maybe two, two weeks after that. Is this too much for you to handle?"

"One or two is nothing for us," Sinh replied with a dismissive wave. "My guy brings in 400 to 500 units at a time from Thailand."

"How much for the half?" the poker-faced informant asked while hiding his glee about the elicited intelligence.

"Forty-two, five," Sinh answered after making a quick mental calculation.

"Doubling what I paid for the quarter is no discount," Lanh said after also doing the math. "Make it an even forty...that'll make up for the shortage."

"If it was short at all, it wasn't *that* short...I'll give it to you for forty-one, five. No less."

* * *

The little guy was early to do the second heroin purchase at the DaLat, seating himself at a corner table amidst the robust lunchtime crowd. The sticky tape holding the Kel in place beneath his loose-fitting shirt irritatingly tugged at his skin, but he didn't dare adjust it for comfort's sake, adhering to my direction not to touch the transmitter because it might affect reception.

The waiter who'd hand delivered the takeout bag containing over six ounces of heroin two weeks earlier approached his table.

"Can I take your order?"

"I already gave it to Ah Sinh," Lanh softly replied. "I'm not here to eat...I'm here to pick up a half unit."

"I know nothing about this," the surprised waiter responded. "Come with me."

He led Lanh into the kitchen and punched in a number on a portable phone, taken from its cradle on top of a stainless-steel counter lined with bowls of bean sprouts, scallions, and dried rice noodles. A cook stood at the stove rapidly working two saucepans, while an aide added ingredients to a big pot of boiling water, both seemingly indifferent to what was happening on the opposite side of the metal divide. Covering the mouthpiece and turning his back on the informant, he said something in Vietnamese to the person on the other end of the line, received his instructions, then handed the phone to Lanh.

"Ah Sinh deeply apologizes," a female voice said, "but he was delayed in Philadelphia on business and won't be back until later this evening. The one with you now will give you a number...call it at five o'clock. I'll tell you more, then," she instructed the informant before abruptly ending the one-way conversation.

Lanh left the restaurant and walked past the parked car containing $41,500 — a different vehicle than the one used during the first heroin buy — and turned the corner onto May Street where the idling Lexus was waiting. He looked back to make sure nobody had followed him, then quickly got in and lay down on the backseat while barking out a familiar order.

"Go! Go!"

***

"What can you tell me?" a punctual Lanh asked the woman after calling the number he'd been given by the waiter, a hardline subscribed to 61 Harrison Street.

"Are you calling from a good phone?"

"Yes, a payphone," he assured her, as I stood next to him in the Holy Cross student lounge hallway recording the conversation.

"Ah Sinh is now in New York. He wants you to contact him there. Take this number."

"Go 'head," Lanh replied after taking the pen and notebook in my hand.

"718-274-2800, room 319. Call now...he's waiting."

I slipped in a new tape, pressed the play/record button, and Lanh followed through with the go-between's directive.

"Westway Motor Inn at LaGuardia Airport." After being transferred to the requested room, a well-traveled cell leader answered the phone.

"Sorry about this afternoon. Unexpected problem in Philly. I'm down here now to pick up the stuff," Sinh disclosed, his voice lowering to a whisper. "It's just offshore. Things are too hot right now and we're waiting for it to get dark before unloading the boat. I'll be back tomorrow with your order. When I'm ready, I'll page you."

Unwitting, real-time intelligence from a high-ranking organizational source about a fog-shrouded, midnight offload of Southeast Asian heroin from a docked ship. It was like something out of a Charlie Chan film noir.

I immediately called my supervisor in Boston, Doug Ross, who in turn reached out to the DEA Asian Heroin Task Force in New York. The New England regional leader of an international organization — *a network that imports up to five hundred units of heroin at a time* — was sitting in an identified motel room waiting for the contraband cargo on a ship to be unloaded. It was too good to be true; a starting point for surveillance to follow what just might lead to the biggest ever seizure of Southeast Asian heroin.

Sinh received the page from Sacramento shortly before midnight, calling back from what he believed to be an untraceable phone in his motel room; the subsequently subpoenaed records confirming it was made to the cell being used by John That Luong. He was told the heroin had been unloaded and was now in a Chinese restaurant not far from the seaport, and that he should contact "Ah Ngai" to arrange pick-up.

After reaching out to the New York cell leader, Ah Sinh and his two-member security team, who'd made the trip with him from Worcester to Philadelphia and on to New York, left their temporary waystation, walked out the front door of the motel and got into a red Acura Integra, a car with a secret compartment bearing Massachusetts plates registered to a Worcester address. It couldn't have been an easier target for the New York surveillance team to pick up on.

Too bad nobody was there to follow them.

Despite his best efforts to convey the credibility of the intelligence, GS Ross was told the Asian Heroin Task Force — or any other overburdened

DEA group in New York for that matter — was unavailable to assist Boston because they were all tied up on other operations.

* * *

Sinh impatiently sat at a table in the DaLat with a full plate of business in front of him. Lanh, the first on his to-do list after just returning from New York, reentered the restaurant after retrieving the green Gucci bag containing something other than a pair of luxury leather shoes.

While Sinh was sorting through the bagful of money on the floor, an Italian looking couple with a hankering for Vietnamese fare walked in. He looked up in alarm and kicked the bag under the table, nervously telling his business associate to take it and meet him outside. They departed the DaLat about a minute apart, leaving behind the takeout order earmarked for Lanh in the kitchen, and the two DEA agents sent in to make observations giving their order to the complicit waiter in the dining room.

Sinh gazed up at the open window above the restaurant and called out a name. The sentinel popped his head out and was told to come downstairs and open the door for them. After being admitted inside and ascending a flight of stairs to a second-floor apartment, Sinh grabbed a brown paper bag — the kind that looked like a supermarket bag just brought in from the car, but its contents hadn't yet been put away — and handed it to Lanh.

"The package prepared for you is downstairs," Sinh said, indicating he didn't think it was safe to do the exchange in the restaurant. "This is the other half that was just broken up. It's not yet weighed and the wrapping's still on it, but it's approximately half a unit of number four white if you want your order now. Otherwise, you'll have to wait until tomorrow."

Lanh accepted the "as is" offer and left the building with a different bag than the one he'd carried in. The substitute half unit of heroin, still shrink-wrapped in embossed plastic with the "Double Uoglobe Brand" label, the name encircled with its logo of two roaring lions sitting on top of the world and certification that the product was "100%" — the purest heroin processed in the Golden Triangle region of Southeast Asia, left no doubt that it had literally just come off the boat, one regrettably missed by DEA.

Chapter 12

"Coast-to-Coast Crime"

July/August 1995

For years, the West Coast criminal network known as "the Company" terrorized Silicon Valley. Highly organized and extremely violent, this group was responsible for a string of armed robberies in the region targeting the bountiful number of computer parts companies that sprouted up in the fertile, high-tech territory. First armed with intelligence from an inside source, then guns that often left maimed or murdered victims in their wake, trained teams of Asian gang members recruited from Stockton, California methodically and viciously executed these heists. Hundreds of thousands of dollars in tiny slivers of processed silicon were taken. These chips were impossible to trace and easily sold on the Asian black market, or to legitimate electronic companies in the US who didn't know, or care, they were purchasing stolen property.

Initially, these robberies were committed with the intention of funding the Sacramento-based heroin operation led by John That Luong, but he found them to be so lucrative, they became more than a mainstay in his thriving criminal enterprise. He increased their frequency in the Valley before deploying other hit teams south to storm the "Silicon Beach" of Los Angeles; north to invade the vulnerable "Silicon Forest" of Portland, Oregon; and eastbound to occupy the Heartland's I-29 computer industries corridor.

Next stop on Luong's cross country continental march: "America's Technology Highway," a concentrated area of computer parts companies along the interstate loops surrounding Boston. Luong's New England regional leader was ready to kick-off another wave of terror beginning with the Digital Equipment Corporation in Hudson, Massachusetts, which supposedly had an inventory of computer chips valued at more than one hundred million dollars.

* * *

Ah Sinh was planning a big birthday bash for himself at his house on Harrison Street in the Union Hill neighborhood of Worcester. He extended an invitation to his newest, favorite client, telling Lanh that most of his people would be there and he wanted to introduce some of them to him. It was an offer the intelligence seeking informant couldn't refuse.

As instructed, Lanh strolled down the long driveway tightly fitted between houses and entered through a back door. He ascended an interior hallway staircase to the second floor, a converted apartment with a spacious spread that Sinh shared with his girlfriend and their two children. It was also the command center for the distribution of massive amounts of SEA heroin, and a safe house for outlaws whenever the need arose. After knocking on the door, Lanh entered the lair of a major Vietnamese criminal organization.

Inside, Lanh met several of Sinh's employees; some he recognized from previous transactions, others who acted behind the scenes, including the mysterious female go-between he'd spoken to on the phone prior to the half unit deal. They welcomed him into the club — everyone, that is, except a squat, muscular, quiet character referred to as "the Enforcer," who kept to himself. The Enforcer's qualifications must have been extremely impressive because he was neither the guy who committed the murder on the West Coast, nor the recent arrival who'd been transferred to Worcester after "shooting somebody in another city."

It seemed the old mill town was an organizational dumping ground for violent criminals on the run.

"I want you to feel comfortable with my people, and my people comfortable with you — just in case I'm not around and you need something," Sinh told Lanh after making the introductions.

"Are you going somewhere?"

"I travel a lot. In fact, I'll be taking a trip in a few days. Gone for over a week. Thanh will be in charge while I'm away," Sinh said, referring to one of the people Lanh just met. "He can get you anything you want."

"I don't mind doing smaller stuff with your people, but if I'm buying whole units, I *only* want to deal with you." Lanh made it clear that the comfort level they'd built up over the course of a year wasn't automatically transferable to someone he'd just met minutes ago.

Sinh understood. "If I'm not here when you're ready to do a unit or more, just page me, and I'll immediately fly back from California."

* * *

Sinh completed his business on the West Coast and returned in less than a week. However, he didn't stick around for long, driving down to New York with security to replenish stock at the Chinese restaurant by the seaport, the network's dispensing center for other cells in the Northeast Region. On the way back, he returned Lanh's page with a page of his own to call his cell phone. During the waning days of beepers and payphones when relatively few carried a cell, his was a closely guarded status symbol for the boss's use, only.

"I'm coming back now and will be there later tonight. Meet me at the usual place at nine. We can talk then."

When the cell leader's car pulled into the Dunkin' Donuts lot, Lanh, as usual, was crouched at the curb; cup of coffee in one hand, unfiltered cigarette staining his fingertips in the other.

"Come on…let's go for a ride," Sinh said to Lanh, who, of course, eagerly complied.

"I'll be ready for one whole unit on Tuesday," Lanh declared as they drove along Main Street towards downtown Worcester. "Maybe two if you give me a better price and take a down payment for the second."

"I don't take partial payments. It's cash on delivery. One will cost you $83,000. If you bought two, I'd lower the price to maybe eighty apiece, but by the time I take care of some other people over the weekend, I'll only have one unbroken unit left."

"Okay, then just the one for eighty."

"Nice try," Sinh replied with a laugh, "but it's a firm eighty-three. If you've got the money for another half, I can give you both for…" Sinh stopped midsentence when he spotted a gray Nissan 200SX waiting at the light on Main at Chandler. "Hold on a second, I gotta talk to this dude," Sinh said while waving out the window to get the other driver's attention. Both vehicles turned from opposite directions and pulled into a parking lot on Madison Street by the Clarion Suites Hotel. "Be right back," Sinh said as he got out of the car.

The "dude" was a painfully skinny Vietnamese male, someone whose distinct appearance Lanh surely would have remembered had he seen him elsewhere. His long, straight, salt and pepper hair hung limply in a silky flow to the middle of his back. The mane was pushed up and tucked behind one ear, which he nervously kept smoothing in place while talking to Sinh. The chance encounter was brief, both operators quickly returning to their respective vehicles and driving into the night on divergent paths.

"Another one of your workers?" Lanh probed.

"Him? No way, just a nerd who's got a big gambling debt with me," replied the cell leader, who also controlled a major booking operation in the city. "He's my inside guy at a computer company we're planning to hit." Sinh's matter-of-fact frankness caught Lanh by surprise. "He knows the security, where the guards are stationed, and how to get into the area where all the memory chips are kept. I've got a team coming in from California to do the job; they've done this before and know which chips to take and how to get in and out quickly."

"There good money in this?"

"Big money! Some of those little suckers go for $400,000 to $500,000 apiece! What we've got planned might net us five mil worth!"

"You done a lot of these?"

"First one out this way, but there's more to come. Hey, you want to get in on this? These chips are really hot on the black market. There's no way to trace them. If you've got somebody in the computer business who can move this merchandise, there's big profit in it."

"Let me check with my people...they're very well-connected."

* * *

August 1, 1995

The cash for the unit buy was too large a sum to have on hand in the office and had to be withdrawn from the Federal Reserve Bank in downtown Boston. The MET money had been exhausted by then, all the new teams throughout the country either spending or appropriating the windfall. But because inroads directly linked to the infamous Ah Sing in Sacramento had never been closer, DEA Headquarters freed up funding from the DOJ Asset Forfeiture Fund.

It took several agents a couple of hours to complete the laborious, handwritten, mixed bill serialization process; the buy money now headed westbound with extra security for the hour-plus trip on the Mass Pike. A surveillance team larger than the norm, but appropriate considering the magnitude of the operation, had already been briefed and units were set up on three known Worcester addresses associated with Sinh.

After briefing the troops, Richie and I remained at the safe site to wire up Lanh and give him final instructions about what he should and shouldn't do, hoping to leave an indelible impression that deterred the free-spirited informant from taking surveillance on an unexpected adventure. With the pilot prepping the DEA plane for takeoff at a local airport on the picture-perfect day, all the pieces were in place for the most expensive buy ever made in the history of the New England Field Division.

It was two hours before the scheduled noontime meet at the DaLat when Lanh's pager vibrated with a coded numerical message: Sinh was at the house on Harrison, but he wanted to meet the informant at the Dunkin' Donuts…now.

"You're not going anywhere until we're ready," I told Lanh. "I don't care if he doesn't like talking on the phone. Call him back and find out what he wants."

After entering the Holy Cross campus center and discreetly attaching the recording device to a payphone on the wall, Lanh punched in the hardline number to the house.

"I can't meet you at that place right now. What is it you want?"

"Something came up and all of a sudden, I'm very busy today. Can we meet earlier?"

"I won't have my end until the time we meet at the other place," Lanh improvised.

"*Shit*…I guess someone else will have to take care of that other thing," Sinh murmured to himself. "Alright, I'll see you then."

No sooner had the call ended, than the unit watching the house on Harrison radioed the red Acura Integra with the secret hide was leaving. Coming into view down the driveway from the back of the house, the car stopped at the sidewalk and waited for traffic to subside before turning left onto the steeply sloping street. The eye, who had to position his car about a block uphill because of the neighborhood's tight layout, counted four heads inside the vehicle, but even with a pair of binoculars, he couldn't see if Sinh's was one of them. However, he did make a positive ID that upped the odds the cell leader was in the car.

His driver and constant companion, "Tu," was the behind the wheel of the car.

The Acura made the turn and one by one units tucked away on adjacent side streets fell into line behind it. Jumping onto I-290, the interstate highway dissecting the City of Worcester, the car cruised for about ten miles before reaching the Mass Pike in Auburn, where the procession then headed eastbound. By then, the DEA pilot had ascended skywards after hearing a moving surveillance was in progress, scrambling to finish fueling and completing his safety checks. He latched onto the red target vehicle below in Framingham, just about the same time the money car with $83,000 in cash for the unit of heroin passed it going in the opposite direction.

At the end of the Pike in Boston, which hadn't yet been extended as part of the massive Big Dig Project, the Acura merged onto the elevated Central Artery and took the exit for Kneeland Street, bypassing the paifang gateway prominently seen from the highway that welcomed all to Chinatown. Parking right in front of a Vietnamese restaurant on the busy Washington Street, as if a space was reserved for the car, the four occupants slipped inside before surveillance could confirm Sinh was one of them. With the network's propensity for utilizing Asian eating establishments to move its heroin, and the cell leader telling Lanh he also made pick-ups from a storage facility in Boston, chances were they hadn't traveled fifty miles just to have a meal.

My supervisor, Doug Ross, who did whatever he could to lighten my overburdened load after Brian was sent off to polygraph school, had taken on the role of surveillance team leader while I remained in Worcester preparing for the buy. As I anxiously listened to the radio transmissions, Doug positioned his troops for a takeaway once the four targets reappeared, which probably wouldn't be long since the unit deal was just over an hour away and it took at least that much time to get back. With the plane circling the downtown area in a holding pattern just outside the tightly controlled airspace of Logan Airport, and the ground units set up to cover all the neighborhood exits, Doug camped out in a space across the street and took the eye on the front of the restaurant. It also became his impromptu command center, as the seasoned veteran started making anticipatory preparations for the next enforcement moves.

Immediately, Doug broke off one of his agents to head directly to the US attorney's office, then located less than a mile away in Post Office Square, to begin writing up a search warrant affidavit for the Chinatown restaurant. Just like the unclaimed opportunity that presented itself in New York two weeks earlier, this was another chance to shutter a major heroin distribution outlet masquerading as an Asian eating establishment.

Only this time it was in his own backyard.

He sought and received the assistance of a second DEA group in Boston, who immediately responded to the call for help. Once the Acura departed with Doug's team in tow, the other group would take their place and maintain a constant watch of the Chinatown restaurant. After the deal at the DaLat in Worcester tied it all together and completed the probable cause, a federal search warrant would be executed in Boston, which with a little luck (and available manpower), might lead back to whatever's left of the offloaded shipment at the Chinese restaurant in New York.

With the groundwork for a grander operation being laid in Boston, fifty miles away I prepared to send Lanh into an inherently dangerous one. The money car—yet again a different one than those used during the two previous heroin transactions—and a special-purpose vehicle with an agent secreted inside its tight quarters, were set up on opposite sides of Park Avenue near the DaLat, both drivers walking away and blending into the commercial area before being picked up. Only one unit in the depleted team was left behind to continue the watch on Harrison. The remaining cars of a once bountiful coverage were hidden in holes along the perimeter of Park, out of sight of Sinh's sentinel in the observation tower above the restaurant.

I was worried about a lot of things, but the weakened surveillance wasn't one of them. Once the rest of the team returned from Boston with Sinh — the deal's facilitator — there'd be more than enough protection if something went wrong. At least that's what I thought until the four travelers believed to be retrieving the heroin failed to emerge from the Chinatown restaurant. An hour of gut-wrenching idleness ticked off the clock without movement or contact from Sinh telling Lanh there'd be a delay. Not knowing what alternative plan Sinh had devised and not wanting to even hint that I knew the cell leader wasn't in Worcester to do the deal, I had no choice but to proceed \with my plan with the units I had.

At exactly twelve noon, as if a synchronized swimming event, all the players moved in unison: Lanh strolled past the parked money car and entered the DaLat; Sinh, who all along was inside the house on Harrison, not in Boston, came down the driveway and got into an arriving gray Chevy Celebrity, which shuttled the cell leader to the parking lot behind the DaLat; and the four targets in Boston came out of the Chinatown restaurant — the only thing picked up the check for an early lunch by the group's leader.

Doug raised the camera resting on his lap and captured the foursome's satiated images. One of them strode through the doorway with the swagger of someone who knew he was important. Head held high with perfect posture, his thick, dark hair was combed straight back, shorter at the sides and meeting a full, clean-shaved face with eyes that squinted in the midday sun. He wore a navy-blue Polo shirt, filled out to define his muscular build and neatly tucked into a pressed pair of khakis, cell phone clipped to the belt. A pair of well-shined, black shoes rounded off a fully polished appearance.

John That Luong hadn't flown cross-country to oversee a one-unit heroin transaction. That was the job of his regional cell leader, which was why Sinh hadn't accompanied him and his West Coast associates to Boston. Sinh's lack of availability might have annoyed the volatile Ah Sing, but it had to be tempered by the fifty-grand in gross profit he'd make on the deal. Besides, it wouldn't affect his plans to usher in a new wave of crime on the East Coast, the first of many projected computer chip armed robberies in technology-rich Massachusetts.

Crisscrossing downtown Boston before dipping into the Callahan Tunnel, the Acura transported the three VIP passengers — Luong, the Cambodian gang leader from Stockton, California, and the computer specialist from Portland, Oregon — beneath Boston Harbor bound for Logan Airport, where they'd greet the other members of the computer chip armed robbery team flying in from California.

After finding a spot in short-term parking, the foursome got out and walked towards Terminal C, loosely followed on foot by an agent who'd driven into the lot right behind them. Inside the terminal they joined up with a group of other people, strangers since no contact was made, who had congregated to await the arrival of TWA flight 192 from Los Angeles via St. Louis. They weren't the only ones lingering about the busy terminal.

Once Doug deduced the Acura was heading to Logan, he radioed the DEA Transportation Group based at the airport and requested they take the surveillance baton from the trailing agent, who'd point out the targets and double-back to his vehicle. Two fresh enforcement faces stood off to the side watching and waiting for their marks to make their connection, hastily concealing muted portable radios beneath jackets, while trying to catch their breath after sprinting from one terminal to the next.

A trickling of first-class passengers filed past the security gate after the flight touched down and taxied up, perking up those on the unsecured side who strained to catch sight of whomever it was they were there to meet. A steady stream of coach arrivals followed, each stopping to be warmly greeted by family or friends, or glumly trudging without fanfare past happy reunions. The next stop for all would be the carousels on the lower level to retrieve their luggage.

Everybody, that is, except the three Asian men who'd traveled light.

"Do you mind if we ask you a few questions?" politely inquired one of the airport agents as he displayed his credentials, both agents pacing step-by-step with the moving targets after determining they had no intention of heading to the carousels. In quintessential profile fashion, the arrivals were quizzed about why three passengers flying all the way from California hadn't checked any luggage. The question was posed more as a curiosity than an official inquiry about suspected wrongdoing.

"I'm sure there's a reasonable explanation. Would you mind sharing it with us?"

It caught the three arrivals off-guard, which, of course, was the objective. A profile stop is designed to peel off a layer of façade, creating a nervousness that exposes a guilty mind, if, in fact, one exists. Of course, this stop was anything but random, but so long as it appeared to be reasonable and occurred within the boundaries of the agents' jurisdiction, it was an ideal guise without raising suspicion it was based upon something else.

The trio looked like they'd been caught with their hands in the cookie jar, as internal panic manifested itself into outward reflections of guilt: an inability to articulate their travel plans, eye contact avoidance, constant movement, faces flushed with fear — one of them even broke out into a sweat, tiny beads of perspiration forming on his forehead as he stared down at fidgety feet — all signs that betrayed their true travel intentions.

Everybody was asked to produce identification. Four displayed driver's licenses with Stockton addresses, one with a Portland address, and Tu had a Massachusetts license with a previously unknown Worcester address. The last of the seven, the dapper one dressed for success, said he didn't have an ID on him and verbally provided what was later confirmed to be an alias with a fictitious California address.

One of the new arrivals finally composed himself enough to spit out their cover story: that they were stopping off to visit a friend who'd recently moved from the West Coast to Lowell, a city with a large Asian population, before continuing to their ultimate destination in Canada. However, he balked when pressed to provide a specific name and address in Lowell.

"Chang Lee..." interjected the Stockton gang leader, as he tried to bail out his clueless crew. "Our friend's name is Chang Lee. We don't yet know his new address; he's going to call us this afternoon at our hotel."

"What hotel are you staying at?"

The gang leader didn't want to hesitate and appear as if trying to cover up something, and his unfamiliarity with the area prevented him from coming up with a plausible lie, leaving him with only one option in response to the question.

The truth.

"The Clarion Suites in Worcester."

Apologizing for the delay and wishing them a pleasant stay, the interrogators parted company knowing they'd successfully completed their mission, while the frazzled hit team led by Luong, who'd made the trip only to oversee the start of a new campaign of terror, realized theirs had just been foiled.

The criminal seven split up into two groups: two returning to the Acura, five to the Budget rental car desk, where the gang leader rented a roomy Lincoln Town Car. Luong stood off to the side and unclipped his cell phone, its recently identified number soon to be monitored by the FBI in San Francisco, notifying those with a need to know of the unfortunate occurrence in Boston.

The entire robbery team had been exposed; there was just too much risk to continue forward with his East Coast expansion plans.

The six visitors stayed one night at the Clarion Suites before flying back to California the next day. Several seventh-floor suites had been registered in the gang leader's name, who apparently was the group's front man, four floors above the one still leased by El Gordo, which during the past week had again started showing promising signs of activity.

* * *

"Get the money and go to the back of the building," the waiter directed Lanh after he'd taken a seat inside the DaLat. "Ah Sinh will meet you there."

The informant came back outside while whispering an update through the Kel, retrieved the bag containing $83,000 from the money car, and followed through with the second part of his instructions. Sinh, oblivious to everything that was happening in Boston, unlocked the backdoor and led Lanh upstairs to the same apartment used during the half-unit deal.

After a cursory count of the money, Sinh told the lookout kneeling on the couch — its backend propped up against an open window for comfort while scrutinizing the busy Park Ave below — to get the package. The worker went into another room and returned with a plastic bag containing 700 grams of pure Southeast Asian heroin. Although the brick had been removed from its Double Uoglobe sealed wrapping applied after processing in Thailand, the printing on the bag itself proved very insightful to its most recent point of origin.

A Chinese restaurant in Brooklyn, New York.

Lanh stoically walked out the front door of the building carrying a different bag then the one he took in, put the final buy of the year-long investigation in the trunk of the undercover vehicle, and true to his unflappable form, got behind the wheel of the car and calmly drove away.

Chapter 13

"Three Days of Reckoning"

August 7, 1995

Six days after purchasing the unit of heroin, Lanh entered Sinh's house on Harrison via the back door at two o'clock in the afternoon and went straight upstairs. Around the block and out of sight, a team of doubled-up DEA agents and Worcester Vice detectives in unmarked cars lined up according to their assigned entry position in the "snake." Most wore bulletproof vests beneath their shirts, upper body protection that made the hot, humid day even stickier, and all had a mandatory raid jacket within reach to visually identify themselves as the good guys. Two miles away, a similarly attired team also lay in wait down the street from the DaLat. Federal search and arrest warrants in hand, both teams were ready to move in on their target locations once the verbal signal was given.

The time of reckoning had arrived.

Complex even in its conclusion, instead of one massive roundup typical of most long-term, federal drug investigations, three strategically staged operations were planned during an intense three-day time-period. Included were proactive lures to keep the leaders of the two biggest heroin organizations in the entire region within reach. Just when both were ready to be reeled in, each was preparing to swim away: Ah Sinh was moving to the western part of the state in Springfield, taking on a bigger role in the international network that would extend his realm of power beyond the boundaries of New England, and El Gordo, the Dominican kingpin, was relocating to Houston to open up a large-scale, multi-drug distribution outlet, both leaving others behind to run their well-established bases in Worcester.

Taking out the lower-level members of an organization without capturing its leaders is akin to removing an embedded tick and leaving the head behind. It allows for the spread of an infectious disease.

The Vietnamese organization was first chosen because of the thin thread connecting them to the Hispanic groups, all of whom were deeply intertwined. No doubt their takedown would be a wake-up call to others in a criminal community known for its scant federal presence, but so long as Lanh's identity was kept a secret until they, too, were rounded up, none could assume it meant the drug-dealing garages and their suppliers would be next.

John That Luong and his West Coast entourage couldn't get out of town fast enough after their robbery plans went awry. Their hasty departure was expected, but not Sinh's, who followed suit on a cross-country flight, kindling concern that somehow he'd connected the dots from Logan to Lanh. But the cell leader came back three days later. At my direction to confirm the primary target was in town so I could proceed with the operational plan, the night before the tentative takedown, Lanh set up a meeting the next day to discuss a two-unit deal with a lofty $160,000 price tag. Sinh seemed free of apprehension.

Sinh's trip to California included some discussion about the foiled computer chip robbery — a too-close-for-comfort interdiction that permanently scuttled Luong's planned expansion in that criminal category. But the primary purpose of Sinh's trip was a face-to-face logistical meeting about major changes already in the works for the New England cell of the heroin trafficking network.

Sinh would soon be overseeing a wider section of New England's interior from his new headquarters in Springfield, while a fresh face would assume his supervisory role in Worcester, a distribution point for the densely populated Northeastern coastline. Thanh Chiem, introduced to Lanh during the birthday party at the house on Harrison, was about to fully take hold of the reins in Worcester. Chiem had come onto the scene only a few weeks earlier and immediately began to familiarize himself with the day-to-day operations; several members of the New England cell referred to him with starstruck awe as Luong's "right-hand man." Chiem was the one who had to relocate after "shooting somebody in another city," causing Luong to adjust his organizational chart by creating a new role of importance for Sinh.

The importance of Chiem's eleventh hour arrival wasn't lost on me or my intuitive informant Lanh; both of us realizing the placement of Luong's top lieutenant in Worcester brought the case even closer to Luong in Sacramento.

With Sinh and Chiem both back in Massachusetts (Chiem had also flown to California for the high-level meeting with Luong) , the regional bosses were in place and the takedown was put in motion. Once the signal was given through the Kel that both high-level targets were inside the second-floor apartment (the heir apparent and his girlfriend had also taken up residence there), the two teams waiting in the wings would spring into action. Chiem was there, but Sinh wasn't, and wouldn't be for several hours, prompting the informant to alter my Op-Plan on the spot.

"What do you mean he's not here?!" Lanh protested. "I just talked to him last night. He told me to meet him here at two! We have important business to discuss! Where is he?!"

"He got tied up in Springfield, but whatever you want, I can take care of it for you," Chiem calmly replied before barking out an order to someone in another room.

"Ming! Get that thing from the cooler in the kitchen and bring it in here!"

A young Vietnamese underling responded to the command, coming into the living room with a small, clear plastic twist tie of white powder.

"Here's a sample from a whole one that's available," Chiem said. "Take it. If the quality meets your standards, you can purchase it today. But unless you *really need it now,* I'd prefer you wait," he said, trying to talk the informant out of buying the unit. "It's good stuff and it will sell quickly — it's just not pure number four. You're a good customer. I don't want to risk losing you with something less than what you've come to expect from us."

"You have nothing fresh?"

"We have a new shipment arriving later this week. Just give me the word and I'll put two aside for you," Chiem responded, apparently informed that Lanh was interested in buying two units of heroin. "I also have a half unit from the last delivery in stock if you need something pure to hold you over. The decision is yours."

"I know my boss is expecting to get *something* today," the cheeky informant replied. "Let me use your phone to find out what he wants me to do."

The little guy knew Chiem wouldn't risk letting someone outside the inner circle talk in an undisciplined manner on an unsecured hardline, especially when the purchase options totaled a weighty three and a half units of heroin. Nor was he about to let him use the cell phone reserved for the Worcester boss's official business; the same one utilized by Sinh, but with a changing of the guard, was now in Chiem's possession. As anticipated, Lanh's request was denied.

"What the fuck! This is how you treat a 'good customer'?!"

"Sorry, man, but we have to be careful."

"You just show up and now you act like you run the show!" Lanh protested. "How do I know I can trust you?"

"You *can* trust me. I can handle whatever you want."

"I just don't *fucking* know you well enough to do this kind of weight," Lanh declared before softening his harsh tone. "Look, there's this restaurant down the street with a payphone. Why don't me and you get something to eat? I'll drive. Then I can find out what my people want and let you know right away. We can talk. Get to know each other a little better. Then maybe next time I'll feel more comfortable dealing with you directly," Lanh said, fully aware there'd never be a 'next time.' "But as far as today goes, I only want to deal with Sinh."

"I just ate. But how about some pool?" Chiem countered. "I got some other business to take care of at the place on Main. It has a good phone you can use. If it's okay with you, I'd like my boy to tag along. On the way there I'll reach out to New York and see if there's something more we can do for you today."

The clever informant agreed. It didn't matter where they went, so long as he could keep an eye on Chiem until Sinh showed up and both were arrested.

Monitoring the Vietnamese exchange and waiting for the slipped-in English signal to send in the troops, I instead had to scramble everybody into moving surveillance mode when Lanh and the two targets left the house in the informant's car, a rental secured by DEA for the sole purpose of getting Lanh to the Harrison house, not traveling with bad guys and taking a ready-for-action entry team with him.

No sooner had they taken off when Chiem paged a number on his cell phone, a call that was returned with a loud ringing response heard through the Kel minutes later.

"I need two, man," Chiem surprisingly answered in English without a hello. Something was uttered on the other end of the line and the conversation, if it could be called that, was over.

"If you are ready with the money today, I can pick up two China white units tonight, but I won't be back from New York until sometime tomorrow." An offer acknowledged by Lanh as he turned the car into a large parking lot off Main Street that ended the short excursion.

Inset at the backend of the spacious U-shaped lot was Mekong Market, an Asian food store specializing in Vietnamese fare, which was attached in row style to another brick building either given permission to be splashed with a colorful mural, or criminally defaced by an unauthorized graffiti artist. Stretching from the street towards the market was the exposed side of a different brick building. The sizable two-story structure housed a string of businesses with entrances on Main — all, that is, except one. Lanh parked the car by that door, which led upstairs to a second-floor expanse filled with felt topped tables, each with an overhead, hanging light illuminating the swirl of toxic cigarette smoke.

Worcester Billiards, a locally known hangout for questionable characters, was crowded for a midafternoon Monday when most people were still at work. Lanh headed straight for the payphone on the wall that took incoming calls, while Chiem and his underling took a table and racked up to start a game. With cue ball strikes and murmured conversations in the background, the informant whispered through the Kel that I was about to receive a page.

"One thing we *don't* want is Sinh or Thanh (Chiem) tripping to New York. Getting *them* is our top priority," I told Lanh after being briefed. "First try paging Sinh. If he doesn't call back, tell Thanh you'll take the half he has in stock today, but stick with the story that you'll only do the deal with Sinh. Try your best to find out when he's coming back to Worcester, but don't be too pushy. It might spook these guys. Once we have Sinh in place, everybody's going down. That includes you, so be ready to come out in handcuffs."

Lanh did as instructed, hanging by the payphone long enough to know there'd be no response to his page, then executing the contingent aspect of his assignment. It prompted Chiem to make several calls on his cell phone, only this time he sought out the privacy not available in the cabin of a car by strolling far enough away to conduct his conspiratorial conversations. When he returned to the table, Chiem simply said, "we're good," chalked up a stick, and took his next shot. Heeding his handler's advice, Lanh probed no further.

Two hours of playing pool and small talk dripped by without a change in status. The entry team that was staked out and psyched up to hit the organization's headquarters on Harrison Street, instead restlessly idled in the parking lot that was big enough, and busy enough, to conceal their conspicuousness, anxiously itching to make arrests after the yearlong federal investigation that so far had seen none.

Then a radio transmission by the sole unit left behind to watch the house on Harrison snapped the prolonged stagnancy.

"The Acura just arrived at my location. Standby, I'm doing a drive-by," the agent reported while vacating his elevated observation post further up the street.

His response couldn't have been any swifter, but by the time he had a clear view down the driveway between houses, nobody was in the car. He double backed and resumed his stationary position, while two other units broke off their inert teams and raced in his direction. But they wouldn't arrive before the Acura was on the move again. As its front end nosed past the edge of the house and stopped to wait for traffic, the sentinel slouched in his seat and got a good look at the only person in the car. It wasn't Sinh, but it was his out-of-pocket driver, Tu, who was also slated for arrest on the day's busy agenda. Despite his desire to follow the car, the eye adhered to directions and remained at his post, watching as the potential fugitive drove away without escort.

The responding units did their best to locate the Acura, scurrying through inner-city streets and checking out known addresses associated with Sinh, but their efforts were in vain. It didn't matter, though, because five minutes later the Acura showed up at Worcester Billiards, Tu going upstairs to snuggle into the little nest of future jailbirds.

Lanh saw Tu coming in and thought Sinh couldn't be far behind, which was when he also noticed he wasn't the only one in the room awaiting an arrival. As the underling (Ming) handed his stick to Tu and moseyed towards the payphone, everybody waiting to hear that their coke order was in stock and ready for delivery watched their dry distributor's movements. After making a quick call and returning to the table, Ming told Chiem "the stuff is ready."

"Is that mine?" Lanh aptly inquired after overhearing the declaration.

"Something else," Chiem responded with a dismissive wave as if the matter at hand was trivial by comparison. "Take the car and get it," he said, returning his attention to Ming. "Bring it to the house, then come back here and wait until it's ready."

Ming, bucking for promotion to the heroin side of the business, left in the Acura driven there by Tu, traveling four blocks down Main Street to the other sleazy Main South pool parlor controlled by the Vietnamese crew, the Queen Bida. He retrieved the package walked over by a runner for the Dominican conglomerate across the street, staying but a few minutes before coming out and heading to his next stop, a house around the corner on Wyman Street, where other young Asian wannabes would cut, weigh, and bag the cocaine for distribution. Thirty minutes after setting off on his assignment, Ming was back in the nest.

The tedious wait for Sinh to show up had just eclipsed the three-hour mark when Lanh's beeper buzzed. The familiar hardline number displayed on its little screen caused him to make a beeline for the payphone, whispering to me on the way that he'd just been paged to call the house on Harrison.

"It's about time! Where have you been?!" Lanh excitedly asked the MIA cell leader. "Stay there and I'll be right over."

"Listen to me…I want you to work with Thanh [Chiem] from now on. You can trust him."

"But I'd rather deal with you."

"You don't have a choice. I'm leaving Worcester tonight…for good."

The permanency of Sinh's words indicated he might be relocating a lot farther away than Springfield. Time was of the essence. With all the players to be arrested now in place, I sent the transmission that put all three teams into action.

"202 to all units…move in now!"

Two lines of cars rolled up to their target locations on Harrison and Park, their occupants getting out in orderly fashion to methodically enter and secure each site before executing three federal search warrants, which included one for the apartment above the DaLat. Contrastingly, the splintered third team at an unexpected and unprepared for location zeroed in like guided missiles straight for the pool hall entrance; cars coming to a halt at haphazard angles, agents and detectives flinging open doors and rushing up the stairs in catch-as-catch-can formation.

The pool room went silent except for the repetitive yelling of "DEA" and "police;" verbal announcements also splayed across the backs of windbreaker jackets. The four Vietnamese men of interest stood and stared at the entrance spectacle from the far end of the hall, where they were soon swarmed and placed under arrest. I forced Lanh to the floor for effect; a gambit to hopefully maintain his cover long enough to scoop up everybody else in the case.

Chiem had the presence of mind to hurl his phone before being arrested; an attempt to put distance between himself and the incriminating device with its stored contact numbers and call history. When a pat-down failed to produce the crucial piece of evidence, I looked around and spotted it on the floor halfway across the hall.

"Whose phone is this?" I loudly inquired of the hushed crowd, holding the phone high above my head. Everybody kept their mouths shut to avoid drawing attention to themselves.

Everybody, that is, except one intrepid, little soul.

"It's his phone," a pre-teen girl volunteered while pointing a resolute finger at Chiem.

Bored with nothing better to do than watch others while her mother played pool and chain-smoked, the child's innocence compelled her to tell the truth.

Trapped and unable to avoid a connection, Chiem blurted out he was only "holding it for somebody else." Since the case put the phone in his *and* Sinh's hands during separate heroin transactions, his statement essentially threw both under the bus. He'd find it equally as difficult to separate himself from the one thousand dollars in cash seized from his wallet, part of the serialized money Lanh paid for the unit of heroin six days earlier.

* * *

The battering ram splintered the second-floor door at the house on Harrison, its wielder stepping aside to let the rest of the team pass while announcing their lawful presence. Ah Sinh, who was standing just on the other side of the door, bags packed and ready to leave for his new home, barely avoided being trampled by the troops. One step away from spreading his poison to another vulnerable city, the cell leader of a worldwide heroin distribution network would instead take up new residence in a federal penitentiary.

* * *

The team on Park Avenue split up into two groups, half going into the DaLat and the other half marching up the stairs to the vacant apartment above it.

While the waiter who'd dished up pricey takeout orders was being arrested in the kitchen, a half unit of 90%+ pure #4 Southeast Asian heroin, 350 grams of compressed powder still shrink-wrapped in the embossed Double Uoglobe plastic straight out of Thailand via New York, was being seized in a second-floor bedroom from its hiding place over a drop ceiling panel.

* * *

John That Luong immediately dropped his latest cell phone after hearing the disturbing news out of New England. First his plans to start up a new wave of computer chip armed robbery terror on the East Coast failed, now one of his more profitable heroin distribution cells had been completely dismantled by DEA, which included the arrest of two of his top lieutenants, people within his inner circle whom he communicated with on a regular basis. The international drug kingpin had to quickly purge himself clean of anything that might tie them together.

But it was too late.

Luong had already been intercepted on an FBI wiretap in Sacramento; conversations that would implicate him in a conspiracy to distribute the unit of heroin purchased by DEA three thousand miles away. It would be the only substantive drug charge law enforcement could muster against the notorious "Ah Sing," which when combined with some thirty-computer chip armed robberies he masterminded in California, Oregon, and Minnesota per his indictment for violating the Racketeer Influenced and Corrupt Organizations Act (RICO), would put Luong behind bars for the rest of his life.

August 10, 1995

On the third floor of the Clarion Suites hotel, an agent quietly slipped into the suite across the hall from the newly-reopened heroin mill to begin the final watch. He put a fresh videotape into the recorder fed from the pinhole camera aimed at the door marked 315, inserted the wired bud from a DEA portable radio into his ear, which prevented anybody on the other side of the uninsulated wall from hearing the chatter of mobile units setting up throughout the city, and settled in for the long haul. It was six-thirty in the morning, an early kickoff for the undercover meet scheduled later that afternoon, but I couldn't chance missing the connection that followed $30,000 worth of high purity Colombian heroin from its point of origin straight into the hands of Rudy Matos.

Six weeks had passed since Rudy and Brian last spoke. After that, Brian departed for polygraph school, Rudy took off to Panama, and the heroin mill at the Clarion Suites shut down. All three major developments put a halt to the evidence-gathering process in the prosecution of Gordo and his gang, although it gave me time to focus on the Vietnamese heroin network also operating in Worcester — a facet of the case that would have *never* happened otherwise. Now with renewed activity at the hotel and Rudy's return, Brian again reached out to the trafficker for the purchase of half a pound of heroin and found a receptive audience.

The Canadian was back.

Sort of.

So long as Brian remained on the grounds of the DEA training facility in Virginia, he was given permission to have telephonic undercover contact in the role established prior to becoming a fulltime student. With Gordo agreeable to doing an eight-ounce deal now that his buffer was back from Panama, the stage was set for an exchange that, once again, would never occur.

Based upon past surveillance, the mill typically opened for business with the arrival of a trusted worker, but this day's first sighting came from within, as the door cracked open three hours after the observation post was occupied and a face previously seen at 46 Florence Street, but never at the hotel, emerged. Gordo's wife, Maria, who was somewhat of an office manager for the organization, taking product orders and arranging money pick-ups before bundling up the cash for courier transportation, placed a tray of trash out in the hallway and quickly ducked back inside before anyone could notice her disheveled morning appearance.

The rest of the family was still asleep inside the two-bedroom suite, crashing after picking up Gordo's father at the airport and celebrating the reunion with a late-night dinner. Gordo's seventeen-year-old stepson and trafficker-in-training would be next to exit the suite, leaving an hour later to get coffee and a box of doughnuts so that everybody could linger a little longer and enjoy the company of the family patriarch, who'd be flying back to the Dominican Republic the next day with $25,000 in heroin proceeds.

When the stone-faced "Loco" knocked on the door with a stack of clean towels he'd been ordered to get from the front desk, family time was over. Gordo had a full day's agenda ahead of him. Two of his more prolific Worcester wholesalers were slated to pick up one ounce "tablets," and the manager of his Providence distributorship was coming up for another thousand bags of "No Fear" stamped heroin, a popular brand in the Rhode Island city.

These allocations would nearly deplete Gordo's fast-moving inventory. Once they were doled out, his new interstate courier, a recent recruit from Esperanza, who'd replaced the discharged Eduardo, would transport the cash collected during the past several days to New York in the Honda with a hide. Gordo and another worker would trail the money car in an already procured rental, where the Big Man would meet with his supplier in Queens — the new Colombian who'd replaced the recently departed one — for another 700-800 grams of heroin.

It was two o'clock in the afternoon when the family filed out of suite 315 en masse. They split up and got into separate vehicles: Gordo and Loco in a red Pontiac minivan rental, Gordo's stepson, father, wife, and six-year-old son in a white Buick LeSabre, a car known to DEA. Rudy had used it three months earlier to deliver two ounces of heroin to Brian.

As the two cars departed, I wondered why someone as smart as Gordo would put his whole family in jeopardy by sleeping where he processed and packaged heroin. Then I realized it was something the cautious Dominican would *never* do.

Which meant the mill was no longer at the Clarion Suites.

Both vehicles traveled in tandem along Main Street with a procession of surveillance units behind them. The parade turned right onto May, passing the Dunkin' Donuts where it all started exactly one year ago to the day. At Florence, the LeSabre made a left, but the rental driven by Gordo continued straight ahead.

I was at the back of the pack in the Lexus with Richie watching as one unit after another turned with the LeSabre as though railcars hitched together, none opting to go with the rental. I frantically tried to get some surveillance cars to switch tracks. But I couldn't break through the nonstop chatter on the radio.

As Richie and I turned onto Park Ave., I continued trying to get other units to break away and catch up with us so we could back off, but I still couldn't penetrate the incessant thread of transmissions as they set up for a takeaway after the LeSabre arrived at 46 Florence. Once we reached Webster Square, the rental turned onto a side street that led to another, a partially paved one that inexplicably dropped into a dirt road.

Gordo parked the rental in front of a little bungalow that proudly proclaimed itself to be "One Wayne Terrace" on an awning that jutted out and over a three-step stoop leading up to the front door, where the Big Man and his worker entered. Richie warned me not to follow the car down the street, which lacked a sign saying it was a dead end, otherwise I would have made the turn and driven right into a hornet's nest of heroin dealers. Instead, I drove by it and stopped behind a tree-covered area that catty-cornered the house, where Richie jumped out of the Lexus and ran into the woods with a pair of binoculars.

The radio roadblock finally cleared, two teams set up at the termination points, while the sentinels inside the Clarion Suites and outside Rudy's apartment on Outlook Drive maintained their watches. With federal search warrants for three of the four locations, and the scheduled delivery time set up by Brian an hour away, all the pieces were on the chessboard. It wouldn't be long before the pawn being moved by DEA headed towards a now exposed kingpin.

Rudy Matos rushed out of his apartment building with typical exuberance on the day of a deal and drove directly to 46 Florence. He bounded up the back staircase while cradling his one-year-old son, his judgment clearly clouded by the profit he'd make off the Canadian. The wholesaler's arrival initiated a ripple of motion. Gordo's stepson hustled down the stairs and sped off in the LeSabre, heading straight for the newly suspected heroin mill at One Wayne, where an Oldsmobile with Rhode Island plates had just arrived. Earlier, its two occupants had been seen at the Clarion Suites knocking on the door to suite 315 before leaving without a response.

No sooner had the stepson gone inside the bungalow, than Loco and another worker came out, taking off in the LeSabre driven there by the teenaged trafficker. As the car turned the corner of Wayne Terrace, Gordo's girth filled the still opened front door's space. Strutting down the stoop with an air of superiority, he stopped and scanned the area for anything out of the norm. Not noticing Richie watching him in the woods across the street, he got behind the wheel of the rental and called out to his stepson and his new primary interstate courier, who hurried out of the house to join him. As the rental with the three targets drove away, somebody else closed the front door of the suspected heroin mill.

Two moving surveillances traveled parallel paths on Main and Park; one following the LeSabre destined for 46 Florence, where Rudy was inside eagerly awaiting its arrival, and the other behind the rental bound for the little bodega on Main known as Sandra's Market, where the money car was being readied for the restocking trip to New York.

At the intersection of Florence and Maywood, far enough away from the house not to inspire flight or the destruction of evidence, yet close enough to credibly testify about its intended destination, the LeSabre was boxed in by two units, felon-stop style. While that was happening, the rental took an unexpected route by turning off Park onto Charlotte Street. It was only two blocks from intersecting with Florence, where Gordo would get a clear view of his delivery car being tossed, which might have taken the team behind him on a panic-filled, dangerous high-speed pursuit. I radioed an urgent directive.

"Stop that rental before it reaches Florence!"

After extracting and detaining the two delivery boys from the LeSabre — a vehicle being seized pursuant to an already signed federal seizure warrant — an agent reached into the car's glove box. He found and flipped an installed latch, freeing the back wall to fall forward and exposing the hidden compartment. Delving deeper into the black hole, he pulled out nine rectangular, one-ounce bars of compressed, neatly wrapped heroin, each cleverly disguised to look like a small bar of hotel soap.

I watched the heroin being seized from the LeSabre and then raced from one motor vehicle stop to the other, passing the entry team filing up the back staircase at 46 Florence on the way, before turning the corner to see a cluster of emergency vehicles clogging the roadway on Charlotte. Spinning bubbles on dashboards and rotating overheads crowning cruisers dizzily ricocheted blue and red lights off neighborhood houses, as the three targets in the rental vehicle stood in the middle of the street, encircled, but not handcuffed.

Everybody on the scene was a little hazy about what would happen next. The surveillance team had completed their mission by stopping the rental before it reached Florence, but nobody knew if there was sufficient probable cause to make warrantless arrests, while those being detained wondered which way they'd be traveling at the crossroads of freedom and incarceration.

I was the only one who could make that call; the only one familiar enough with every piece of evidence collected over the past year and how it related to the faces in a complex conspiracy. I alone watched all the comings and goings from suite 315, reviewing each segment of film ad nauseam. Based upon a vast amount of circumstantial evidence, that suite was being used as nothing but a heroin mill.

But now the mill along with all those familiar faces had moved to a new location, a belief that would soon be determined with certainty, where the delivery car with over half a pound of heroin had simultaneously departed with the rental. The two in the LeSabre had been arrested, and Rudy would soon be joining them, but the fate of the three standing in the middle of Charlotte Street hung in the balance.

Immediately recognizing the faces etched in my mind and immortalized on the tapes, I placed each one of their owners under arrest. Gordo looked stunned as two pairs of handcuffs had to be latched together behind his massive back to connect a pair of thick arms. He'd twice outsmarted state systems in Brooklyn and Lawrence, leaving behind breadcrumbs of untraceable aliases to track. Both times he'd fled back to the Dominican Republic, only to reenter the US a wiser and more powerful trafficker with a new name in a new city.

It was different this time. He'd be facing a strong, federal case as the leader of a sizable and dangerous organization, and as a foreign national who wouldn't hesitate to skip out on justice by again fleeing to the DR, that meant there'd be no bail. Gordo had to face the inevitable fact that his Houdini reign of drug terror had come to an inescapable end.

The kingpin had been captured.

Checkmate.

* * *

The door at the top of the stairs exploded after demands to open it went unanswered. One defendant was already in custody outside the house, arriving at 46 Florence in a Lincoln Town Car just prior to the entry team's snaked approach. When the Dominican wholesaler, who was out on state bail for possession of heroin with intent to distribute, reached the first step leading up to the second-floor apartment and saw what was coming behind him, he tossed away three rubber-banded bundles of money; cash he admitted was payment for the ninth ounce of heroin seized from the LeSabre (the other eight earmarked for Rudy).

Gordo's wife Maria, Rudy, and Rudy's infant son were the only ones inside the apartment. Rudy was immediately arrested, but the case against Maria hadn't yet been made, so she remained free, although she'd later be charged in a superseding indictment.

Rudy asked if the child's mother could be called to pick up the baby, who was crying, frightened by the loud noises. Nobody answered the phone at the apartment on Outlook Drive, so a message was left, which apparently "Sasha" received, because fifteen minutes later she showed up at the house in her brand-new, red Acura Integra and was also taken into custody. The arresting agent was sympathetic to her pleas to let her go for the baby's sake, but she didn't have the authority, nor the inclination, to ignore the warrant issued for Mayra Lopez after she'd been indicted by a federal grand jury for conspiracy to distribute heroin and crack cocaine.

It was a shame that neither parent of the baby turned over to the state fully weighed *all* the consequences of loss against the illegal windfall of gain.

No drugs or monies were found at 46 Florence, but despite clever efforts to conceal them from being discovered, inconspicuous records seized from the inner pages of a book on a shelf would prove even more damaging to Gordo. The ledger, along with other corroborative evidence and cooperator testimony, would prove he was responsible for the distribution of at least twenty-two kilograms of high purity Colombian heroin during the past year. A staggering amount of dope which when further cut by others in the trickledown trafficking chain, parlayed into almost three times that amount on the street. To Gordo's chagrin, he'd discover that relevant conduct for crimes uncaught are considered in the federal sentencing guidelines.

* * *

"DEA! Police! Open the door!"

I loudly issued the command while pounding on the front door of One Wayne Terrace. Lined up behind me was a slapdash team put together from other already-executed entries made throughout the city. This one was different, though, because it hadn't yet been authorized by the court. Time was of the essence. Many now detached tentacles of Gordo's organization still squirmed free following their leader's arrest. It wouldn't take long before word got back to whoever was inside the house. Exigent circumstances called for securing the premises before crucial evidence was destroyed, then applying for a warrant to search the newly identified, suspected heroin mill.

The response from within was the echoed sound of somebody running; first towards the door, then away from it. This unspoken, panicked message clarified that he or she had no intention of honoring the order. I stepped aside to let the Worcester detective with the battering ram do his thing, which allowed the rest of the team to pour through a breached entranceway.

The team spread out to clear the small, two-story structure \as I continued to loudly, and repetitively, announce a police presence — lessening the odds that we would be mistaken as intruders, but never eliminating the possibility of a violent encounter in a dangerous profession where nothing should be taken for granted.

"Drop it! Come out with your hands up!"

The detective issuing the directive stepped back after opening a first-floor closet door at the base of the stairs. His arms were extended in a classic push-pull grip, his service weapon aimed at a figure skulking in a dark corner of the closet. With milliseconds to determine what the suspect held in his hand, which with too much hesitation might be the last snap decision he'd ever make, the object was dropped. A cell phone hit the floor and ended the brief, tense showdown, but not before the worker guarding the mill, who didn't have time to make it back upstairs to retrieve the .380 handgun in the bedroom, pushed the send button on the cell with a "911" emergency message. Moments later, the beeper seized from Gordo when he was arrested on Charlotte Street vibrated in my pocket.

There was nothing inside the house that made it a home; no furniture, wall hangings, rugs, curtains (the black sheets over the windows didn't qualify) or personal effects of any kind. The kitchen cabinets and drawers were just as barren; no canned or boxed goods, plates, glasses, utensils or cookware. The refrigerator was empty, too — it wasn't even plugged in. Only two stained, bare mattresses for overnight security, one plopped on each floor without bedframe or covers, and every piece of paraphernalia that formerly resided at the Clarion Suites Hotel was in the house.

The sole purpose of One Wayne was to process and package significant amounts of heroin for distribution. Everything needed in a heroin mill operation was splayed out on an extension table in an upstairs bedroom, several folding chairs around it as workstations for the assembly team. A big pile of heroin, several bottles of inositol cut and multiple boxes containing thousands of blue glassine bags, almost four hundred filled before the worker came downstairs to take a break from the tedious insertion process, were on display.

It was a treasure trove of no-doubt-about-it evidence: strainers, pestles, bowls, and food processors to mix the heroin with cut; rectangular metal molds in the exact shape of the ounce tablets purchased from Rudy — a signature separating Gordo from every other dealer selling loose powder heroin; and a massive cast iron vise to compact his unique little bars of "hotel soap" into one solid piece. Each one of these items was caked with powder that tested positive for heroin.

There were also digital scales for precise weighing; packaging materials consistent with those used in the undercover purchases; and stamps with ink pads depicting Gordo's bagged brands.

Additionally, there was proof that tied it all right back to suite 315 at the Clarion Suites. In the closet sat the large piece of wheeled luggage and the oversized duffel bag — both containing traces of powder that tested positive for heroin — used to transport everything from the former mill to the current one…a move captured on videotape two months earlier.

It was all one big exclamation point on a day's complete package of solid evidence needed to totally dismantle the Roberto "El Gordo" Portes organization.

* * *

August 11, 1995

At the early morning hour often referred to in law enforcement circles as "O-dark thirty," one hundred and fifty agents, troopers, detectives, and police officers representing a bevy of federal, state, and local law enforcement agencies trickled into the Auburn command center to begin the final phase of Tune-Up's takedown. The day's path to its goal was uncomplicated. Without any primary defendant placement or drug seizure contingencies, they would simultaneously serve arrest, search, and asset seizure warrants at dozens of Worcester locations, while teams set up in New York to concomitantly hit their targeted sites.

Everybody was in uniform or wearing a raid jacket, the name of their respective agency or the generic "police" / "federal agent" prominently splashed across the back, cloth badge visually announcing their authority on the front. It was a boisterous bunch that sipped cups of coffee and wolfed down doughnuts courtesy of the host agency. Most of the cops in the crowd were unknown to me, assigned by their department to participate in the roundup; others familiar from working with them during the course of the case, some bleary eyed from the previous evening's activities that ended only a few hours earlier. A significant victory that had shuttered a different kind of factory in the old mill town.

Some of the day's defendants were sound asleep when arrested, including the leader of Locomotion Auto Repairs' drug distribution center, Rey Barnes, and Rudy Matos' crack source of supply, Julio Santana, the money laundering owner of J&M Telecommunications.

Not everybody to be arrested was an unresisting sleepyhead. Marla Barnes and her fugitive partner, Ricardo Smith, put up a fight by barricading their Brooklyn apartment. But seven flights up with no place to run, they'd also be taken into custody without further incident when the door was opened with a little blunt force.

A few fugitives slipped through the cracks that day, but coordinating with the US Marshals Service, most would be located and arrested. Milton Morales, the crack dealer who'd fled Brooklyn's "Dead Zone" after murdering two of seventeen Santiago brothers during a family feud, was one of them. He'd be tracked down on a frigid November night by a tenacious Richie Burgos at a Worcester house on Erie Street, but not before being first found by a would-be Santiago-gang assassin, who twice shot but failed to kill Morales as he used a payphone on a Manhattan street.

There'd be additional waves of indictments in the wake of Tune-Up's takedown after a flood of cooperation. Foremost on the list was Gordo's former protégé turned Worcester County's King of Coke/purveyor of Nigerian trafficked heroin, Luis "Luichi" Pena. Luichi fled the country in fear of being next after everybody around him was taken down, only to be nabbed on a Customs lookout at Logan Airport after thinking it was safe to return and pick up where he'd left off — a call straight out of his mentor's playbook.

In total, nearly fifty rotten-to-the-root teeth were extracted from a mouthful of traffickers.

But there was still one more bad tooth I was aching to pull.

Chapter **14**

"Second Chance" Guaynabo, Puerto Rico

January 1996

Good fortune did not greet Richie and me during our first trip to Puerto Rico. Our fugitive hunt abruptly ended when the Policia de Puerto Rico extradition agent assigned to help us find Jose "Flaco" Garcia instead found himself arrested, the leader of a rogue gang of cops whose protection of Cali Cartel drugs included murder. Enough of a cooldown period had passed since the splash of the case's takedown. Flaco was now a dual jurisdictional fugitive, and Richie and I returned to Puerto Rico with the assurance that this time around, federal resources would be committed to our mission.

When we arrived at the DEA San Juan office that morning, two task force groups merged together were busily preparing for a big operation somewhere on the island. We were met by Javier Pena, the acting assistant special agent in charge (Acting ASAC), a mouthful of title temporarily granting him greater authority until DEA's Career Board made a permanent selection for the vacant post. He led us into the Task Force 1 group supervisor's office, which technically was still his office, plopping down in his old, familiar chair behind the desk. Richie and I sat opposite him, as did Fernando Feliciano, one of Javier's agents who was filling in for his boss as the acting group supervisor (AGS). Fernando probably preferred his newfound seat of power occupied for the past month and a half, but today found himself ceding to the entitled whim of rank.

Javier expressed how sorry he was to hear about what happened to us during our first trip. "Puerto Rico's crazy enough without having to deal with something like that," the acting ASAC said. A sympathetic apology I sensed was sincere rather than lip service from a ladder climber. He guaranteed things would be different this time, that finding our fugitive would be "the division's top priority."(San Juan, the flagship of the Caribbean Field Division, was part of the Miami Field Division at the time.) Fernando would be our main point of contact, he said, nodding to the AGS, who silently soaked in his marching orders, his boss telling him to assign a DEA task force officer to work fulltime with us for the length of our stay and designate an agent to assist whenever requested.

"I've also touched base with the Marshals Service. They've agreed to provide additional help," he added, rounding out a sufficiently staffed arrest team. "If you need anything else, reach out for Fernando. He'll make sure you get it."

"What happened before is water under the bridge," I said, not being totally honest about the scars that still stung. "We've developed several new leads about this guy's possible whereabouts and some old ones we never got the chance to follow up on. From what we hear, he's picked up down here where he left off in Worcester. Maybe he's popped up in one of your groups' cases. If possible, I'd like everybody in your office to look at this mug shot," I said while removing an eleven by fourteen-inch photo of Flaco from my black bag. "I also have a stack of smaller photos. Maybe you could encourage your people to take one and show it to their CI's."

"Most of the office is outside getting ready for an operation today," Javier replied, motioning to the packed house of planners visible from the centralized, fishbowl office. "How about we go out there now and take care of that?"

Outside the office, Javier instantly silenced his troops' chatter with a "Listen up everybody." They obediently stopped what they were doing and gathered around the well-respected leader.

"These agents are here from Boston to arrest a dangerous fugitive who as of right now is our top priority." He went on to give an abbreviated version of our first trip and how he wanted them to take a good look at a photo we had, as I held high the mug shot of Flaco before pinning it on a cork board. "Maybe he's a target in one of your investigations, or you've seen him during surveillance. Copies of this photo will be on the secretary's desk. Please take one and show it to your CIs. If you or any of your informants recognize him, let one of these agents know right away. I'd like you to do whatever possible to help them get this guy."

Javier finished up by wishing his people luck on their own operation, and the crowd disbursed. Most looked at the displayed mugshot, while a few grabbed a pocket-sized photo before all formed back into small, clamorous teams that continued planning their day's strategy.

Over the mass of huddled heads from the far end of the spacious group, I saw Fernando parting the crowd, heading toward Richie and me with our latest island guide. We were introduced to Miguel Ortiz, an angular, gangly-limbed TFO who sported thick glasses on an oily face plastered with an infectious smile.

After mapping out our stops for the day with Miguel — who, like his predecessor, only spoke Spanish — the three of us set off on a new adventure. But on the way out of the office, another TFO pulled Miguel aside and whispered something that caused the guide to lose that infectious smile. They then waved Richie over to join them, and, once again, I was on the outside looking in. A minute later, Richie broke away to give me an update, uttering the same words he'd said by the Customs shack at the edge of San Juan Bay during our first trip. The déjà vu then slipped into *The Twilight Zone.*

"He recognizes Flaco!"

"You're kidding me," I said. "Is he a target in one of his cases!?"

"No..." an incredulous Richie replied, "Flaco is his nephew!"

Task Force Officer Gil Garcia stood there looking as if he, too, had been transported into another dimension. Just like the proverbial deer caught in the headlights, he was unsure which way to turn, as his mind tried to process the conflict his heart felt between loyalty to family and dedication to duty. What emerged was something of a hybrid, a combination of TFO Garcia and Uncle Gil.

"He's living in Guaynabo, but you don't have to worry about a thing," Gil said with Richie translating. "I'll take care of everything. I'll bring him to you."

His declaration was meant to be a comfort, but all it did was make me worry. There was no way he was going to convince his brother's son, a dangerous drug trafficker on the run from a fifteen-year state jail sentence *and* a federal drug indictment, to voluntarily surrender.

"Maybe it's best if you just tell us where to find him and we'll take it from there," I replied, hopefully appealing to Gil's common sense. "I promise he'll be arrested as safely as possible. We don't want to see him or anybody else getting hurt."

"No...I'll take care of everything myself. I'll bring him to you," Gil repeated his mantra accompanied by a blank stare directed toward no one in particular.

The emotionally distressed TFO lacked the objectivity and clarity of mind to plan his own nephew's arrest, but I felt this wasn't the time to press the issue or alienate him by going over his head. Gil held all the cards. He could either lead us straight to Flaco or send the fugitive deeper into hiding.

* * *

Guaynabo is part of the metropolitan San Juan region, a diverse twenty-seven square mile municipality with some one hundred thousand residents. It extends from the northern section of the island with its bustling central business district near the Caribbean Sea, to its southernmost interior barrio of Sonadora with a suburban/rural mix that's home to La Marquesa Forest, a six-hundred-acre national park some might call a tropical jungle. According to Gil, it was also where Flaco now called home.

Fernando told me that Gil wouldn't be available to help us until the DEA San Juan operation was done for the day. Since ASAC Pena made it clear that our fugitive operation was the division's "top priority," and Gil was part of the San Juan operation's support team, not the undercover in the case, I was disappointed. However, I rationalized the contradictory decision. Despite being promised otherwise, I couldn't expect the busy Caribbean office to drop everything for us.

It took most of the day, but once Gil fulfilled his duties and returned to the office, he led a six-man arrest team on a twenty-mile trek to a small parking area at the outer edge of La Marquesa. The isolated site sat at the base of a hilly terrain overrun with thick, overhanging vegetation. So dense was the foliage, it shrouded the hot, setting sun and umbrellaed us in a cool, dark shadow.

Gil said the lot wasn't far from where Flaco resided. The disclosure was tempered by his refusal to divulge anything else about his nephew — the fugitive's address, his phone number, the car he drove — all information Gil admitted to knowing but wouldn't share, despite several requests to do so.

"He's staying at a house up the road. I will drive there by myself. If his car is there, that means he's home."

"And if it is, what will you do then?" I asked through Richie.

"Don't worry. I'll take care of everything."

"I hope you're not thinking about trying to convince him to come down with you, because he won't. I understand he's family, but we know a different side of him that you've never seen. Somebody has to go with you. You can choose whoever you want, the rest of us will wait here. If his car's there, just come back and we'll figure this out together. But let's be clear here...you're not going up there alone."

The entire team, a loquacious bunch of happy Spanish speakers until then, went silent as Gil defiantly stared at me. Only the squawk of camouflaged tropical birds could be heard, as Gil dug in his heels and fumed at the audacity of my challenge.

Everybody else knew he shouldn't be involved in making the arrest, but no one wanted to say it out loud. They had no interest in confrontation, internally hoping Gil would come to his senses without their involvement. The tension, more palpable than the thick, jungle humidity, finally snapped when one the two US marshals assigned to the operation spoke up.

"Hey, we've worked together in the past. Right? You know you can trust me. Why don't the two of us head up there together? If we see his car, we'll just swing around and come back here to talk it out. Nobody will follow us. Okay?"

The anger in Gil's face softened, and his rigid, combative posture slackened; signs that perhaps he'd finally realized his normally-sound investigative judgment had been clouded by his fervent family connection.

"Okay," he whispered in resignation. The marshal placed a consoling hand on his hunched shoulder, then led Gil to his car and the two of them drove uphill together.

Whether or not the marshal's presence deterred an impulsive act would never be known, because Flaco's car wasn't there. With dusk rapidly fading into darkness, staking out unfamiliar tropical territory without the benefit of streetlights, or even paved roads for that matter, seemed unwise, so the operation was suspended for the night. The arrest team would reconvene early the next morning at the base of the same hill in Guaynabo.

Everyone, that is, except Gil, who was told he would not be involved in the operation.

While he and the marshal were on their recon mission, the rest of the team discussed the task force officer's conflict of interest. Everybody agreed that once it was known where the fugitive lived, his emotionally torn uncle should be cut out. Gil seethed, thinking I'd tricked him into revealing his nephew's location, but then backed down after learning from the others that it was a unanimous group decision.

* * *

I was starving, so the first thing on the agenda after returning to my hotel room was to order room service. Then I began writing up the Op-Plan for the next morning's arrest. Dinner would arrive simultaneously with a phone call that would not only kill my appetite to eat it, but also the enforcement proposal being prepared.

"Change in plans, bro," Richie said. "Miguel just called me and said that Gil called him to say he told his brother we're looking for Flaco."

"Wait a minute…you're telling me Flaco's father knows his son is a fugitive and that we're down here to arrest him?"

"Yep...and get this. Gil's set up some harebrained scheme at his house tomorrow morning. I wanted to get the scoop directly from Gil, but Miguel told me not to bother because he wouldn't talk to me, that he (Miguel) was the only one he somewhat trusted."

Uncle Gil had unilaterally come up with an Op-Plan of his own. He'd contacted his fugitive nephew directly at a phone number he declined to share and arranged for Flaco to pick up his father (Gil's brother) early the next morning at an address Gil refused to disclose. They'd then drive to Gil's home in Guaynabo for a "breakfast meeting," where Gil would announce some sort of "family medical emergency." Once Flaco was locked inside the house, Gil would signal the team waiting outside to come in and make the arrest.

Gil not only guaranteed a vacant hilltop house when the arrest team arrived at Flaco's residence as planned, it also created a possible hostage situation by trapping a violent criminal in a corner with a family he might now view as a bunch of betrayers.

Gil was a renegade who couldn't be corralled by me or influenced by any of his Puerto Rican peers. His immediate supervisor had to be notified, the point of contact guaranteed by Acting ASAC Pena to provide whatever assistance was needed. Instead, what I got was an earful from Fernando that left me further slack jawed.

"So, what do you want me to do about it?"

"What do I want you to do about it!? You're his supervisor! This guy's gotta be reeled in! He's out of control! He's too conflicted to think with a clear mind!"

"What did you expect? It's his family we're talking about. You're lucky he said anything in the first place…I know I wouldn't have. I don't really care about you or your fugitive, but whatever you do, make sure there's an Op-Plan on my desk tomorrow morning and approved by *me* before doing it." Then he hung up the phone, leaving me sitting on the edge of the hotel bed totally dumbstruck.

'I don't really care about you or your fugitive.'

Words in stark contrast to those of the Miami Field Division and its San Juan office, who'd assured the already once shell-shocked visitors from New England that finding Flaco would be their *top priority*. It was flat out insubordination. Fernando had been given a directive to provide all the necessary support requested of him; an order he chose to defy by responding to my plea for help with a resounding *'Fuck you.'*

There was no obvious explanation for Fernando's animosity; no history existed between him and me. We'd never even spoken prior to that morning meeting. Perhaps his authority as the acting group supervisor felt usurped by his boss's take-charge intervention, which was meant to safeguard the fugitive seekers from being wronged again, but instead manifested into an insecure hostility that Fernando directed at the cause of his perceived slight. Whatever the reason, it was clear that the obstacle of a DEA agent's arrogance had now replaced one of police corruption in the quest to find Flaco.

I considered moving up the chain of command but decided otherwise for fear of what else I might encounter at the signpost up ahead. So, I completed my Op-Plan, or at least one based upon the information Gil chose to share with Miguel, went down to the lobby and faxed it to Fernando's desk for review in the morning, then returned to my room and double-locked the door before daring to close my eyes.

* * *

Richie and I picked up Miguel at the DEA San Juan office the next morning and headed out to meet the others in Guaynabo. According to the Op-Plan, which Fernando did approve, the guide was supposed to be in a separate surveillance car, but a shortage of government vehicles prevented him from being issued one.

When Richie, Miguel and I arrived at the meet location, behind a supermarket in a busy business district about five miles from Gil's house, the two US deputy marshals were already there. Despite being requested otherwise, the marshals came in one car, which further reduced the number of mobile units to three. The last member of the arrest team, the DEA agent designated to assist whenever needed, hadn't yet shown up, so Miguel paged him to determine his ETA while the rest of us went over the plan.

Like many places in crime-plagued Puerto Rico, the windows of Gil's house were barred. A wrought iron fence added another layer of security around the perimeter, enclosing most of the property that sat at the edge of La Marquesa National Forest. A wide expanse of swampland provided the final piece of protection, a watery barrier that merged with solid land at the back end of the premises.

The house was situated on a dead-end street at the bottom of a very steep hill. The paved roadway ended there, merging into a verdant valley overgrown with dense woodland and tangled vegetation. It was impossible to set up with an eye on the front of the property, or at least without being noticed, so one unit would be parked about three blocks uphill with an unobstructed line of sight over the rolling hills created by leveled, intersecting streets; far enough away not to be seen, but close enough to detect movement in or out of the driveway. A rover car would confirm any observations by doing a drive-by, while the third unit sat behind the supermarket, a location Gil told Miguel would provide a clear view over the marshland to see the back of his house with a pair of binoculars.

Just prior to his arrival at the house, Flaco was instructed to call from his cell phone so that Gil could come out and unlock the gate at the end of the driveway, a normal practice whenever visiting. After he and his father pulled into the parking area, the gate would be reclosed and key-locked, thus imprisoning the fugitive...along with his family.

While Gil's wife prepared breakfast for the morning meeting (she was not privy to the plan), Gil would step out onto the back deck and discreetly doff his cap to the unit watching from the far side of the swamp — the visual signal that it was time to move in. That car would drive the five-mile U-shaped loop around the wetlands to join up with the others, at which time Miguel, who was the only team member with a cell phone, would call the house. Gil emphasized it should be the *only* telephonic communication with him to avoid any suspicion that something was afoot. He'd come out to open the gate, supposedly for another arriving family member, and let the team in to make the arrest.

The marshals took a tree-shaded observation post behind the supermarket, while Richie, Miguel and I sat uphill from the house, unable to avoid the morning's direct, hot sunlight. Even with the air-conditioning on full blast, our white Chevy Cavalier rental quickly turned into a sweatbox. The third unit with the DEA San Juan agent would be the rover by default. However, he was an hour late and hadn't yet responded to multiple pages or repeated radio transmissions. I worried that Flaco would arrive before everybody was set up, but the anxiety of a bareboned, insufficient coverage abated when Miguel's cell phone rang.

"Ask him how far out he is," I said while continuing to squint through a pair of binoculars. Richie translated and Miguel made the inquiry, but instead of relaying a response, the go-between silently reached over the front seat and handed me the phone.

"Sorry, but I thought you knew," apologetically said the bilingual DEA agent. "Fernando took me off your operation. He said I wasn't needed. Because you had the marshals with you, he was going to take away Miguel, too, but I think I talked him out of it."

Fernando had eliminated another mobile unit without even having the decency to tell me. He'd rejected, or more probably didn't bother to consider, that part of the Op-Plan that articulated the possibility of a moving surveillance and a felony stop. Now, dwindled from five units to two, each set up five miles apart and separated by a swamp, the vehicular arrest contingency was no longer an option.

The two units left standing maintained their watches for another uneventful hour. According to the information Gil chose to feed Miguel, Flaco and his father should have already arrived, which made me wonder if the fugitive had ever been set up to show up in the first place.

"This has gone on long enough! Richie, tell Miguel to call Gil and have him call Flaco. Find out why he's not here yet."

Not having any control over the operation and needing to go through three layers of task force officers just to make a phone call had pushed my patience to the limit. It only worsened when Miguel refused to make the call because Gil told him not to contact him unless it was an emergency.

"I don't give a shit what Gil wants! You tell him to call the house *right now* or I'm gonna shut this thing down!"

The anger in my voice needed no translation, as Miguel punched in the number on his cell; the loyalty for his fellow TFO's wishes overruled by an enraged need to know.

"Gil told Miguel that he's not going to call Flaco," Richie apprehensively relayed after the call ended.

"Why not!?"

"Because Flaco called him…*over an hour ago*! He said he got delayed in traffic on the way to pick up his mother!"

In an ill-advised plan that was quickly spiraling into the absurd, this was the first mention of Flaco's mother's involvement. Supposedly, the fugitive picked up his father in Guaynabo before traveling halfway across the island to get his mother, who lived apart from her husband, calling his uncle on the way back to tell him they were running late. Flaco's notification was a common courtesy that Gil failed to extend to the anxiously awaiting arrest team.

Incredulous, I just shook his head. "Wow! Better let the marshals know what's going on. Tell Miguel to give them a shout on the radio."

It should have been a short transmission, nothing more than a status update, but it evolved into a rapid fire, Spanish-speaking exchange that made me wonder what they could possibly be talking about. When the portable radio went silent, Miguel and Richie looked at one another with the same shocked expression on their faces.

"You're not going to believe this," Richie said. "We have to take the marshals' place behind the supermarket."

"Why?"

"Because they went for breakfast! They said to page them if anything new develops."

"*What!* Call them back and tell them to stay where they are!"

But it was too late. The marshals had turned off their portable radio and shoved it under the seat of their car. Miguel paged them to call his cell phone, sending out several "911" messages, but neither responded. The deputy US marshals officially responsible for capturing the federally declared fugitive had abandoned their post in favor of flapjacks and coffee.

Miguel tried calling Gil again to tell him to forget about the signal, to let him know there was only one car out there, and that he should call him when it was time to make the arrest, but the headstrong TFO leading the operation by the nose didn't answer the phone. With no other options to contact Gil other than knocking on the front door, I hit the gas and sped around the swamp to the business district five miles away, hoping to find the marshals in a nearby restaurant and convince them to rejoin the operation. There weren't any in the plaza where the supermarket was located, and not wanting to waste time expanding the search, I steered the rental to the back of the store and began peering through binoculars from a new location.

Gil was right about one thing. It *was* the perfect place to watch the back of his house over the flat, stagnant marsh, although I wondered how he came to know that. I regretted not canceling the operation earlier. It was too late now; I couldn't abandon Gil's family to face the consequences alone after Flaco found out he'd been set up. Then I thought without a second unit nearby, we were too far away to quickly respond if something went wrong.

Something went wrong?! Everything about this has gone wrong!

"Richie, tell Miguel to call Gil again. He needs to know we're going back to the house and that nobody will be watching the back deck from here. When Flaco arrives..." I stopped midsentence when I saw movement on the far shore.

It was Gil.

He was giving the arrest signal.

I swung the car around and hit the gas, zigzagging past a "T" shaped loading dock on the side of the supermarket before reaching the plaza parking lot. A gap in cross-traffic allowed for a quick left out of the lot through a red light, as once again three agents raced through the streets of Puerto Rico in pursuit of Flaco, only this time without the aid of a blue bubble to pave the way. Headlights flashing and horn beeping, the Cavalier veered around other cars, their surprised drivers yielding to the rental not viewed as an emergency response vehicle, but one driven by a crazy, impatient driver.

Once beyond the outskirts of the business district, the Cavalier connected with a wider loop road around the swamp, which headed upwards and away from the valley. Several free-flying miles were traveled before intersecting with Gil's street at its highest elevation, where a left turn started barreling the car back downhill. There were several cross streets in the plunge; dead ends to the left that led back to the swamp, causing the speeding car to scrape bottom and go airborne, each flight landing with a frame rattling thud.

I stopped the car a block short of our destination and Miguel was in the process of calling Gil to come out and open the gate, when someone ran from the driveway, looked up the street, and turned the other way into the dense forest of La Marquesa.

"It's Flaco!" Richie exclaimed.

I floored it until asphalt met jungle, where the Cavalier came to a skidding halt in a swirling cloud of dust. Richie had his door partially open during the skid, waiting for the forward lurching to stop before jumping out and following the same path taken by the fugitive, who'd already been swallowed up in a tropical tangle of green. I shouted for Miguel to radio for backup and keep an eye on Flaco's car at the end of the driveway, which arrived after we'd left to find the noshing marshals, then got out and joined Richie in the foot pursuit.

Thick overhanging growth instantly eclipsed the sun, getting darker as I went deeper into the jungle. I ran as fast as I could trying to catch up with Richie, who was somewhere up ahead but nowhere in sight, maneuvering around clumps of plant life and leaping over dead, fallen ferns, careful not to land wrong on the tropical terrain and buckle an ankle.

The heavy breathing of someone else running should have indicated I was gaining ground, only it was coming from behind me. I stopped and spun around expecting to be ambushed by a lying-in-wait Flaco, but instead encountered a gasping Miguel.

"What the hell are you doing here!?" I demanded to know while trying to catch my own breath. "I told you to stay with the car and call for help!"

Miguel screamed back with just as much irritation in his voice, only I had no idea what he was saying. We stood in the middle of nowhere staring at one another; both drenched in sweat from the adrenaline-fueled jungle sprint, unable to communicate as the chatter of tropical birds gleefully mocked our dilemma.

The language barrier left a gaping hole for Flaco to double-back and escape. It also meant Miguel hadn't called for backup, because in his haste to jump out and join us in the pursuit, he left both the radio and his cell back at the car.

"Richie, I'm gonna get more troops out here!" I yelled into a sea of verdant. "You're not alone, Miguel's coming up right behind you!" I then poked a finger in the TFO's chest, pointed deeper into the jungle and pushed him off in Richie's direction.

Rapidly retracing my steps until clearing the canopy of leafy trees, I looked down Gil's driveway and saw Flaco's car was still there, then angled towards the rental haphazardly stopped in the middle of the street, three doors flung open wide. A glint of bright sunshine reflected off something metallic on the ground by the front passenger door, which at first, I thought was the portable radio dropped by Miguel, before realizing he'd exited the Cavalier from the backseat on the other side of the car.

It wasn't the radio.

It was a handgun.

As I bent down to pick up the 9-millimeter, thinking it tossed by Flaco to avoid being caught with the gun, I heard somebody running behind me, the footfall on asphalt louder as it got closer. Dropping to the ground and whirling around while extending the gun already in my hand, I again expected to see the fugitive, or maybe even his uncle, whose loyalties were in deep question after he'd fallen off the wrong side of his conflicted fence, facilitating the foot chase by leaving the driveway gate unlocked after failing to convince his nephew to surrender, but to my shock again found myself face-to-face with a confused Miguel.

He didn't realize I wanted him to continue the pursuit, which was when I realized the gun in my hand wasn't jettisoned by Flaco. Gil's driveway was too far away. That left only one logical conclusion: it was jerked free from Richie's holster when he bailed out of the recoiling car.

Richie was alone in the jungle chasing a desperate and dangerous criminal.

And he didn't even have a weapon to protect himself.

* * *

The winded Worcester detective emerged from the shadowed coolness of the forest into a flora-filled field of bright sunshine. There was a river up ahead that divided the land, where he stopped to catch his breath in the thick, humid air that made it difficult to breathe even if he hadn't been running. His lungs burned and quads felt glue-infused, but despite his best effort to close the gap, he never caught sight of the fleet-footed felon once he'd fled into the jungle, although he believed he'd kept the pace and Flaco was somewhere nearby.

He bent over at the river's edge, hands on knees wondering what happened to Miguel. After hearing his partner's message of reassurance, he thought the guide would have caught up with him by then. It was easy to get lost in this tangled maze of vegetation; Richie was unsure if he'd even be able to navigate his own way back to the road.

Where he stood was an uprooted, thick-trunked tree that had fallen across the river, spanning its width to create a natural bridge that Flaco could have accessed. It looked sturdy enough, but he hesitated with concern about patchy spots of slick-looking algae, not to mention being unsure about taking the chance on his still unsteady sea legs.

As he pondered his path, Richie heard a rustling noise behind him and turned expecting to see Miguel coming out of the forest. He couldn't believe his eyes when instead from the underbrush emerged a wild boar.

The creature was huge! It had to weigh at least three hundred pounds with massive shoulders that tapered down to a bristly back and hindquarters that ended with a limp pigtail. Shifty eyes in an oversized head with a long snout and sharp protruding tusks stared down the unwelcome visitor. The threatening overture made Richie nervous as he reached for the gun in his holster, only to discover it wasn't there.

What happened to my gun!?

The boar dug its snout into the ground and tossed a gauntlet of dirt in the air, then belted out a loud squeal and charged its target.

Richie was no longer the hunter.

He was the prey.

Making a split-second decision of self-preservation rather than choice, Richie jumped onto the tree and ran across the river, somehow maintaining his balance on the slimy surface without slipping into the watery divide. He leapt onto the far bank with the intention of staying in full stride, but instead landed with a squish and got sucked up in mud. Grabbing a branch on the dying tree to extricate his body, he could only pray that the boar wasn't about to gore its helpless victim.

* * *

I picked up the portable from the backseat of the Cavalier and tried calling for help, but the battery was dead, so I reached for Miguel's cell phone, which the TFO had just clipped back onto his belt, only to have my hand slapped away, the rejection coming with a stern look and an angry utterance that by its tone was a warning not to touch.

I thought the worst, that island corruption had again raised its ugly head and Miguel was protecting his fellow TFO. Never did I consider the possibility that the straight-shooting, deputized detective on loan to DEA from the Policia de Puerto Rico was overreacting to a strict policy regarding authorized cell phone use. Prior to their ubiquity, at a time during their infancy when the high cost of use was charged by the minute, these department issued cell phones were frequently misused for personal reasons.

Rebuffed, I dashed towards Gil's house hoping to find the law-abiding side of him home, only to discover that the gate left open for Flaco's escape had been locked while the fugitive was being chased through the jungle. I tried to convince Gil to come out and let me in to use his phone, but my gate-rattling, loudly announced call for help went unanswered.

Somehow, I had to make Miguel understand we needed assistance to find Richie, whose safety was now the operation's only real objective. It was a fool's errand to venture back into the jungle on foot ourselves, only to find we were lost with him. A coordinated ground and aerial search team had to be called in.

Simplistically adding "o's" to words and pantomiming as if playing a party game, whatever I said or did apparently registered, as Miguel's eyes lit up with comprehension.

The TFO took the phone out of its holder and made a call, to whom I didn't know, then gave an enthusiastic thumbs up that help was on the way.

Until the cavalry arrived, we frantically cruised the streets adjacent to the jungle's edge on the chance Richie might wander out someplace other than where he went in. Stopping at gaps in the thicket, which were far and few between with a view not much deeper than the face of the forest itself, I stopped the car and we got out, each alternately and repeatedly yelling the missing detective's name, then quietly listening for a response. A little coqui frog playfully answered back, but there was no reply from the intended recipient.

We then moved upwards from the shadows of the jungle to the point where land touched the sky. I again got out of the car and began scanning the panoramic scene with my binoculars, hoping to detect any movement that might provide the search team with a starting point. Miguel saw what I was doing and followed suit, as the accidental partners stood side-by-side after finding a way to communicate. But our efforts were fruitless; neither's enhanced vision was able to penetrate the vast awning of treetops.

We slumped to the ground in defeat, our backs propped up against the side of the rental with nothing more to do but worry and wait for the troops' arrival. The quiet tranquility of the cool, high altitude provided a meditative atmosphere that had a calming effect. It allowed for a clearer mind that made me realize forty minutes had passed since Miguel called for help. The air should be filled with whirring rotor blades and screaming sirens by now.

I pointed to my partner's cell phone, raised an extended thumb and pinky to my ear and said, "Fernando." Without resistance or hesitation, the TFO punched in a number. Once he'd gotten the acting group supervisor on the line, Miguel handed the phone to me.

"Do you know we've got an emergency situation down here?"

"So, I've been told. Miguel called his department and they contacted me," Fernando replied with obvious annoyance that another agency had been involved. "Deploying a tactical unit with a helicopter seems like an overreaction. Why *the hell* did Richie chase this guy into the forest in the first place?"

I initially thought the delayed response was caused by something lost in translation, but Miguel understood me. He'd called in an "officer needs assistance" to his parent department — the Policia de Puerto Rico — who immediately mobilized a search and rescue team, but according to protocol, they contacted DEA for final approval as the lead agency in the operation before dispatching the units.

Fernando told them to stand down.

"You *knew* we needed help and you stopped it from coming? Are you *fucking* for real!? You listen to me, and you listen good…you better get a helicopter up in the air and some ground units rolling right now! Because if anything happens to Richie, this is all gonna fall on *YOUR…FUCKING… HEAD*!"

* * *

Richie pulled himself out of the muck and turned around expecting to see the charging boar, but thankfully it stayed on the other side of the river, proudly snorting and wagging its tail in triumph after successfully defending its territory. The pursuer-turned-pursued knew the wild pig wouldn't let him go back the same way he'd come, so Richie had no choice but to go deeper into the jungle with the hopes of finding another way out.

He entered a big field of tall grass that stood several feet higher than his modest height. Unable to see anything beyond what was right in front of him, he stepped with caution while on the alert for snakes. He hated snakes, and the tropical landscape had plenty to offer. Even so, as he grasped for the phantom weapon in his empty holster, Richie wondered what he'd do if he actually encountered one.

The lack of a visible horizon disoriented the wanderer, who blindly trudged through the field with a lost sense of direction, not knowing if he was heading towards safety or going deeper into danger. But then a sound in the distance, faint at first but unmistakably familiar, gave him hope that help was on the way. He stood still and listened to the harsh sirens that grew louder as they got nearer. Then he heard the whirl of rotor blades and looked up to see not one, but two helicopters. He wildly waved his arms to get their attention, but the engulfing grass camouflaged his presence and prevented him from being seen, as both choppers veered off to begin their search in another part of the jungle.

The sirens acted as a homing device, as Richie recalculated his route through the reeds and followed the sound until reaching the river further downstream, well beyond the realm of the boar. Sloshing across a narrow gap and reentering the thicket of tropical overgrowth, he worked his way through the dense darkness until emerging from the jungle on a perimeter street, just as the Cavalier serendipitously turned onto it.

"I lost my gun, and I was chased by a big pig!" Richie blurted. The meandering detective was bruised, muddied, and disheveled, his perfectly combed hair now a frazzled mess, but otherwise no worse for wear.

"It's good to see you, too, my friend," I chuckled. "Don't worry about your gun, I have it. You dropped it when you got out of the car. A big pig, huh?"

"It was huge, bro! This thing was grunting and squealing, and it wanted to shish kabob me!"

I couldn't help but laugh even harder. "You can tell me all about your pig story later, first we have to let everybody out here know you're okay."

"But don't let them go, bro! Flaco's still in there! This may be our last chance to get this guy!"

After sidestepping the perils of nature and somehow navigating his way out of the jungle, all the tenacious fugitive hunter wanted to do was head back in to finish the job.

On a portable radio with a fresh battery passed to me by one of the responding units, the good news about Richie being found was greeted by a condescending voice that made me fume all over again. Fernando, on scene and taking charge of the operation after covering his exposed ass by authorizing the mission, didn't ask if Richie was unharmed, nor did he address a request for the search team to continue looking for the fugitive. Expressing nothing but indifference, he simply wanted to meet me in front of Gil's house.

When the rental arrived where the chase began, Fernando, his arms folded in defiance and his face sporting an expression that was anything but contrite, stood at the end of the driveway alongside one of the satiated marshals. Gil was there, too, although he was separated from the other sinners by a still locked security gate — wrought iron protection against retribution for his betrayal should anybody be so inclined.

Despite the tension that simmered to the surface, I decided this wasn't the time or the place for a confrontation. Avoiding discussion about all the reasons why Fernando had undermined the mission and callously put Richie's life in danger, I instead focused on finding the fugitive, again requesting the response team remain on site.

A straight-faced Fernando told me the helicopters had "another mission to respond to" and were "no longer available." He said searching on foot without them would be futile, that the brush was just too thick, adding that Gil said his nephew "knows the forest like the back of his hand" and it'd be "like looking for a needle in a haystack."

Over Richie's vehement objection, I agreed with Fernando's reasoning for not continuing the search. It would have further jeopardized safety, so I agreed that ending the operation was the right thing to do. I didn't know then that his convincing rationale for walking away when we were so close to success was based on a lie.

The Rapid Action Team of the Policia de Puerto Rico didn't have another emergency response call. In fact, they *wanted* to stay and continue the search for Flaco. After corruption had stained their department's reputation and scarred the fugitive hunters from New England, both had been given a second chance to get it right. But after Richie was found and Fernando's self-preservation motive for authorizing the rescue mission was satisfied, the arrogance of an acting group supervisor told the specialized unit their assistance was no longer needed.

For the second time, Richie and I would leave Puerto Rico without the fugitive we'd come to arrest; betrayed again by those we trusted to help us find Flaco, who remained free to continue his unlawful ways.

Chapter 15

"The Quality of Life"

February 1997

How do you measure the impact of a drug organization on a neighborhood?

Government officials typically answer this question by citing the number of arrests made and total amount of drugs, money, and weapons seized at the conclusion of a long-term federal investigation. A press conference is often the forum, as stone-faced agency heads huddle around microphones spouting off canned catchphrases like "won't be tolerated," "make an example of," and "send a message to" — restricted in what they'd really like to say by rules of discovery, risks of compromise, and/or concern for witness safety.

Operation Tune-Up was no exception.

Though statistics *are* an indication of a successful drug enforcement operation, how much of an impact they actually have in a neighborhood can only be projected. Time is needed to make that determination, and the only ones truly qualified to make it are the people living and working in the affected community. Unfortunately, that part of the story is seldom told, leaving the public to remember forgettable names lacking the "sexiness" of traditional organized crime figures, metric weights with no relatable meaning, and the long-lasting image of boastful bureaucrats. It spawns disinterest in some ("just another drug bust") and reinforces cynicism of government in others, both of which stir up feelings of failure in the so-called "war on drugs."

A year and a half after the August 1995 arrests, William T. Breault, an outspoken community activist and longtime Worcester resident, was given the opportunity to tell the other part of the story. Breault was the founding father and chairman of a civilian association called the Main South Alliance for Public Safety, which for years had been fighting to reclaim Main South from the drug dealers and dregs of society who'd overtaken the neighborhood. It was a vociferous position of leadership that often put him at odds with an overwhelmed and under-resourced police department waging the same battle.

When Breault testified at the sentencing hearing of Roberto "El Gordo" Portes, who'd been jury-convicted of being the mastermind responsible for most of the heroin distributed in Worcester, he made victims' rights history. It was the first time ever in the United States that an entire neighborhood was recognized as a "crime victim," and a spokesperson allowed to give a victim-impact statement, a voice previously reserved only for individuals affected by specific acts of violence or financial fraud.

Breault told the court how heroin wreaked havoc upon his community, both socially and economically, attributing it and in the same breath crack cocaine as the primary cause for Main South's shuttered storefronts, burnt out residential buildings, plummeting property values and abandoned playgrounds. He cited Castle Park as an example. The tree-lined urban oasis, once a safe place for families to enjoy the swing sets, tennis courts and hiking trails, had turned into a shooting gallery for junkies and a hangout for drug dealers, gangbangers, and prostitutes. Afraid of going into the park, residents stopped using it.

"They were cooking there, they were sleeping there," Breault said. "People stopped using the park. Nobody wanted to go in there."

He then shocked the court with startling statistics: during an annual cleanup of the park by the community association just prior to Tune-Up's takedown, over seven hundred used syringes were collected. When another cleanup was conducted a year later, fewer than ten needles were found. The neighborhood celebrated what *they* decided was a victory in the war on drugs by holding a picnic in the park — *five hundred families gathered for the event.*

Fear had been replaced by a long-forgotten sense of freedom in Main South. Residents once again felt safe to venture outside, as if a long-lingering storm system had finally been swept out to sea. Immediately after the roundups, the once plentiful supply of heroin became near non-existent, and at the time of Breault's testimony, this drought had lasted the better part of two years. A phenomenon of absence, especially for a city the size of Worcester. As a byproduct, the source-less street predators abandoned their entrenchments and the violent crime rate plummeted. A community's firsthand evaluation echoed by the Worcester PD and DA's office; two agencies that discovered a full house of cooperation beats a pair of territorialities any day.

"There were a lot of people in that operation that we could never get for years," said Vice & Narcotics Sergeant Thomas J. Gaffney, a police department spokesperson who publicly praised the unprecedented progress. "Those guys were the main source."

"Operation Tune-Up was highly successful," added the district attorney, himself, John J. Conte. "It dismantled three highly-organized groups of drug dealers in the city who have not been replaced." The DA was so impressed that he laid out a long missing welcome mat at the county door for DEA to establish a permanent presence in the old mill town.

Breault credited Operation Tune-Up for a community revival that many saw as a miracle. A prolonged dearth of drugs that stimulated Main South's business growth, rising property values, increased interest in owner-occupied residency, and the overall quality of life. A true victory in the war on drugs — not because DEA said so, but because the neighborhood, itself, did.

With organizational pipelines terminated for Gordo's Colombian heroin, "Ah Sinh" Ta's Southeast Asian heroin, and "Luichi" Pena's Nigerian trafficked heroin originating in the Golden Crescent region — the three main areas of the world producing the illicit product — it literally dried up the drug in a long-infected American city, giving one inner-city neighborhood a rare chance to heal from the throbbing pain of non-stop distribution and drug-related violence.

Of course, Tune-Up didn't permanently eliminate heroin in Worcester. So long as there's demand, there will always be supply; the only way of reducing both is by building a seawall of demand reduction education at a young age that protects impressionable minds from the high tides of abuse, addiction, and death. Otherwise, nothing is learned from epidemics like the one that blossomed then or the fentanyl crisis it morphed into today. The susceptible will continue taking a path of no return, and history will ceaselessly repeat itself.

In the meantime, there will be victories if law enforcement and the communities they're sworn to protect work as one. Feelgood results that don't just put bad guys behind bars, but also free the innocent victims unjustly imprisoned by them.

I was proud knowing this investigation was one of those victories; inspiration as I saddled up and rode off to the next MET deployment in another drug-plagued New England community.

Operation Tune-Up had reached its conclusion.

Well, almost.

Chapter 16

"Last Chance"

January 15, 1998

Richie Burgos and I stood on the darkly lit catwalk peering out a one-way window mirrored on the terminal side. A passenger's manifest doesn't always reflect reality in a world of aliases, so we visually combed the crowd of early morning travelers for the fugitive's face, just in case he'd slipped back into the States and was rendezvousing with the woman about to board a nonstop flight bound for San Juan, Puerto Rico. New York agents from the JFK Airport Group were scattered around the departure gate, wired bud filling an ear, ready to make the arrest once told the target had been sighted.

It had been almost two and a half years since the takedown of Operation Tune-Up. Everybody arrested and indicted in the case had been adjudicated through the criminal justice system by then, but there was one defendant who hadn't even started the process. That's because the dual-jurisdictional fugitive, Jose "Flaco" Garcia, hadn't yet been apprehended.

The woman being watched inside the terminal was the girlfriend Flaco left behind. Richie knew her from his many visits to the Worcester County Courthouse; he there on police matters, she an employee of the court. Their casual acquaintance took an investigatory turn after Flaco was declared a federal fugitive. With the impactful case very much in the public eye, both in the press and on the streets, there was nothing to lose as he questioned her several times about Flaco's whereabouts, making it clear that withholding information could result in a charge of harboring a fugitive. Her response was always the same: she'd had no contact with Flaco ever since he took off in the middle of his state trial for cocaine trafficking.

According to one of Richie's reliable sources, that was a lie. Allegedly, they'd spoken with each other on a regular basis ever since Flaco fled, and she was looking forward to a long-planned vacation with her fugitive boyfriend in Puerto Rico when things cooled down. The intelligence was given enhanced credibility by the pen register attached to her Worcester phone, which showed a recent outgoing call to an untraceable cell with a Puerto Rican exchange in close juxtaposition with one made to a local travel agency. A subpoena revealed that she'd booked a flight on American Airlines from New York to San Juan that morning.

There was no obvious logistical reason for her to fly out of JFK instead of the closer Logan Airport in Boston, so after setting up a surveillance with DEA New York, Richie and I drove down the night before her scheduled departure — just in case the fugitive shifted hiding places and was now staying with his brother in the Bronx, who was also being monitored for contact by way of pen register. But nobody met her at the airport as she boarded the plane alone, which taxied from the gate on time at 6:20 A.M.

After Richie notified the US Marshals Fugitive Task Force in Puerto Rico — which had a team on standby pending the outcome in New York — and gave them the girlfriend's physical description to continue surveillance once the plane landed in San Juan, there was nothing more for us to do but wait for a return call. So, we left the airport and found a place to have breakfast before heading back to Worcester.

The drive was an uneasy one; small talk and classic rock thinly veiling the anxiety of knowing this was our last chance to find and arrest Flaco. It was somewhere on the Merritt Parkway in Connecticut when Richie's cell phone rang. The timing was right, as was the language when he answered the call: Spanish. The plane should have touched down by then; all the passengers disembarked and on their way to some tropical island retreat.

As the thump of intermittent wipers brushed away a light drizzle, I tightened my grip on the wheel, along with the hope that Flaco had been picked up at the airport. I was optimistic, though cautiously this time, battle-scarred by the bizarre events during the other two attempts to capture the fugitive in Puerto Rico; his freedom first enabled by a corrupt cop protecting the Cali Cartel, then by an arrogant agent, a conflicted uncle, and a wild boar.

Eyes focused on the road, I didn't know what Richie was being told, but based upon his animated reaction before ending the call, I sensed an old adage right around the bend.

Three time's a charm.

"We got him, bro!"

Author's Note

A purer and more "user friendly" form of heroin began its epidemical march during the 1990s when Colombian heroin joined ranks with its evil counterparts from the Golden Triangle and Golden Crescent regions of the world. This potent product and its synthetic cousin, fentanyl, are primarily responsible for the current crisis of today, claiming many casualties while leaving behind devastated family members and friends bobbing in the wake of addiction. It's a crisis that touches all of us on one level or another.

Law enforcement will continue to fight the trafficking organizations responsible for the manufacturing, importation, and distribution of drugs, both on America's front lines and in the trenches of our infiltrated communities. Like Operation Tune-Up, there will be other battlefield victories that make for safer places to live and an improved quality of life, albeit not forever as was the case in Worcester's Main South neighborhood. The "war on drugs" will never be won unless demand reduction education better arms future generations of susceptible souls. They are the foot soldiers who will ultimately curb the flow of use, abuse, and addiction with weapons of deep-rooted resolve and rejection.

Though its narrative format reads like fiction, A Peek Under the Hood is a true story, painstakingly written with accuracy from my original notes, in-depth interviews, comprehensive background research, and an eidetic memory. It is real, at times raw. I have minimized gruesome criminal details, street monikers some may deem derogatory, and salty language. If any still found what was included to be offensive or disturbing, I apologize, but removing it all dilutes too much reality of life on the streets. I also made some detail changes to protect law enforcement tactics/techniques, the continued safety of undercover agents and cooperating witnesses, ongoing investigations, and classified information, but they do not alter this story's truthful path.

Acknowledgments

Stepping outside the boundaries of your investigative comfort zone and working with another law enforcement agency – a federal one – is a path of coordination shunned by some police departments. I'd like to thank the entire Worcester PD Vice & Narcotics Unit for opening their minds and sharing their knowledge and expertise, especially Richie Burgos, Mark Coyle, Tom Gaffney, and Brendan Harney; the city Gang Unit, including current Chief of Police Steve Sargent, who continued that productive partnership beyond Operation Tune-Up; and then Chief of Police Edward Gardella, who encouraged cooperation by requesting the first ever DEA Mobile Enforcement Team ("MET") deployment in New England. They all broke down barriers and showed what happens when local and federal forces unite against a common foe.

I'd also like to thank all the original members of the New England Field Division's MET team and other contributing agents from the Boston office, notably Mike Boyle, Clem Fisher, "Ned" Dailey, Paul Gazzara, Elvin Laboy, Nancy Morelli, "Phil" Muollo, and Brian Tomasetta; the most supportive DEA supervisors in the world, Jack Mahoney and Doug Ross; and the other agencies that participated in the case, including ATF ("Butchy" Tortorella), the US Marshals Service (Dave Taylor), Massachusetts State Police (J.R. Martinez), and the Royal Canadian Mounted Police (Bill Larison), who without his cross-border dedication to duty, Operation Tune-Up would have never been born.

With dozens of federal defendants successfully prosecuted in the operation, and another hundred plus taken down in subsequent Worcester County cases, which led to the establishment of a DEA office in Worcester, assistant US attorneys Heidi E. Brieger, Allison Burroughs, David Hennessey, Jack Hodgens, Kevin McGrath, Michael Ricciuti, and Emily Schulman all deserve the public's thanks for their dedication to justice.

Finally, I'd like to thank my network of advisors and critics, guides who provided direction as I navigated a path to the book's completion: first and foremost my dear friend, Tony "Mr. Smoothie" Fiotto, who unfortunately couldn't stick around to share in the joy of its fruition, Paul Fazio, Maryanne Galvin, Eben Howland, the late Mary Ellen "Mel" Hurley, Sheila Kelleher,

Sylvester Ryan, and Steve Lyons, and a special acknowledgment to Robin, whose love and devotion unwaveringly supported me along this long and winding road.

About the Author

Michael Pevarnik is a thirty-year veteran of federal and local law enforcement who retired in 2009 from his role as a supervisory special agent with the Drug Enforcement Administration. He was the case agent for "Operation Tune-Up," a history-making investigation that virtually eliminated heroin for the better part of two years in New England's second largest city.

His casework as a field agent and supervisor with DEA's Mobile Enforcement Team, an elite group based in Boston that deployed to dismantle deeply rooted organizations in drug related, violent crime plagued communities throughout the six-states of New England, earned the author more than two-dozen awards, including the DEA Administrator's Award (Providence, Rhode Island); US Attorney's Award in the District of Massachusetts; the New Hampshire State Police Colonel's Award; and the Organized Crime and Drug Enforcement Task Force Award in the Districts of Connecticut and Maine. He later oversaw the division's Asset Forfeiture Group, established its Financial Investigations Team, and restructured its Recruitment Program.

A former police officer/detective with the Montclair, New Jersey Police Department, the author has a Bachelor of Science degree (Magna Cum Laude) in criminal justice and accounting from William Paterson University. He is also a graduate of the Essex County New Jersey Police Academy and the DEA Academy in Quantico, Virginia.

To learn more about the author and his career, visit his website at www.michaelpevarnik.com.

More Nonfiction from Rootstock Publishing:

Alzheimer's Canyon: One Couple's Reflections on Living with Dementia by Jane Dwinell & Sky Yardley

The Atomic Bomb on My Back by Taniguchi Sumiteru

Catalysts for Change: How Nonprofits and a Foundation Are Helping Shape Vermont's Future ed. by Doug Wilhelm

China in Another Time: A Personal Story by Claire Malcolm Lintilhac

Collecting Courage: Joy, Pain, Freedom, Love — Anti-Black Racism in the Charitable Sector eds. Nneka Allen, Camila Vital Nunes Pereira, & Nicole Salmon

Cracked: My Life After a Skull Fracture by Jim Barry

I Could Hardly Keep From Laughing: An Illustrated Collection of Vermont Humor by Don Hooper & Bill Mares

A Judge's Odyssey: From Vermont to Russia, Kazakhstan, and Georgia, Then on to War Crimes and Organ Trafficking in Kosovo by Dean B. Pineles

The Language of Liberty: A Citizen's Vocabulary by Edwin C. Hagenstein

A Lawyer's Life to Live by Kimberly B. Cheney

Nobody Hitchhikes Anymore by Ed Griffin-Nolan

Pauli Murray's Revolutionary Life by Simki Kuznick

Preaching Happiness: Creating a Just and Joyful World by Ginny Sassaman

Red Scare in the Green Mountains: Vermont in the McCarthy Era 1946-1960 by Rick Winston

Save Me a Seat! A Life with Movies by Rick Winston

Striding Rough Ice: Coaching College Hockey and Growing Up in the Game by Gary Wright

Tales of Bialystok: A Jewish Journey from Czarist Russia to America by Charles Zachariah Goldberg

Uncertain Fruit: A Memoir of Infertility, Loss, and Love by Rebecca & Sallyann Majoya

Walking Home: Trail Stories by Celia Ryker

You Have a Hammer: Building Grant Proposals for Social Change by Barbara Floersch

To learn about our Fiction, Poetry, and Children's titles, visit our website www.rootstockpublishing.com.

CPSIA information can be obtained
at www.ICGtesting.com
Printed in the USA
JSHW021903160723
44764JS00001B/7

9 781578 691487